The Second Homeland

India is my second homeland. I was once again a child there after Poland.

—Wieslaw Stypula
Warsaw, Poland

I often toyed with the idea of applying for Indian citizenship,
since I was born in Karachi in 1944.

—Janusz Dziurinski
Connecticut, USA

Balachadi was the happiest time of my childhood. How can we
ever repay the kindness that we received.

—Marian Raba
Leicester, UK

The Second Homeland

Polish Refugees in India

ANURADHA BHATTACHARJEE

with the Chronicle of Franek Herzog

SAGE www.sagepublications.com
Los Angeles • London • New Delhi • Singapore • Washington DC

First published in 2012 by

 SAGE Publications India Pvt Ltd
B1/I-1 Mohan Cooperative Industrial Area
Mathura Road, New Delhi 110 044, India
www.sagepub.in

SAGE Publications Inc
2455 Teller Road
Thousand Oaks, California 91320, USA

SAGE Publications Ltd
1 Oliver's Yard, 55 City Road
London EC1Y 1SP, United Kingdom

SAGE Publications Asia-Pacific Pte Ltd
33 Pekin Street
#02-01 Far East Square
Singapore 048763

Published by Vivek Mehra for SAGE Publications India Pvt Ltd, typeset in 10/12 Minion by Diligent Typesetter, Delhi and printed at Saurabh Printers Pvt Ltd.

Library of Congress Cataloging-in-Publication Data

Bhattacharjee, Anuradha.
   The second homeland : Polish refugees in India / Anuradha Bhattacharjee ; with the Chronicle of Franek Herzog.
       p. cm.
   Includes bibliographical references and index.
   1. Polish people—India—History—20th century.   2. World War, 1939–1945—Deportations from Poland.   3. World War, 1939–1945—Deportations from Soviet Union.   4. Refugees—Soviet Union—History.   5. Refugees—India—History—20th century.   I. Herzog, Franek.   II. Title.

DS432.P67P65   940.53'145—dc23   2012   2012003291

ISBN: 978-81-321-0707-1 (HB)

The SAGE Team: Shambhu Sahu, Shreya Chakraborti, Anju Saxena and Dally Verghese

Disclaimer:

Sections of Franek Herzog's memoirs were printed as a book in Polish by the Town of Lubaczow, Poland, in 2006, published by Kresy Museum in Lubaczow, editor-in-chief mag. Zenon Swatek. The title of the work in Polish is *Na Tulaczym Szlaku, Kronika Rodziny Herzogow 1866-2000* (*The Way It Was—Chronicle of Herzog Family—1866–2000*). Copyright held by Franek Herzog.

Dedicated to the children—our future:

Abhimanyu (late) and Aishwarya Bhattacharjee,
Stephen, Cassandra and Gregory Verbeke

Thank you for choosing a SAGE product! If you have any comment, observation or feedback, I would like to personally hear from you. Please write to me at contactceo@sagepub.in

—Vivek Mehra, Managing Director and CEO,
SAGE Publications India Pvt Ltd, New Delhi

Bulk Sales

SAGE India offers special discounts for purchase of books in bulk. We also make available special imprints and excerpts from our books on demand.

For orders and enquiries, write to us at

Marketing Department
SAGE Publications India Pvt Ltd
B1/I-1, Mohan Cooperative Industrial Area
Mathura Road, Post Bag 7
New Delhi 110044, India
E-mail us at marketing@sagepub.in

Get to know more about SAGE, be invited to SAGE events, get on our mailing list. Write today to marketing@sagepub.in

This book is also available as an e-book.

━━━━━━ ℘ ℭ ━━━━━━

Contents

CREO

List of Tables

☙❧

List of Maps

☙❧

List of Photographs

❦

Section 1: Arrival

1. The last postcard from Father (Lieutenant Colonel F Herzog) from Starobielsk
2. Polish boys in Bandra, 1942

Section 2: India Years

3. Franek, Balachadi, 1942
4. Tadek Herzog and Henry Bobotek, Balachadi, 1943
5. Marian Rozanski, Jerzy Dobrostanski, Franek Herzog, Zbigniew Suchecki, Jerzy Krzyszton, Steven Balaram and Mrs Janina Dobrostanska, Balachadi, 1945
6. End-of-year report for 1943–44 from Balachadi
7. End-of-year report for 1945–46 from Balachadi
8. The youngest children at Balachadi with Indian caretaker, 1942
9. Dr Ashani, Mr Joshi, Fr Pluta and Polish nursing staff, Balachadi, 1942
10. Sabina Kotlinska's picture, 160, Rama Varma (Appan) Tampuran, War Publicity Officer, 'Cochin', 1944
11. Programme sheet of a function by the children, Balachadi, 1944
12. Jam Saheb with Polish children, Jamnagar, 1944
13. Polish refugees arriving from Russia, 1942
14(a). Letter from a complete stranger (front)
14(b). Letter from a complete stranger (reverse)
15. Book on Indian theme developed by Madam W Dynowska
16. Franek (extreme left) and Jerzy Krzyszton (extreme right) with two Portuguese scouts in Goa, 1947

Section 3: Reminiscences and Reflections

Cover Photos

- Front cover, main spread: Tadeusz Dobrostanski, Quetta, 1942; courtesy of Tadeusz Dobrostanski
- Front cover, bottom right: Polish girls with Wanda Dynowska and Subramaniam; courtesy of Jan Seidlecki
- Front cover, bottom left: Polish children at the beach in Balachadi, 1943; courtesy of Tadeusz Dobrostanski
- Back cover: The last postcard from Father (Lieutenant Colonel F Herzog) from Starobielsk; courtesy of Franek Herzog's collection

List of Abbreviations

∾

AAN	Archiwum Akt Nowichy (Polish acronym for 'The New Archives')
API	Association of Poles in India
BNA	British National Archives
COP	Chamber of Princes
DP	Displaced Person
GOI	Government of India
HMG	His/Her Majesty's Government
IRCR	International Committee for the Red Cross
IRO	International Refugee Organisation
ITC	Interim Treasury Committee
IWC	Imperial War Council
JRA	Jewish Relief Agency
KGB	Komitet Gosudarstvennoy Bezopasnosty (Committee for State Security)
MERRA	Middle East Relief and Refugee Administration
NAI	National Archives of India
NCWC	National Catholic Women's Conference
NKVD	Narodnyi Kommissariat Vnutrennikh Del (People's Commisariat for Internal Affairs)
NWFP	North West Frontier Province
PAI Force	Persia and Iraq Force
PCG	Polish Consul General
POW	Prisoner of War
PUC	Polish University College
RAF	Royal Air Force
UNRRA	United Nations Relief and Rehabilitation Administration
WVS	Women's Voluntary Service
ZPP	Związek Patriotów Polskich

List of Appendices

༆

भारत का राजदूत

ســفــيــر الــهــنـــد

AMBASSADOR OF INDIA

21st March, 2009

Foreword

⌘

From time to time those of us who were posted at Warsaw came across the members of 'Jamnagar Club' functioning under the aegis of Indo-Polish Friendship Society, who recalled that they had been in India as children during the 1940s and narrated some very happy memories. It was difficult for us to put their experience in perspective of the context of the World War II and relegated the incident to one the many mass movement of displaced people at that time. They mentioned places like Jamnagar and Kolhapur, but since we could not exactly relate to the events under discussion, we merely carried out the obligatory social exchange.

The event caught the imagination of one of my colleagues who thought these people were Jews and he narrated it to Dr Kenneth Robbins, a Jewish Indologist at Washington in 2000, who promptly published a journal article saying that these people were not Jews but Roman Catholics. The puzzle only deepened.

In 2002, Anuradha contacted us at the Europe-East Division of the Ministry of External Affairs in New Delhi, when I was serving as Joint Secretary, seeking information about these Poles from our sources. During the meeting it transpired that she already knew more about these people than we knew in the Division. It was a pleasant surprise to see her in Warsaw in early 2003, where I was the Ambassador of India, by then, with a group of journalists who had been invited to Warsaw by the Polish Government. She was relentlessly researching her project, which was by then a doctoral dissertation.

P.O. Box 1727, Ruwi, PC 112, Muscat, Sultanate of Oman
Tel: (+968) 2468 4512/ 2468 4513, Fax: (+968) 2469 8291, Email: hom@indemb-oman.org

Slowly, we had begun to understand the association of the members of the Jamnagar Club with India. 2003 being the golden jubilee year of the diplomatic relations between India and Poland, I was obliged to attend many functions, one of which was the biennial meet of the Association of Poles in India 1942–48 (API), the bigger club that the 'Jamnagar Club' had merged into, which also had chapters in several countries and many members. During the reunion, I met Rev. Z. Peszkovski and heard about the Katyn Forest and related events by which the members of API had reached India. He was the only surviving adult from that time who could put the events in perspective for me.

Later, we read the diligently researched thesis and its findings surprised us pleasantly—a unique Indian initiative during extremely trying times—another beautiful example of the nobility of the Indian character and spirit. An idea about a film on the subject was mooted by some of us, but unfortunately, it did not see fruition due to budgetary constraints.

I am delighted to introduce this account which not only introduces the Indian people to some of the lesser known aspects of the WW II, but also does us proud by bringing out the generosity of the Indian people in spite of passing through hard times themselves. This work is a tribute to the spirit of perseverance. I hope some readers will be inspired and motivated to make a film on the subject.

Happy Reading !

(Anil Wadhwa)
Ambassador

P.O. Box 1727, Ruwi, PC 112, Muscat, Sultanate of Oman
Tel: (+968) 2468 4512/ 2468 4513, Fax: (+968) 2469 8291, Email: hom@indemb-oman.org

Acknowledgements

CRRO

This work would not have been possible without the help of several people. First of all, I would like to thank Mr Hiranmay Karlekar, Consultant Editor, the *Pioneer*, for encouraging the idea of a book and suggesting that the subject be pursued as a doctoral study when no academic work to build the proposed story around, could be located in Indian academic circles.

I am grateful to Dr Shridhar (alias Raja) M Dixit, Department of History, University of Pune, for accepting to supervise my work, in spite of my not having a background in historical studies. His bold and opinionated stand gave me the confidence to continue. He made my dream of a book on the subject his own, and put his weight squarely behind me. Both, Mr Karlekar and Dr Dixit, held my hand whenever I faltered and kept me firmly anchored to and focused on the work I had begun, especially after a personal tragedy.

Gratitude is also due to Meenakshi Rao, features editor, the *Pioneer*, who published the first article that I had culled out, after initial research, which led to this work to be transformed from a minor journalistic venture to a serious academic pursuit.

It is to this wonderful new tool of communication—the Internet—that I owe my ability to have carried out this study. Without it, even a lifetime would not have been adequate to be able to put the fragments of the story together. The help and encouragement of the members of Kresy-Siberia discussion group on the Internet, is particularly noteworthy. To the moderator, Stefan Wisniowski, who I met personally only in June 2011, I extend my very grateful thanks. He answered several questions patiently, introduced me to the group and took great pains to help me locate some of the 'shy or silent' members. Several of those members in turn shared the memories and resources that have made up the body of this work, especially

Tadeusz Dobrostanski and Stanislaus Harasymow. Tadeusz introduced me to Dr Kenneth Robbins and Franek Herzog in the USA, Henry Baczyk and Stanislaus Harasymow in Australia and Wieslaw Stypula in Poland—all over the Internet—each of who contributed significantly to this work. Stanislaus let me have his handwritten and printed books from the period, besides a letter reproduced in the work. Barbara Charuba of Canada, introduced me to Stefan Klosowski when he was scheduled to visit India and to the Association of Poles in India, London, and offered constructive suggestions several times. Zygmunt Mandel contacted Dr Robbins and me voluntarily and added a whole new dimension to the work.

My gratitude also goes to my London friends from the Association of Poles in India 1942–48, and its president Jan Siedlecki.* Members of the Association took time and assisted me on visits to various archival institutions, often booking a few files for my use on their own reader's ticket, so that no valuable time was lost in procedural matters. They were: Teresa Glazer, who took me to the British Library to see India and Oriental Collection; Karol Huppert, who accompanied me to the Polish Institute and Gen. Sikorski Museum, which houses a unique collection of Polish documents; Eugenia Maresch, member of the Anglo-Polish Historical Committee, who shared her knowledge and experience in accessing Polish Refugees documents kept at the British National Archives at Kew (formerly Public Records Office) and Wiesia Kleszko, the secretary of the Association, for being so helpful in locating people and their addresses. Jan and Wiesia also made the introductions as a prelude to setting up appointments and subsequent meetings.

To Roman Gutowski, and all members of Association of Poles in India (API), Warsaw Chapter, I owe a lot. They not only hosted me in their homes at short notice, but also shared memories, memorabilia and insights while answering my myriad questions. Roman made it possible for me to meet all members of API, Warsaw, especially Fr Peszkovski, the sole surviving adult from the period.

Princess Hershad Kumariji of Nawanagar and Colonel Vijaysingh Gaikwad helped me with the Indian side of the story and local links in Jamnagar—Balachadi and Kolhapur, respectively. Major General Vikram Madan of the Indian Army identified Balachadi as the place where there is a Sainik School with a wartime history, when I was perplexed about

* Jan Siedlecki, Fr Peszkovski and Aneta Naszynska departed while this book was under production.

the location of the erstwhile camp. To the librarian of Sainik School, Balachadi, Mr Atul Desai, and the then Principal Wing Cdr. VK Kaushal, I owe gratitude for letting me peruse the historical material housed there—especially the paper written by Dr Kenneth Robbins and copies of documents from British Library-India and Oriental Collection that Ken had placed there, after publishing the said paper in the *Journal of Indo-Judaic Studies* in 1998. Ken later asked me to join him as research associate, which kept me afloat financially for this extremely expensive project whose links were scattered all over the world, besides enhancing my portfolio of research papers.

Dr Krzysztof Majka, the Ambassador of Poland and Ms Margaret Wejsis-Golebiak, Counsellor at the Embassy of Poland in New Delhi made it possible for me to visit Warsaw on a study visit, which added great value and dimension to my work. The Charles Wallace India Trust (CWIT) granted me a small fellowship to visit London and peruse documents there. I extend my gratitude to the archivists at all the archives: National Archives, New Delhi; Tata Central Archives, Pune; Kesari-Maratha Sanstha, Pune; State Archives, Kolhapur; The New Archives, Warsaw; British Library-India and Oriental Collection; British National Archives and Polish Institute and General Sikorski Museum, all in London. The librarians at Sapru House Library, New Delhi, and Rajputana Rifles Centre Library, New Delhi, deserve special mention for making available to me old and rare books. Many thanks are due to Ms Nayana Bose of the United Nations High Commission for Refugees (UNHCR), New Delhi, who patiently explained to me nuances of refugee matters.

I would fail in my duties if I did not thank Aneta Naszynska, Danuta Pniewska and Mirka Gutowska, who hosted me in their homes during my two visits to London and Warsaw, respectively. Stanley Whittlesey, Alicja Edwards, Eugene Bak, Casimir Majewski and Wieslaw Stypula sent me books that helped to shed light on the dynamics of the period. Lech Lesiak pointed in the right direction to be able to source two critical books. Richard Alford of the CWIT presented me with 'Deportation…' by Keith Sword when I had given up all hopes of locating the work with authentic figures. API Warsaw and London presented me with two limited edition books published in Warsaw: *Exiled Children* and *Schooling in Wartime Exile*, which are cornerstones to the study and examples of the changing political orientation in Poland and the growing interest of the new generation in the history that was kept under wraps for so long.

No academic work is possible without borrowing from predecessors. This work stands on the shoulders of titans: Professors Norman Davies,

Ian Copland, Kieth Sword and Bisheshwar Prasad. The context for this work is developed by excerpting the fruit of their labour.

I also owe gratitude to Sheta Shaha, who read this manuscript and offered advice on structure and continuity, Professor Atul Tandan of Mudra Institute of Communications, Ahmedabad, India, for letting me have the time and space to see this work to its logical fruition and Rekha Natarajan of SAGE Publications who has guided the entire publication process since inception.

Last but not the least, my heartfelt gratitude to my family: my son late Abhimanyu, who believed in the project, but did not live long enough to see it realised; my daughter Aishwarya, who bore my frequent physical and mental distance from her with cheer; my husband, Ajoy, who put up with all my demanding work and travel needs; my parents, though not in the physical realm anymore, late Lieutenant Colonel Monindra K Mukherji and Mrs Usha Mukherji, who taught me never to stop seeking the truth.

There are many who I may have missed out here, but their contribution is just as important. To them all and many others I express my deep gratitude. The responsibility of all omissions and errors is my own.

Anuradha Bhattacharjee
Ahmedabad/Noida

Introduction

∽≈∾

An official Kremlin document sent to the European Court of Human Rights in 2010 suggests hopes of Russia acknowledging responsibility of the Katyn massacre in 1940 may be disappointed. In a response to a lawsuit by those seeking Russia's rehabilitation of the Katyn victims, the Russian government said there's no certainty the Polish victims were even shot, while generally Russia is not obliged to conduct an investigation into what it calls 'the events'. To the rehabilitation calls, the answer is 'nyet'.

—Marcin Sobczyk, *Wall Street Journal*, 6 April, *2010*

*I*n 2010, when Vladimir Putin invited his Polish counterpart to jointly commemorate the 70th anniversary of the Katyn Massacre—scheduled for 10 April, there was hope that Russia was trying to redefine its official stance on the Stalin-ordered killing of about 22,000 Polish military officers and intellectuals by the Soviet secret police and Stalin's tool of repression, the infamous NKVD, during the Second World War. Some kind of a long awaited reconciliation was expected when Putin was to deliver his speech at the forest near Smolensk in the presence of Polish officials. However, events did not play out as expected. The plane carrying the Polish President, Lech Kaczynski, his wife Maria Kaczynska and 94 top officials of the country from all services and sectors crashed near Smolensk, killing all aboard. Once again the country was left virtually headless with the death of its crème-de la crème, in a sad echo of events 70 years earlier. Katyn had claimed the best of Poland the second time round.

In 1990 Boris Yeltsin had handed over a batch of documents from the Stalinist era accepting Soviet involvement in the matter. In 1993 Rev

Msgr Zdzislaw Jastrzebiec Peszkovski, Pope's home prelate since 1970, who had been a prisoner at Kozielsk in 1940 as a prisoner of war published his book *Memoirs of a Prisoner of War of Kozielsk*, where he gave a figure of 4,403 Poles shot at Katyn, from a Soviet document dated 14 May 1940. He was the force behind the commemoration of Katyn in 1995. He had been the Priest of Katyn since then.

After narrowly missing being executed in Katyn, he joined the Polish Army in the East, upon formation in 1941, and reached India in 1942 as scoutmaster for the young Polish children being hosted in India in the Princely States of Jamnagar and Kolhapur.

The Western world has at all times played a cover-up role in the discussion of Katyn massacre and other savageries of the USSR, in a bid not to antagonise Soviet Union, especially after the importance of Poland as an ally faded after it capitulated completely under the dual invasion on 1939. According to historian Norman Davies, unofficial or classified UK documents concluded that Soviet guilt was a 'near certainty', but the alliance with the Soviets was deemed to be more important than moral issues; thus the official version supported the Soviet version, up to censoring the contradictory accounts.

According to some standard sources, in 1943, the *Katyn Manifesto* was published in English in London by Count Geoffrey Potocki de Montalk. He was arrested by the Special Branch and sent to an agricultural camp in Northumberland. In the United States, a similar line was taken, notwithstanding that two official intelligence reports into the Katyn massacre were produced that contradicted the official position. In 1944 Roosevelt assigned his special emissary to the Balkans, Navy Lieutenant Commander George Earle, to compile information on Katyn, which he did using contacts in Bulgaria and Romania. Earle concluded that the massacre was committed by the Soviet Union. Having consulted with Elmer Davis, the director of the Office of War Information, Roosevelt rejected the conclusion officially, declared that he was convinced of Nazi Germany's responsibility, and ordered that Earle's report be suppressed. When Earle formally requested permission to publish his findings, the president issued a written order to desist. Earle was reassigned and spent the rest of the War in American Samoa.[1]

A BBC programme directive dated 2 July 1940 states: 'Please keep an eye on programmes dealing with Russia. Ironical or derogatory remarks about Stalin and speculation about Russia's motives and probable action are thought to be equally undesirable, at present.'[2] No revocation of this directive could be located and is probably in effect even today. The independent broadcaster has been deaf and mute on the subject.

According to Laurence Rees, a producer of a series on the Second World War for BBC, author and senior visiting fellow, London School of Economics and Politics,[3] in Britain, many newspapers, notably Lord Beaverbrook's *Daily Express*, were hugely supportive of the Soviet war effort, and the fact that George Orwell could not get his brilliant satire on the Soviet state, *Animal Farm*, published during the War suggests that there was little appetite, to say the least, for balancing material about the horrors of life under Stalin. The greatest white-washing of Stalin goes to a film made in 1943 by Warner Brothers called *Mission to Moscow*, based on a book written by the former US ambassador to the Soviet Union, Joseph Davies. *Mission to Moscow* was condemned as crass pro-Soviet propaganda in the 1950s, but during the War it was a hugely influential piece of work. And it is not as if the British and American governments did not know the truth about Stalin's murderous regime.

Rees continues that not only did they learn how brutally Stalin's forces were behaving in occupied territory as early as 1940, but the US president at the time, Franklin Roosevelt, and British Prime Minister, Winston Churchill, even went so far as to suppress information which pointed to the fact that Stalin and his secret police had orchestrated a mass murder—the killing of thousands of Polish officers in the forest of Katyn. Rees concludes that the trouble is that the legacy of these 'expedient lies' has still not entirely left us.

Peter Novick[4] opines the Holocaust did not loom large in the thinking of the American people either during or immediately following the Second World War, but became a central concern among Jews and other Americans approximately 20 years later, with the rise of Zionism. He continues that the thinning of Jewish identity needed to be countered and many advised that the Holocaust was not properly 'seared into the memory of a generation born after WWII'.[5] The millionaire who provided most of the original funding for the Simon Wiesenthal Center told a reporter that it was 'a sad fact that Israel and Jewish education and all the other familiar buzzwords no longer seem to rally Jews behind the community. The Holocaust, though, works every time'.[6] He details the turning away from social activism by a large layer of Jewish intellectuals and media, and the development of 'identity politics', all of which, he contends, contributed to the rise and diffusion of the Holocaust.

Since no comparable identity politics was at play in the UK or USA during the period, the Soviet backed communist government in Poland, and the Cold War ensured that the Polish experience under the Soviets during the War and the ensuing migration to India and other countries remained under wraps.

Thus, the passage through India of the Polish population surviving the Soviet *Gulags*, having lost most of their menfolk to Katyn, has remained under the carpet for all these years. This work is the result of a decade's relentless pursuit of details from fragments scattered all over the world and a largely self-funded research.

This work traces the passage through India of Polish people who have suffered the greatest unrecognised human rights violation of our times after Soviet forces marched into and occupied Polish territory to the east of the River Bug on 17 September 1939.

The description of the arrests, transportation to the Soviet Union and life in the camps by the last of the aging survivors is often sub-human. No trial against the perpetrators of the crimes has ever been held, no one convicted and no compensation paid, unlike the Nuremberg Trials where the Nazi perpetrators of the Holocaust were brought to book. The event remains like an untreated wound amongst the victims and their families. The subject of Stalin's crimes against the Polish population still awaits its true author, as files still remain classified in countries of the former USSR.

Since the USSR had ended the War as an ally, Western historians overlooked its activities against Poland in conjunction with Nazi Germany in the earlier part of the War. As a Russian journalist once put it, 'The Soviets deported the Polish people and the Western historians deported the event from history,'[7] with the events not finding a mention in the media. Poland herself had a puppet communist government, supported by the USSR till 1989. The Indians, euphoric with the hard-won independence from British rule and subsequent nation building, did not go into the details whether the Poles who had been in India were Jews or others. The event has, therefore, remained in the memories of only those people who had been associated with it personally.

The Indian context is new to most. In 1991, the author, who was then a journalist with *The Times of India*, met an elderly Polish lady married to a medical officer from the Indian Army in Pune. This sparked off the author's interest in the subject. The lady had been introduced as a survivor of the Holocaust, but during the three-hour interview she spoke about starvation and hard physical labour in the camps of Siberia. She continued with the journey through Kazakhstan and Uzbekistan to join the Polish Army being formed, its evacuation through Persia and war-duration domicile of the civilians in India.

Knowledge about wartime European history was limited and the story was not published at that time. However, the notes of the powerful story of human endurance and grit remained, only to be revived a decade later after a visit to the United States Holocaust Memorial Museum in 2001. Some minor publications there indicated the Soviet invasion and occupation of pre-war Polish territory and deportation of over a million Polish civilians to Siberia and Kazakhstan.

A reference to the archival files in National Archives in New Delhi revealed that India was a transit destination for the Jewish population fleeing Europe in the face of Nazi tyranny. The Polish Legation in Bombay was working overtime in conjunction with the Jewish Relief Agency (JRA) to provide travel documents and other support to the Poles reaching India and helping them to travel onwards to their chosen destination of Palestine or the USA.

Tucked within those files is also the story of another humanitarian and refugee crisis of great proportions—that of Poles (Jewish and non-Jewish) deported to the USSR finding their way to India by the industry of the then Polish Consul General to India, Dr Eugenisuz Banasinski. His efforts found resonance amongst several Indian Princes. Jam Saheb Digvijaysinhji of Nawanagar, who was also the Chancellor of the Chamber of Princes and thus the representative of India in the Imperial War Cabinet, opened the doors of his State to the first batch of 500 orphaned Polish children in a unique first.

It emerges that the Polish population has suffered not only the Holocaust targeting the Jewry under the occupation of Nazi Germany, but also annihilation of the civilian population under the Soviet Union, which targeted the educated Polish people without prejudice to religious faith, racial origin or class. In some Polish circles, the event is referred to as 'Gehenna', an archaic term for hell. The complete civilian population of the region east of the River Bug, popularly known as the eastern borderlands or 'Kresy' region of pre-1939 Poland, was herded off in cattle trains into the depths of Siberia and Kazakhstan by the Narodnyi Kommissariat Vnutrennikh Del (NKVD or Peoples Commisariat for Internal Affairs), a forerunner of the KGB—the secret police of the occupying Soviet forces—in four major waves. The dates common to a large number of survivors worldwide are:

- 10 February 1940: The people deported were the First World War veterans, forestry workers and rich farmers.
- 2 April 1940: Families of police officers, army officers and soldiers and people fleeing the Nazis from the western side of the country.
- 3 June 1940: People fleeing the Nazis, landowners and civil servants.
- 4 June 1940: Saw the deportation of the remaining people of every category mentioned earlier.

In the first few days of Soviet occupation, the political and social personalities of Poland were detained. The NKVD or Soviet Police arrived with lists, which had been prepared in advance, and arrested members of parliament and senators, local mayors and heads of district administration, all eminent landowners and owners of factories, all people engaged in official activities, chief justices, priests, public prosecutors and members of the constabulary, including simple policemen. Poles and Ukrainians, White Ruthenians, Lithuanians and Jews, landowners and farm-hands, factory owners and workers, officers and other ranks, judges and tradesmen, Roman Catholic priests, Protestant ministers and Jewish Rabbis were all torn away from their homes by the NKVD and sent to Soviet prisons and camps.

Their deportation was followed by the forcible removal of their wives and families, old people and children as well as civil servants, school teachers, physicians, small landowners, employees of cooperative services and all types of professional and communal organisations, to the deserts of Kazakhstan or the Siberian wilderness. In the latter case, usually the whole family was deported—grandparents, parents and children. On a given night, known in advance only to the authorities, the dwellings of these unfortunate people were surrounded and invaded. They were given 20–30 minutes to pack, and then sent out of their homes. After that, they had to endure an average of three weeks of journey crowded into cattle trucks, dirty, hungry and exposed to the hardships of severe frost in the winter or equally unbearable heat in the summer. During these journeys, babies died, old people passed away and epidemics spread, so that the transport parties arrived at their destination having lost a large part of their original number. Once there, the deportees were put to heavy physical work, which claimed further victims.

Once in the collective camps or *kolhoz* of Siberia or Kazakhstan, the work was backbreaking physical labour. Franek Herzog's diary presents a glimpse of the back breaking physical work that they had to do, from the filter of a child's memory.

The Polish deportees were sent to distant geographical locations for varying lengths of time, dependent upon the date of their arrest and deportation. Initial transports were directed towards Siberia and later ones towards Kazakhstan. Once in the Soviet Union, their immediate fate was largely determined by the people who controlled the local *kolhoz*es. Most Poles refer to the region beyond the Ural Mountains as 'Siberia.'

The people were forced into labour such as tree felling and woodcutting, digging holes, snow clearing, brick making, milking and shovelling grain. Living conditions and access to accommodation and food varied from *kolhoz* to *kolhoz*, as did relations with the Soviet authorities and local inhabitants. Some families were able to establish limited contact with relatives back in Poland and were assisted by periodic parcels of food or money; others had to rely solely on the possessions they had been able to take with them. As many deportees had been given little time to pack, their ability to supplement meagre rations or share of *kolhoz* earnings through the sale or exchange of personal possessions varied greatly.

The prisoners of war were sent to Kolyma, near Kamachatka peninsula, to mine gold in minus 70 degrees centigrade without adequate clothing or food. 'Kolyma means death. One can stand it for one year, at best two…. There is only the frost reaching 70 degrees centigrade, scurvy, constant hunger and the bayonet or the bullet of a warder's rifle. While you could scoop up gold with a spoon, there was no food anywhere', sums up Anders,[8] under whose aegis the Polish Army was formed later in the Soviet Union.

The treatment of the Poles by the Soviet Union between 1939 and 1941 is still an unfamiliar story to many people. At the time, news of what was going on barely reached the West, and later in the War, when Britain and the United States became allies of the USSR, discussion of the episode was discouraged as tactless. The true story that emerged in fragments in the post-War years was actively discouraged as several historians have noted. It was completely overshadowed by the more spectacular and better-publicised savageries of the Nazi occupation of Poland and the rest of Europe, because they had been committed by the defeated Nazi forces, whereas Stalin had provided the much-needed support to contain the Nazis and finished the War as an ally. Yet, it was no less brutal or cold blooded. Stalinist USSR, woefully short of manpower at the time, had imposed a journey to the lumber camps of Siberia and collective farms of Kazakhstan on 1.7 million Polish people—a life of slow death from cold and starvation, as at the same time the Nazis were experimenting with Auschwitz or Treblinka. Historian Norman Davies says, 'Who is to say which was the more humane?—the effect was much the same. Of the estimated two million Polish civilians deported to Arctic Russia, Siberia and Kazakhstan in the terrible railway convoys of 1939–40, at least one half were dead within a year of their arrest.'[9] Almost no one in the West considers (Stalin's) crimes to have been evil in the same visceral way that they feel Hitler's crimes to have been evil.

The *Gulag* is an integral part of both Soviet and Russian history and it is inseparable from European history. The Soviet and Nazi camps were built at roughly the same time. Hitler knew of the Soviet camps and Stalin knew of the Holocaust. At a very deep level, the two systems were related.[10] No one wants to think that the Allies defeated one mass murderer with the help of another.[11]

There seems complete official coordination in the deportation. Regions or destinations were pre-arranged for the deportees of a certain period. While most of those deported on 10 February 1940 were sent to Siberia and Archangelsk regions, the people deported later found themselves in the wilderness of Kazakhstan and regions close to Mongolia.

Ironically liberation for many people came after Germany attacked the USSR in Operation Barbarossa in June 1941 and the signing of the Polish–Soviet Military Agreement on 14 August 1941. That Agreement paved the way for the formation of a Polish Army on Soviet soil, under the command of General Wladyslaw Anders, who was till then held a prisoner of war in a jail outside Moscow.

On 22 August 1941, General Anders promulgated his first orders to the army. He called on all Polish citizens to do their duty by joining the colours of the White Eagle. He also decided on creating a Women's Auxiliary Service.[12] After the signing of the Agreement, an Amnesty was declared—for crimes never committed—and more and more Polish people released from prisons and concentration camps began to report to Moscow. Their physical condition was bad. Later, it was decided to move the Polish Army camps to Jangi Jul in Uzbekstan in the warmer south regions of the USSR. Endemic infectious diseases such as typhoid, dysentery and malaria plagued the whole region.

The estimated quarter of a million Polish troops who had been 'interned' in the Soviet Union had been largely forgotten by the West. After their first dramatic appearance on centre stage at the beginning of the War, they had fallen into a no man's land because, technically, they were not prisoners of war, as the Soviet Union had never declared war on Poland. Later sources have estimated that the number of people killed in Katyn exceeds 22,000.

By the time of the Soviet–Polish Agreement in July 1941, Stalin needed all the help he could get, and from August 1941, Polish officers were allowed to scour the USSR collecting their countrymen for the army. In the process, they contacted many of the Polish families who had been 'resettled' throughout the USSR.

The news of the Amnesty reached many Poles indirectly, often by accident, as narrated by Danuta Pniewska in the chapter 'Transit Camps'. Zofia Mendonca recalled seeing a few well-dressed men talking to the camp authorities a few days before the guards vanished and they found themselves abandoned at the camp. Several scholars maintain that many impediments were placed in the way of those seeking identification papers which would give them the freedom to travel south. Thus, slowly and reluctantly, the gates of the Siberian and Asian camps swung open, and hundreds and thousands of Poles—soldiers, women, officials, priests and even orphaned children—began to make their way towards centres where the new Polish army was being gathered. Many had already died.

The personal recollections of those who survived indicate the relief they felt when news of the Amnesty reached them, but also detail the hardship they encountered in their efforts to escape. It was a period characterised by uncertainty, hunger, starvation, disease and daily confrontations with death, both of strangers and loved ones. These experiences have etched themselves into the minds of those who witnessed them. Stefan Klosowski recalled travelling in all sorts of transport—sledge, barge, train, carts and walking over long distances—in their quest to reach the Polish Army collection centres. Many people died during this trek to freedom marking their routes with their own graves.

In their emaciated state, the people contracted infectious fevers and thousands died on the way or at the Polish Army camps at Guzar and Kermine in South USSR. Of 14,000 people in the camp, 6,800 suffered from malaria and typhus; 3,000 had died in Kermine camp and 4,000 in Guzar.[13]

By July 1942, the Soviets were encountering internal disturbances. There was evidence of the terrible and bloody liquidation of the rising of Turkomen and Uzbeks by Budienny. Towns and villages were seen with all the buildings in ruins, and the people spoke about the slaughter of thousands and deportations to concentration camps of hundreds of thousands. Some of the younger men were able to escape to Afghanistan (see Map 1).[14]

According to Anders, the Soviets wanted to exclude Ukrainians, White Ruthenians and especially Jews from leaving the Soviet soil. The Polish Army was told not to include Jewish civilians in their convoys. After his personal intervention, the Soviet government decided that only those Jewish civilians could leave Soviet soil that had members on active service in the Polish Army.[15] Several Jewish soldiers from Anders' Army deserted when they were stationed in Palestine several months later, Menachem Begin, later the premier of newly born Israel in 1948, among them. Many civilians were taken over by the JRA in Persia, for repatriation to Palestine. And yet about a dozen children reached India

Map 1: Polish people scattered across the USSR

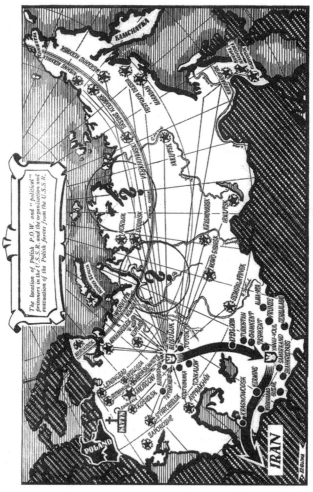

Source: W Anders, *An Army in Exile*, London, 1949, pp. 56–57. Courtesy of The Battery Press Inc.

with the group of orphans, only to be removed to Palestine in the following weeks, as evident from Zygmunt Mandels documents reproduced in Appendix 14.

The thesis, from which this work is prepared, began with building up the fragments of information collected from varied sources—reminiscences and personal memorabilia of the last remaining aging survivors or their descendents, some declassified archival documents from archives across the world and incomplete details from several books. An authoritative work has to be awaited still, as vaults in several countries are yet to disgorge their contents.

India, though not sovereign at the time and not at all prosperous, became the first country in the world to accept and offer war-duration domicile at her own cost to the hapless Polish population rendered homeless and subsequently stateless by the events of the world's worst war till date. In 1942, the end of the War was nowhere in sight and the first batch of 500 children were to be maintained from charitable funds to be raised in India. The rest, as they say, is history and this work attempts to chronicle it.

In chronicling this study, the primary sources used are: archival files in National Archives of India, New Delhi; The British Library, London, formerly the India Office Library; British National Archives, Kew, formerly Public Records Office; The Polish Institute and General Sikorski Museum, Kensington, London; and The New Archives, Warsaw. Oral history technique has been used for interviews with several survivors in London and Warsaw, mostly recorded on videotape and with those in the USA, Canada and Australia over extensive e-mails.

The secondary sources used are published books and articles obtained from auction sites, borrowed from personal collections and biographies sent often by the authors themselves or people mentioned in those works. The Association of Poles in India (API), Warsaw and London chapter, gifted two limited edition books, *Exiled Children* and *Polish Schooling in War-time Exile*, published by the Photographic Archives of Poland, to the author, respectively. A complete list of sources is given as Bibliography.

The wonderful new tool of communication—the Internet—has greatly facilitated this study. A search on the Internet yielded a starting point, from where, by reference, one by one, the survivors were contacted. Most testimonies are gathered from people who are comfortable with written English and Internet technologies. There are many people who could not be contacted and testimonies obtained due to their lack of either skill. This left out a large group in Poland and possibly several others in other parts of the world. All communication for this study was carried out in English, thus including only bilingual Polish survivors. Official communication between the Government of Poland and Her Majesty's Government was conducted in English, as is borne out by the availability of archival files. Internal communication between the Polish government-in-exile and its consulates in Kuibyshev, Tehran and Bombay (Mumbai) could not be benefitted from as they are in Polish. Some informal translations were obtained with the help of the Embassy of Poland in New Delhi.

A few crtical turn of events have made this work possible. First was the acceptance as a member into the Kresy–Siberia discussion forum by the moderator Stefan Wisnioski and his introducing me to Mr Tadeusz Dobrostanski, based in Melbourne, Australia. Dobrostanski had spent his childhood in Balachadi along with his older brother Jerzy and mother Janina Dobrostanska, who was one of the guardians. He shared his fabulous collection of pictures from the period and in turn introduced me to his childhood friend from Balachadi, Franek Herzog, based in Connecticut, USA. Herzog's diary is the 'voice of the witness' of this history and forms an inherent part of this work. Both of them introduced me to Wieslaw Stypula and Roman Gutowski in Warsaw, Poland when I was going there to research the work. Gutowski, in turn, escorted me personally to meet Reverend Z Peszkovski, the last surviving adult from the period. Barbara Charuba introduced me to Stefan Klosowski when he was making his 'pilgrimage trip' to India. The president and secretary of the API 1942–48, Mr Jan Siedlecki and Mrs Wieslawa Kelszko respectively, introduced me to Daniela Szydlo and Marian Raba, all of who added to the dimensions of this work.

Peszkovski had narrowly missed being executed in Katyn, had joined Anders' Army upon its formation and later found himself in India as Scoutmaster for the young boys in the Polish camps of India. He said he had had the opportunity to meet Mahatma Gandhi during one of the latter's visits to Panchgani and was deeply influenced by him. He took the path of non-violent struggle against the communist structure imposed on Poland after the War.[16] He became a man of religion and philosophy and went into the folds of the Church after demobilisation and kept the struggle up for the cause of his brother officers in Katyn (one of who was Lieutenant Colonel Franciszek Herzog, the late father of Franek Herzog), thus linking India to that event, too.

This history has become the cornerstone of bilateral relations between India and Poland. *Tulacze Dzieci* was the official gift of the Government of Poland to the President of India and Queen of England during their respective official visits to Poland.[17] A school named after His Highness Maharaja Jam Saheb Digvijaysinghji of Jamnagar is one of the better private schools in Warsaw since 1995. 'The students of this school will be the custodians of this valuable history,' noted Professor MK Byrski, Dean of Department of Indology, University of Warsaw, and former Ambassador to India.[18]

NOTES AND REFERENCES

1. Benjamin B Fischer, 'The Katyn Controversy: Stalin's Killing Field', Studies in Intelligence, https://www.cia.gov/library/center-for-the-study-of-intelligence/csi-publications/csi-studies/studies/winter99-00/art6.html. Retrieved on 10 December 2005.
2. Programme Directive No. 19, http://www.bbc.co.uk/archive/ussr/6717.shtml. Retrieved on 1 October 2010.
3. Laurence Rees, http://news.bbc.co.uk/2/hi/uk_news/magazine/7719633.stm. Retrieved on 30 September 2010.
4. Peter Novick, The Holocaust in American Life (US: Houghton Mifflin Co., 1999).
5. Ibid., 187.
6. Ibid., 188.
7. Comment in the visitor's book on documentary film A Forgotten Odyssey, screened in London in 2001. Produced and directed by Jagna Wright and Aneta Naczynska, London.
8. W Anders, An Army in Exile (London: Macmillan, 1949), 71.
9. N Davies, Heart of Europe (London: Oxford University Press, 1984), 67.
10. A Applebaum, Gulag (New York: Macmillan, 2003), xxxiii.
11. Ibid., xxii.
12. Ibid.
13. R Umiastowski, Poland, Russia and Great Britain 1941–45—A Study of Evidence (London: Hollis & Carter, 1946), 48.
14. W Anders, An Army in Exile, 110.
15. Ibid., 112.
16. Videotaped interview to author, Warsaw, March 2004.
17. Fundacja Archiwum Fotograficzne, Polish Schooling in War-time Exile (Warsaw: Fundacja Archiwum Fotograficzne, 2004), 17.
18. Personal interview to author, Warsaw, March 2004, reiterated in New Delhi, September 2005, when he was visiting Professor of Sanskrit at Jawaharlal Nehru University, New Delhi.

A Brief Historical Background

Poland has, at various times, been described as the heart of Europe due to its central location in Europe and its tragic history which have had a bearing on most or all of Europe. According to Norman Davies, Poland was scientifically and culturally a vibrant country that was granted the Catholic symbol of the Sacred Heart of Jesus by the Vatican in 1765. Amongst the most famous Poles, three names stand out—Nicolas Copernicus (1473–1543), Jan Kochanowski (1530–84), the poet to whom the senior branch of Slavonic literature can be attributed and Jan Zamoyski (1542–1605), chancellor and the chief architect of Poland's 'noble democracy'. The country shows a long tradition of democracy and religious tolerance, embodied even in its early constitutions. Catholics, Orthodox, Armenians, Jewish and Muslims coexisted peacefully in Poland since at least 1573 by the passing of the epoch-making Statute of General Tolerance promulgated by the Confederation of Warsaw while the rest of the continent was torn by Wars of Religion.

Poland's borders have been changing in different periods of history and the country has been wiped off the map on several occasions. It has been a battleground and its territory and lands divided between the kingdoms of Germany, Russia and Austria several times. Poland had been partitioned by its powerful neighbours from 1795 to 1807, 1874 to 1918 and again from 1939 to 1945.

The country had emerged after an oblivion of 123 years after the Great War in 1920. Yet, 19 years later, it vanished from the map again, wiped out under the dual occupation of Germany and Russia and re-emerged after the Second World War with a different set of boundaries (see Map 2). Few nations in the last 300 years have seen more military action than the Poles. In the 18th century, as in the 20th century, Polish lands regularly provided the arena for Europe's wars on 'the Eastern Front'. In the 19th

Map 2: Poland's changing territory

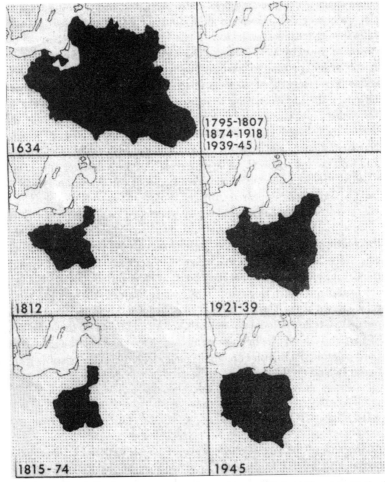

1634

1795-1807
1874-1918
1939-45

1812

1921-39

1815-74

1945

Source: N Davies, *Heart of Europe—A Short History of Poland* (London: Oxford University Press, 1984), 354.

century, they supplied the armies of the German, French, Austrian and Russian empires with countless officers, volunteers and conscripts.

Though separated into three parts just before the Great War, or the First World War as we now know it, Poland preserved her idea of a national unity. She remained, wrote Maitland, 'three undigested fragments in three stomachs'.[1] The Poles, under Austrian and Prussian rule, had some chance of expressing their nationality, but not those under Russian rule. Siberia had welcomed its influx of Polish deportees periodically throughout history. In July–August 1914, when Europe entered the ordeal of the Great War, Poland did not exist in any practical sense. It did not exist on any map of Europe. Twenty or thirty million people, who called themselves Poles, lived as subjects of the Russian Tsar, the German Kaiser or the Emperor King of Austria. There was no one alive at that time who could remember the time when Poland had been an independent state. Warsaw and Wilno (Vilna) were provincial cities of Russia; Danzig (Gdansk) and Posen (Poznan) were flourishing cities of Prussia and Krakow and L'wow (Lemberg) were part of the Austrian Empire. The 'Polish Question', one of the recurrent bones of contention in 19th century, had all but disappeared from the diplomatic agenda. Yet, the Great War transformed the map of Europe and rescued Poland from oblivion.

After the War ended, Poland obtained some territories to the west and the south, but her boundary to the east was always a matter of debate. The boundaries in the past had never been defined by ethnicity, though the Great Powers had studied ethnic data at Paris and produced a boundary for Poland which represented the eastern limit of purely Polish territory. Known as the 'Curzon Line', it stretched roughly from Punsk, in the north, to Grodow-Vlodava, north of Kholm and, thence, to the boundary of Eastern Galicia. The line was named such as it had been suggested by Lord Curzon, the British Foreign Secretary in 1919, as the possible frontier of Poland on the east.

The Second Republic

At the end of the Great War, a wave of Polish nationalism swept the region and Josef Pilsudski, the front runner of the movement, who had been a German prisoner in Magdeburg Castle, was released and helped to be installed as the Premier of the newborn state ahead of an allied takeover of Poland. The Republic, which Pilsudski took control of on 11 November 1918, had no frontiers, no established territory, no government, no constitution and no international recognition. Most Poles agreed that it was just a reincarnation of the old Republic which had been destroyed at the end of the 18th century. For this reason, it is now referred to in Polish history as the 'Second Republic'.[2] Six border wars were fought in three years against Germany (in Posnia and Silesia),

Czechoslovakia, Lithuania, western Ukraine and Soviet Russia (1919–20). The Treaty of Riga of 18 March 1921 divided the borders between Poland and the Soviet Republic. In fact, the Treaty of Riga completed Poland's territorial struggle and established diplomatic relations on a note of satisfaction. With this, she acquired a population and territory about double of what was recommended by the 'Curzon Line'. There were some 27 million people, including White Russians, Ruthenians, Ukrainians and Lithuanians. The Red Army had suffered the only unredeemed defeat in its distinguished history.

Subsequently, the war veterans were settled in these newly acquired eastern borderlands with grants of land. The region was called 'Kresy' or eastern borderlands and it was assumed that those who had helped to regain it for Poland would be the most conscientious in safeguarding the territorial interests too.

Pilsudski presided over the constitutional period from 1921 and survived a coup in May 1926. Colonel Walery Slawek became the prime minister and Colonel Josef Beck the foreign minister in 1932. Ignacy Paderewski, the concert pianist, came to Warsaw to serve as the first parliamentary prime minister. Marshal Pilsudski retained two key posts himself— Inspector-General of the Armed Forces and Minister of War.

The economy was stable and Polish cultural life saw an explosion of literary and artistic talent. There was no enforced ideology. Pilsudski was the object of much adulation and affection. Faced with the rise of Stalinist Russia on one border and Nazi Germany on the other, he formulated the 'Doctrine of Two Enemies'. Poland was to uphold proper relations with both neighbours, but to ally with neither. To this end, he had signed two ten-year pacts of non-aggression—one with the USSR on 25 January 1932 and its sequel with Nazi Germany on 26 January 1934. Poland's predicament in the late 1930s was far from enviable. A location between Hitler and Stalin provided the least comfortable location on the globe. To combine with one or the other was equally distasteful and equally dangerous.

The Molotov-Ribbentrop Pact

When Molotov replaced Litinov in May as the new Soviet foreign minister, all the preconditions of a Nazi-Soviet Pact had been brought into place. With a Franco-British military mission still nominally negotiating an Anglo-Franco-Russian Treaty in Moscow, the Soviets were already negotiating with Berlin. In July, Ribbentrop, the German Foreign Minister, let it be known in the Kremlin that there were no problem matters that could not be amicably solved.

The Nazi–Soviet trade talks in July 1939 changed gears. It emerged that the Germans had designs on Western Poland and, in due course, on Western Europe and Scandinavia. The Soviets had designs on Eastern Poland, the Baltic States and Bressabaria. A public pact of non-aggression between Nazi Germany and the Soviet Union was signed in Moscow by Ribbentrop and Molotov on 23 August 1939. A secret protocol defined the territorial arrangements, including the prospective partition of Poland along the rivers Narew, Vistula and San. Notwithstanding the renewal of the British Guarantee, Hitler was free to launch the attacks on Poland with impunity. He ordered the *Wehrmacht* to march within the week. It marched on 1 September 1939. Hitler justified his act by alleging that Poland had already mobilised and had committed hostile acts against Germany, including the persecution of Germans in Poland.

The outbreak of the War was made possible by the secret protocol of the Non-Aggression Pact between the Nazi Reich and the Soviet Union, signed in Moscow by Ribbentrop and Molotov on 23 August 1939, also known as the Molotov-Ribbentrop Pact. By this protocol, the two contracting parties envisaged a joint attack on Poland and the Baltic states and the division of the territory between themselves. According to Norman Davies, it is doubtful if without the assurance of Soviet collusion, the *Wehrmacht* could have risked a unilateral attack on Poland.

The first phase of the War began with the invasion of Poland and ended with the fall of France. It began without declaration or formality with the attack by the German Air Force on 1 September 1939 on Polish military targets, airfields, military bases, training centres and railway junctions and the march of the German Army on the same day. At the dawn of 17 September, in accordance with the secret protocol of 23 August, Soviet troops crossed the eastern frontier of Poland and took up positions already agreed with Germany. The remaining Polish forces were trapped and compelled to surrender either to the Soviets or to the Germans.

The September campaign in Poland was fierce, but brief. Isolated from the direct assistance of their French and British allies, surrounded on three sides by German forces in East Prussia and Slovakia as well as on the western frontier and vastly outmatched in manpower and equipment, the Polish Army had little hope of victory. Also threatened, as it proved, by the Soviet Red Army in the east, it had little chance of even protracted resistance.

In many instances, they fought with heroism till they were vastly outnumbered and then had to start retreating. The Poles inflicted over 50,000 casualties on the *Wehrmacht* and were still fighting hard when the entry of the Soviets sealed their fate. In September, the Western Allies had not fired a single shot in Poland's defence. The last Polish unit in the field capitulated at Kock on 6 October 1939. The Second Republic was dead within one quarter of a century after 1914.

Thus, the whole of Poland passed under the occupation of Nazi and Soviet forces. The Polish government and High Command took refuge in Romania and on 30 September 1939, a new government was constituted abroad under General Sikorski, first in France and later in England. On the western side of the Nazi–Soviet demarcation line along the Bug and the San, the Germans established a 'General Government' with its headquarters in Kracow. Many districts of pre-War Poland, including Suwalki, West Prussia, Wielkopolska and Upper Silesia, were directly incorporated into the Reich. On the eastern side of the demarcation line, in 'western Byelorussia' and 'western Ukraine', the Soviet authorities staged some kind of a plebiscite to demarcate the people's wish for annexation into the USSR. The district of Wilno (Vilnius) was generously handed to Lithuania. Poland was neatly partitioned. In the opinion of its conquerors, so ably expressed by the Soviet Foreign Commissar, Molotov, by that time it had ceased to exist. The arrangements were crowned by the German-Soviet Treaty of Friendship of 28 September 1939, which also provided for the joint action against the expected Polish resistance. During this era of close Nazi–Soviet collaboration, both partners pursued similar policies towards their Polish charges. Both sides were guilty of atrocities. The Germans shot 20,000 civilian hostages in Bydgoszcz alone and burned synagogues. The Soviets massacred prisoners in the gaol of Vinnitsa. Both sides subjected the population to police screening for undesirability. The Gestapo followed racial guidelines, consigning some two million Polish Jews to closed *reservaten* or ghettoes and dividing the Aryan population into *Reichdeutch* (German citizens born in the Reich), *Volksdeutch* (German nationals) and *Nichtdeusch* (everyone else). In the Extraordinary Pacification Campaign (*Abaktion*) of 1940, some 15,000 Polish priests, teachers and political leaders were transported to Dachau or shot in the Palmiry Forest. The first experiments were made in euthanasia, in the selection of children for racial breeding, in slave labour schemes and in gas chambers.

The Narodnyi Kommissariat Vnutrennikh Del (NKVD or People's Commissariat for Internal Affairs), a forerunner of the Komitet Gosudarstvennoy Bezopasnosty (KGB), followed guidelines based on their own idea of class analysis, assigning some two million people associated with the professions or with pre-War state employment to forcible deportation. Both sides arrested many thousands of political prisoners and when convenient, exchanged them. The Gestapo received German 'criminals' and Jewish agitators in return for communists and Ukrainians. Both sides were engaged in trade—Russian oil flowing into Germany through Poland in support of the invasion of France and the Battle of Britain. Both sides were happy to make frontier adjustments, such as the Soviet purchase of Suwalki, as they were reluctant to interfere in each other's military adventures.

Hitler did not interfere in Stalin's attacks on Finland, the Baltic states and Romania. Stalin did not intervene in Hitler's conquest of Denmark, Norway, Holland, Belgium, Luxembourg and France. Each side, in massive propaganda campaigns, praised the achievements of the other. Each side was working with equal vigour for the reduction of the Poles to the condition of a leaderless, friendless nation.

Indeed, in the light of the subsequent reversal of policy, Norman Davies argues that at this stage, the Soviet terror in many ways exceeded that of the Nazis. The Stalinist regime had a head start on the Nazis in the techniques and logistics of terror, having upped the necessary machinery during the recent purges in its own country. At a time when the Germans were still refining their preparations for Auschwitz or Treblinka, the Soviets could accommodate a few million Polish and west Ukrainian additions to the population of their 'Gulag archipelago' with ease. Although they preferred to condemn their victims to a long slow death from cold and starvation—in contrast to the Nazi method of summary murder—who is to say which was the more humane? The effect was much the same. Of the estimated two million Polish civilians deported to Arctic Russia, Siberia and Kazakhstan in the terrible railway convoys of 1939–40, at least one half were dead within a year of their arrest.[3] The Soviet crimes of this vintage are symbolised by the fearful name of Katyn—a name which clearly arouses as much guilt in the Soviet Union as revulsion in the outside world.

Katyn

Katyn is the place where 4,200 Polish officers from the Kozielsk camp were killed in Stalin's way. They called it special action; by some kind of law, it was not necessary to have any normal procedure for sentence of death but only an order, 'Kill them', was enough.

It is so unbelievable as it was the worst thing that could happen in the world. This place is testimony that it is possible to kill people without even trying to show why or for what reason. This was one of Stalin's new style of killing people—called Katyn. It is the name of the place where they were killed and we didn't know whether there was only one Katyn or more [such summary executions]. Altogether about 15000 people were killed and being a survivor of that horror, everybody was asking me for as many details. It was the worst possible thing but since I was a Polish officer, they believed whatever I was telling them, however terrible.

—Lieutenant Z Peszkovski, Warsaw, 2004[4]

During the Nazi–Soviet partition of Poland in 1939, more than 180,000 Polish prisoners of war (POWs) fell into the hands of the Red Army. Ordinary soldiers were sent to labour camps and officers were separated and sent to three special camps—Kozielsk (near Smolensk), Starobielsk (near Kharkov) and Ostashkov (Kalinin district). They numbered 15,000 in all and included a large number of reservists, as well as customs officers, police, prison guards and military police. All three camps were under the NKVD control, and all prisoners were subjected to detailed interrogation[5] and Soviet propaganda. In the course of April and early May 1940, convoys of prisoners under the NKVD guard left the three camps for unknown destinations. Daily lists of those who were to travel were telephoned from the NKVD in Moscow. Those leaving Kozelsk travelled through Smolensk and were unloaded at a small town called Gniezdovo.

Once Polish–Soviet diplomatic relations were re-established in July 1941, the Polish authorities immediately began searching for officers to staff the new Polish units being formed in the USSR (Anders' Army). Despite the personal intervention of General Sikorski, the Soviet authorities denied any knowledge of the missing officers, claiming that they had all been released under the general amnesty extended to Poles. On 2 December 1941, during the meeting between Sikorski and Stalin, Stalin even suggested that the prisoners may have escaped to Manchuria.[6]

In April 1943, the Germans released the news that they had discovered a number of mass graves in the Katyn forest near Smolensk, which they believed to be those of Polish officers murdered by the NKVD. They formed just one part of a much larger group of over 15,000 Polish officers—prisoners, professionals and reservists—who had disappeared from Soviet captivity in the spring of 1940 and whose fate was otherwise unknown. Almost all of them were educated professionals—doctors, civil servants, teachers, etc. Each one had his hands wired behind his back and a bullet in the base of his skull. It was later confirmed that the 4,400 bodies were those of prisoners from the Kozelsk camp.[7]

The Nazis announced that the crime had been committed by the Soviets and the Soviets the converse. Forensic examination of the bodies proved that they had been in the ground for about three years, a period when the region was under Soviet control. The discovery of the graves led to dramatic repercussions in the diplomatic field. When the Polish government in London approached the International Red Cross in Geneva with the suggestion that an international commission examine the graves, the Soviet government broke off diplomatic relations with the Poles. In July 1946, those conducting the Nuremberg trials, pointedly refused to apportion blame for the Katyn massacre, despite Soviet attempts to portray it as yet one more Nazi atrocity.

In April 1990, on the 50th anniversary of the date it was committed, an official Soviet announcement confirmed that the NKVD had been responsible. The prisoners from the three camps had been handed over to the NKVD boards in Smolensk, Kharkov and Kalinin for execution. In the summer of 1990, two further mass graves were found at Kharkov and Miednoye (near Kalinin). Just over two years later, in October 1992, the Russian President, Boris Yeltsin, handed over documents to the Polish authorities which proved beyond doubt that the crime had been carried out under the direct orders of Stalin and the Soviet Politburo.[8]

Operation Barbarossa

Operation Barbarossa, Hitler's attack on the Soviet Union, which was launched from the *Wehrmacht*'s position in Poland on 22 June 1941, ended the Nazi-Soviet Pact in one mighty treacherous blow. It drove the Soviets from eastern Poland within two weeks and extended the Nazi realm into the depths of the Soviet Union. For the next two years, the Nazi grip on Eastern Europe was complete, and even then, was slow to crumble. The German's New Order in Poland could be constructed without serious disturbance. The General Government, now enlarged to include the District of Galicia with the city of Lemberg (L'wow), was to serve as the principal laboratory for the Nazi's ambitious social experiments. According to the outlines of the Generalplan-Ost, the Nazis aimed to redistribute the entire population between the Oder and the Dnieper. German settlers were to be introduced by the millions. The Poles were destined either for Germanisation, where suitable, or for expulsion beyond the Urals.

One encouraging change, from the Polish point of view, took place in the Soviet policy. Having worked with Hitler in the joint suppression of all things Polish, Stalin now turned to the Poles for a common front against Germany and proposed an alliance with Sikorski. Diplomatic relations were established on 30 July 1941, and a military convention was signed on 12 August of the same year.

The USSR stated its readiness to form a Polish Army in the Soviet Union to grant an amnesty to all Polish internees (for crimes never committed) and to annul the provisions of the Nazi-Soviet Pact regarding Poland. Pravda even announced that the western frontier of the USSR, as fixed in 1939 in conjunction with Hitler, was not necessarily final. Constant difficulties arose on every simple issue of Polish–Soviet relations, especially over arrangements for the Poles in Russia. No satisfactory explanation was forthcoming to queries about the 15,000 missing officers. But at the height of German arrogance in Poland, it was far preferable for the Poles to be pitted now against just one enemy instead of two.

Regrouping of Polish Army

The Polish government's military forces were scattered across the length and breadth of Eurasia. It took an immense feat of organisation to co-ordinate their activities and replenish the depleted cadres. In the initial period following the September debacle, the main concentration of some 85,000 men arrived in France from units gradually released from internment in Romania and Hungary. Sikorski's 'Polish Army in France' included two military divisions, the Podhale Rifle Brigade of General Bohusz-Szyszko, the Armoured Brigade of General Stanislaw Maczek and an Air Force Division of fighter squadrons. It served under French command at Narvik and in the French Campaign of May–June 1940. Another concentration, the 'Polish Army of Levant' consisting principally of General Kopanski's Autonomous Carpathian Brigade, had assembled in French Syria. The remnants of the Polish Navy, three destroyers and two submarines, which had escaped from the Baltic with incredible ingenuity with the Merchant Marine, were already in British ports. The fall of France caused near catastrophe. Most of the Polish units in France were taken into German captivity, but some crossed into neutral Switzerland or Spain, and approximately one-third succeeded in extricating themselves by a hair-raising evacuation to Great Britain. The Polish Air Force Division escaped via North Africa. Kopanski's Brigade defied its French superiors and marched from Syria into British Palestine.

All the survivors of the Polish Armed Forces were now under British command. Churchill, Sikorski and Charles de Gaulle shared the distinction of being the only Allied leaders who 'fought on'. Yet, they all needed a long period of recuperation, which the soldiers were granted but the airmen and sailors were not. In the Battle of Britain in the autumn of 1940, Polish fighter pilots eventually made up 20 per cent of the Royal Air Force's (RAF) strength. Two exclusively Polish Squadrons—302 (*Poznan*) and 303 (*Kosciuszko*)—alone accounted for 109 Luftwaffe 'kills' (12 per cent of the total). Their 'loss-kill ratio' of 1:9 was unsurpassed. The Polish Navy was sent off immediately on Atlantic patrol. The Polish code breakers broke the Enigma Code that went on to decrypt the intercepted German messages, which eventually led to the rout of the German forces.

The Army was rebuilt more slowly. In 1941, the Polish–Soviet military convention permitted the formation of the 'Polish Army in Russia' under General Wladyslaw Anders. This decision launched one of the epic odysseys of modern warfare. Polish refugees and deportees who had withstood the rigours of Stalin's Arctic camps or of Siberian exile and the famine of Kazakhstan drifted into the collecting centres at Buzluk on the Volga and at Totskoie and Tatistchev. The camps were a bunch of tents pitched in a forest where the men had no boots or shirts. During his first visit to the Totskoie camp, Anders found 17,000 emaciated soldiers covered with ulcers resulting from semi-starvation and dressed in the tattered relics of old Polish uniforms.[9] He then insisted that the camps be moved to the warmer regions in south USSR, where they could be supported logistically by the British authorities from Persia.

The Polish troops collection centres moved to Yangi-Yul in Uzbekistan and Polish deportees continued reaching there, using all modes of transport available, but mostly on foot. They often marked their route with their own graves. In some cases, the transport was not allowed to stop at the Polish Army collection centres and was sent further south on the pretext that they should await the arrival of the Polish troops there. The deportees were sent by rail to Turkestan and from there by boat along the Amu Darya for forced labour.

Whole convoys were forced to leave their trains and were left stranded on the Steppes without any supplies. The Soviet authorities were taking the line that once the Poles had been liberated from prison or labour camps, there was no further obligation on the part of the Soviet authorities to provide for them.[10] There was no possibility of buying food in the USSR, and anyone deprived of rations simply starved to death. Sometimes it was possible to barter some clothes for food, but after two years in captivity, few possessed any clothing suitable for exchange.

Other collection centres were organised at Guzar and Kermine, which attempted to house, feed and extend medical help to the tens of thousands of Polish deportees reaching the collection centres. Over a million people of value to the nation had been drained from Poland by the Soviets without prejudice to their racial origin, class or religion. Poles, Ukrainians, White Ruthenians, Lithuanians, Jews, landowners, farm-hands, factory owners and workers, officers and other ranks, judges, tradesmen, policemen, Roman Catholic priests and Protestant ministers and Rabbis were all torn away from their homes, absorbed by the monstrous machine of the NKVD and sent to the Soviet prisons and camps. Their deportation was followed by the forcible removal of their wives and families, old people and children, thereby 'beheading' the community, making it an inert and amorphous mass of humanity.[11]

The death rate at the makeshift hospitals in Guzar and Kermine camps were very high on account of exhaustion, typhus and dysentery. There was a hopeless inadequacy of food, medicines, accommodation, linen or even soap, yet the doctors toiled on, rising many times over their duty and capabilities. It must also be mentioned here that there was an acute anti-Semitism in the USSR. The Bolsheviks did not allow any formerly Jewish member to rise to a high position within the party. All Ukrainians, White Ruthenians and Jews were blocked from joining Anders' Army in formation by not being allowed to leave the camps. 'What is the case of the White Ruthenians, Ukrainians and Jews to you? You want only Poles', asked Stalin to General Sikorski and Anders during one of their discussions[12] about the troops. While Sikorski maintained that they were an integral part of Polish society before 1939, Stalin insisted that they had taken part in plebiscites and had become Soviet citizens.[13] Everything—food, uniform, weapons and all military equipment—was in short supply in the Soviet Union. In March 1942, after endless obstructions by the Soviet authorities, 77,200 military and 37,300 civilians, including 15,000 children, crossed from Krasnovodsk on the Caspian Sea to Pahlevi in British-controlled Persia. The troops and civilians were those who bore allegiance to the Polish State without prejudice to their denomination. There were several Jewish men in the Army and children in the orphanages who were later moved to Palestine by the JRA from the various centres for the Polish deportees in Persia and India.

By 1941, the USSR had joined the Grand Alliance, and the presence of a large number of people to testify about the harrowing conditions in the USSR became an embarrassment to the British, thus, this side of the war history remained classified till the last decade of the 20th century.

Indian Princely States

A series of events had developed in India, geographically distant and virtually unrelated to Poland, to come together in this unparalleled historical episode. Most of India had slipped under the British rule by 1857, yet there were several Princely States subservient to the British Crown, with severely curtailed powers, who provided a haven for Polish people affected by the destruction that was the Second World War. The only thing common between the Poles and India at that time was Britain. While Britain had declared the famous Guarantee of Poland in 1939, she was struggling to retain Ireland, India and Palestine for the Crown. With each war in Europe, Britain's grip on India was loosening and Indian nationalism was asserting itself more and more, seeking the departure of the British.

Though the Indian rulers had signed away most of their independence vide the peace treaties concluded with the British, by the 20th century they began rallying together in various ways to gain back some of their lost independence, sometimes in conjunction and at other times in opposition to the nascent Nationalist Movement. One such state was Nawanagar, which had been catapulted to a fairly important position in the relatively newly formed Chamber of Princes, a body of the Princely States for their negotiations with the British overlords.

Princely India and the First World War (1914–18)

The policy of laissez-faire with the Indian Princely States was launched on 1 November 1909, with a speech by Lord Minto at Udaipur. During the First World War, the princes had the resources and expertise to make a valuable imperial contribution not only at the all-India level but also at the international level. Some dozen regiments of the State's Imperial Service Troops saw service in the Middle East and France, while the Maharajas of Bikaner, Nawanagar and Idar; the Raja of Akalkot and the Nawabs of Loharu and Sachin all spent time at the battlefront (see Map 3 for India's political landscape).

Several Princely States contributed money and munitions generously. Tiny Sangli donated ₹75,000 directly to war funds and invested ₹0.5 million in war bonds; Nawanagar contributed the equivalent of half a year's revenue from the public fisc and the Jam Saheb another £21,000

Map 3: India: Political, 1858–1947

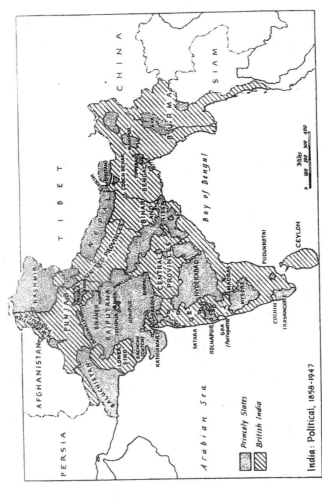

India: Political, 1858–1947

Source: L James 'Raj: The Making & Unmaking of British India', in Ian Copland (ed.), *The Princes of India in the Endgame of Empire 1917–47* (London: Cambridge University Press, 1997), 329.

out of his own pocket; the ruler of Bikaner in 1916 gave the equivalent of his 'entire Privy Purse allowance for one year' while the ruler of Rewa offered his entire hoard of jewels. At the same time, the rulers helped out on the propaganda front, lending their names to recruitment drives and weighing in on the governments' side against elements opposed to war on ideological grounds. Ganga Singh of Bikaner felt that their views should be heard not only in paramountcy issues but to be treated 'as *somebodies* in the ... Indian Empire'.[14] He also felt that India was ripe for 'furthur political ... advance'. Early drafts of the princely programme advocated annual conferences at Delhi, but later versions went well beyond this to advocate the setting up of permanent machinery for the exchange of opinions and ideas between the Princely States and British India. Sayaji Rao of Baroda and Ranjitsinghji of Nawanagar were quite vocal in pressing for such changes while the Secretary of State, Austen Chamberlain, gave the idea of regular conferences a cool reception. Already, he averred, the rulers were exhibiting a dangerous 'tendency to meddle with the affairs of British India ... collected at Simla', and they could easily end up becoming 'tools of Opposition'.[15] Pressed, he sanctioned a further conference in 1917.

The Montagu Declaration of August 1917 pledged that, henceforth, British policy in India would be directed at 'the gradual development of self-governing institutions';[16] further, it stated that Montagu himself would visit India that winter to draw up, in concert with the Viceroy and in consultation with interested parties representing a broad cross section of Indian political life, concrete recommendations for a limited devolution of power.[17]

An ad hoc 'committee of four' Princely States consisting of Ganga Singh of Bikaner, Ranjitsinghji of Nawanagar, Bhupinder Singh of Patiala and Jey Singh of Alwar was constituted to draft a common set of proposals to put before Chamberlain. Montagu did not disappoint. Five months later, the princes' main demands were included in the joint recommendations on constitutional reforms forwarded by Montagu and Chelmsford to the British government. The Chamber of Princes (COP) was launched with glittering ceremony at the Red Fort on 9–10 February 1921. It was to have 120 seats and advise the Viceroy on all 'questions affecting Indian States generally or which are of concern either to the Empire as a whole or to British India and the States in common'.[18] Maharaja Ganga Singh of Bikaner was the founder chancellor of the COP in 1921 and continued till 1926. He was a war hero and signatory to the Treaty of Versailles. Ranjitsinghji of Nawanagar was an active member of the COP and often filled in for the ailing Ganga Singh of Bikaner. He even represented the COP during the League of Nations meetings at Geneva.

In 1938, Jam Saheb Digvijaysinghji of Nawanagar, successor to Jam Saheb Ranjitsinghji, took over the chancellorship of the COP from Maharaja Bhupinder Singh of Patiala, on the latter's demise. He was 42 years old and had been on the throne of Nawanagar for only five years and in the Standing Committee for barely two. Most people thought he lacked sufficient political experience, but he proved to be a surprise. He was not only warm and decent like Ranjitsinghji before him but also had a gift for politics, was energetic and a good public speaker; he had a healthy streak of political realism or as Leo Amery, Secretary of State for India, put it, he had 'practical common sense'.[19]

India and the Second World War

War broke out in Europe in September 1939 and spread quickly. On 3 September 1939, Australia, India and New Zealand, being British colonies, also declared war on Germany. Jam Saheb Digvijaysinghji was a member of the Imperial War Council (IWC), by virtue of his position as the chancellor of the COP in India. He had served in the Army during the War of 1914–18. In fact, as the chancellor of COP and a member of the IWC, he was following the footsteps of his predecessor Ranjitsinghji who had also been the representative of the COP to the League of Nations Conference in Geneva. It is believed by the Polish people that Digvijaysinghji, who was one of the nephews and contenders for the throne of Nawanagar at the time, was a frequent visitor to Ranjit's estate in Geneva and had met Dr Ignacy Padrewski, the famous pianist, there. Padrewski later became the first prime minister of newly born Poland after the First World War at the behest of Marshall Pilsudski.

The outbreak of the War also allowed the princes to dramatise their loyalty to the Crown. Travancore built at its own expense a patrol boat for the Indian Navy; Bhopal spent its entire stock of US securities on the purchase of American fighter planes; Jodhpur contributed money for a Halifax bomber; Kashmir donated 18 field ambulances; Hyderabad, not to be left behind in any way, paid for three squadrons of war planes. Altogether, the cost of war materials provided by the states down to 1945 exceeded 5 million pounds.[20] In addition, the states made numerous direct grants of cash and gave generously of their land, buildings and workforces for war purposes: Mysore handed over all state-owned

buildings in Bangalore for the use of the Army. Nawanagar started a torpedo training school. Gwalior converted its Hattersley Mills in Bombay
to the webbing for parachutes and Bikaner built a military hospital. By
1945, Hyderabad had spent ₹52.7 million on war-related projects and
Bhopal over ₹20 million.

Again, the *darbar*s made an important indirect contribution to the
war effort by actively promoting it among their subjects. Considerable
official pressure—up to and including threats of reprisals—was applied
to induce subjects to part with cash.[21] By the end of 1944, over 300,000
men from 59 states had signed up for military service and 15,000 more for
war-related jobs in industry—a higher per capita response than any of the
provinces of British India except for Punjab—while some ₹180 million
had been contributed by the people from the states in subscription to
government war bonds and securities and donations to the Viceroy's War
Purposes Fund—again a result that put British India to shame.[22]

By 1940, India had become a transit point for the Jews escaping Nazi
persecution in German-occupied Poland and other regions. The Polish
Consulate in Bombay, through the Polish Relief Committee and the JRA,
extended succour to the Polish escapees reaching India.

It is believed by Jam Saheb Digvijaysinghji's children, Jam Saheb
Shatrushalayasinghji and Princess Hershad Kumari, that it was during
one of the IWC meetings that he met Dr Ignacy Padrewski, the former
Polish Prime Minister, who was also attending the meeting as a Special
Invitee. Padrewski appraised the British government about the condition
of the Polish civilian population in the USSR and the urgent need to
evacuate them. General Wladyslaw Anders, commander of the Polish
Army being formed in the USSR, and Professor Stanislaw Kot, Polish
ambassador to Kuibyshev (wartime capital of the USSR), continually
pressed the government-in-exile. While the British remained in dilemma
on the matter, Digvijaysinghji, in the typical *darbari* style, offered to host
the orphaned Polish children in his state.

> I can't tell you with certainty, but what we were told was that my father
> used to know some of the Polish people, especially one their most famous
> pianists, when he used to spend time at Ranji's chateau in Switzerland as
> a boy. During the lunch breaks of one of the IWC meetings in London, he
> heard the details about the circumstances of the Polish children—that they
> had nowhere to go, no country was willing to receive them etc. and offered .
> to take on their responsibility. It apparently upset the British Government
> because they were not quite in tune with this offer. So, he said that he was
> not asking them but inviting them to Nawanagar as his guests. Finally after

a lot of correspondence etc., which I learnt later from Col. Clarke, that it was finally said that 'you can receive them and we cannot agree about them being looked after by the State'. He said, 'they will be my personal guests'. They were actually paid for from his allowance or whatever it was called in those days but not from the State Treasury.

—Hershad Kumariji, daughter of late His Highness
Jam Saheb of Nawanagar[23]

The Nawanagar offer was grabbed by the Polish. The Polish Ambassador to India, Eugeniusz Banasinski, moved quickly to have this scheme, called the 'Tashkent Scheme', approved by the Government of India (GOI) and arranged that six trucks taking relief supplies to the USSR would evacuate the children by a hitherto unused land route, setting to rest British concerns about stretching military supply lines further.

Evacuation of the Polish Army from the Soviet Union

As thousands of volunteers arrived at the Polish reporting stations in the USSR to join the Army, a huge number of civilians were also pouring in. Despite the general hunger, the military took up caring for the civilians, particularly the children. The estimated 75,000 children in various Polish centres in Russia needed instant help after the 'amnesty'. To create an adequate number of proper institutions would have required a huge outlay of money and an army of educators, neither of which was possible there under the circumstances. With much effort by the Polish Army and the Polish Embassy in Kuibyschev, 139 orphanages and nurseries had been established in which approximately 9,000 children found shelter. Those whose lives were most threatened were given preference. They were housed in wooden or clay huts or tents. There were no beds, no toilet facilities, no soap and no food or medicines. Their primitiveness bordered on utter poverty, yet these relief institutions, substituting for a home, carried on their assignments, attempting to save its occupants from hunger, offering some kind of roof over their heads and attempting to safeguard them from disease. Dysentery and typhus were rampant. Caring for these children, who were dying one by one of infectious diseases, hunger and the stress of orphanhood was a major concern for the Polish authorities. The testimony of Zofia Morawska, in charge of one such orphanage, is available on the Internet.

Once aware that the Polish Army was supporting a large number of
civilian population with their assigned rations, the Soviets, citing difficulty in feeding the Polish Army, cut the scale of their rations. The mu-
tual distrust between the Polish and the Soviets grew to the point that
the newly formed Polish Army was asked to leave the USSR. News of the
proposed evacuation precipitated a feverish stampede towards the south
from all the collective farms and factories, wherever the Poles were working. Even the Social Service officials began leaving their posts in order to
be included in the assigned quota. Fear of losing what was probably the
only chance of being evacuated overcame even the fear of new arrests,
with which the Soviets were likely to stem the tide of people southwards.
There was horrendous panic and disorganisation as there was no guarantee that they would reach the evacuation points in time. Finally, only
115,000 people, 77,200 military personnel and 37,300 civilians, including
15,000 orphans, could leave. The civilians were mostly military families.
General Wladyslaw Anders, under whose aegis the Polish Army in the
USSR had been formed, issued an order that the transports had to include as many children as possible, including the gravely ill, even if they
had to be brought to the trains carried in someone's arms.

General W Anders wrote in his autobiography:

> Soldiers had shared their poor rations with the civilians, who had gathered
> under the wing of the army for protection, knowing that they could only
> survive in that way. Hundreds and thousands of Poles had already perished
> in transit and reserve centers. I accordingly gave orders that any Pole who
> reported should be included in the military transport, and all nurseries
> and orphanages.[24]

Churchill was 'told about the disappearance of a large number of officers
and the urgent need of securing the evacuation of Polish children, for
they could not be expected to survive another winter. Churchill then said
he had given orders for the women and children to be received from the
USSR together with the troops'.[25] The evacuation took place through two
points—Ashkabad and Krasnovodsk—on the Soviet border to Meshed
and Pahlevi, respectively, in neighbouring Persia, where they were received by British, Indian and American troops who made all the arrangements of food, tented accommodation and onward transportation for
them. Persia was neither a British colony nor a theatre of war. She had
declared her neutrality to both the Axis and Allied forces at the beginning
of the War but was occupied by the British and the Soviet forces due to
her rich and vital oil resources.

NOTES AND REFERENCES

1. AJ Grant and H Temperley, *Europe in the Nineteenth and Twentieth Centuries 1789–1950* (London: Longman, 1980), 159.
2. N Davies, *Heart of Europe—A Short History of Poland* (London: Oxford University Press, 1984), 115.
3. Ibid., 67.
4. Quoted from a video recorded personal interview to author taken at Warsaw in March 2004.
5. Treatment, style of interrogation and summary trial described in detail in S Rawicz, *The Long Walk* (Connecticut: The Lyons Press, 1988).
6. W Anders, *An Army in Exile* (London: Macmillan, 1949), 85.
7. K Sword, *The Oxford Companion to WW II*, ed Dear and Foot (London: Oxford University Press, 1995), 508.
8. Ibid., 508.
9. W Anders, *An Army in Exile*, 63–64.
10. BNA, CAB/111/310, Interdepartmental Conference on Polish Relief held at the Foreign Office on 29 October.
11. W Anders, *An Army in Exile*, 65–66.
12. Ibid., 89.
13. Ibid., 89.
14. Ian Copland, *The Princes of India in the Endgame of Empire 1917–47* (London: Cambridge University Press, 1997), 35.
15. Chelmsford collection, 2, Chamberlain to Chelmsford, 24 November 1916, cited in Ian Copland, *The Princes of India*, 36.
16. Ibid.
17. Ibid., 37.
18. Constitution of the Chamber of Princes, NAI, F&P, Secret Reforms, June 1920, 11–16, cited in Ian Copland, *The Princes of India*, 41.
19. Amery to Linlithgow, 13 November 1942, TOP, III 251, cited in Ian Copland, *The Princes of India*, 189.
20. Ian Copland, *The Princes of India*, 185.
21. Ibid., 185.
22. Ibid., 185.
23. In a personal interview to the author. Subsequent quotes in this book are from the same.
24. W Anders, *An Army in Exile*, 101–02.
25. Ibid., 123–24.

Arrival

❧

Franek's Odyssey

CRRO

It was a warm April day in Bombay as a carriage pulled up in front of a huge bungalow in Bandra. Major Pullers, a general physician of the British Army, stepped out of the carriage and walked into the bungalow. Typically he saw his patients at the hospital, but this was an extraordinary assignment. Some weeks ago he had been asked by headquarters to set up a small clinic with about six nursing staff in this bungalow. He was greeted at the door by a small dignified lady, Kira Banasinska. She was the delegate for Red Cross in India and the wife of the Polish Consul General (PCG), who is also the dean of the diplomatic corps in Bombay.

They shook hands warmly as Kira led Major Pullers to his office in this building.

'How was the journey? Have they taken it well?'

'Well quite', Kira replied, 'what with all the sweets and fruits they have been receiving since reaching Quetta a week ago.'

'So how many children do you have here now?' Major Puller continued.

'We have about 170 here now. We hope the rest will follow soon.'

'Oh that's a number! Have you been able to have them all deloused?'

'We've been doing that since they were in Meshed.'

'Very well! Getting the hygiene in place is the very first step. Now we start checking them for other problems. Have you managed to get a good contractor for your food supplies? Getting the right nutrition into them now onwards will make all the difference.'

'Let us hope the damages to their bodies are not irreparable. In God and you we trust.'

'In God. The way you've got them here is nothing short of miraculous.'

'Our Lady is very kind. You know they celebrated Easter Mass in the deserts using the back of one of the trucks they were travelling in as the altar.'

The doctor has the look of incredulity as he turns from Kira to look at his first patient of the day—a small thin boy, a little over three feet in height dressed in loose khaki shorts, a white vest and a pair of open sandals. He is one of the tiny heroes who had somehow managed to reach a Polish orphanage in Russia, often trekking tens of miles and then the 5,000 kilometres' road journey from Persia to India. His complexion is sallow and the cheeks are sunk but a pair of grey eyes look up at the doctor from sunken sockets. A week's stubble of dark hair could be seen coming up on his head.

Major Pullers motions him inside with a pat on his head and asks, 'What is your name?'

It is only after Kira translates the question into Polish that the doctor receives a reply, 'Franek Herzog, son of Lieutenant Colonel Franciszek Herzog, 10 years old', in a heavily accented voice.

The mention of the rank strikes a deep chord in Major Puller. He thinks to himself, 'So this is what an orphaned son of a Polish brother officer looks like.' He glances at the long line of children waiting to be examined and gets to work immediately.

After a thorough examination of the skin, joints and stomach, aided by his questions translated into Polish by Kira, Major Pullers sends Franek to the hospital for rest, observation and a diet rich in iron and calcium for two weeks. His next patient is not so lucky. He suspects she has tuberculosis. She will be spending some months in a sanatorium in a nearby hill station under observation.

Over the next few days, he has seen them all and there are 20 cases of suspected tuberculosis, 11 cases of whooping cough, 41 cases of septic tonsils, 44 cases of scabies and other skin diseases, a third of them needing dental treatment and almost half beginning to show signs of scurvy.

The rooms in the bungalow are reorganised such that the children with skin diseases are in three rooms, the ones with whooping cough are in one, separated from those with suspected tuberculosis. Those with septic tonsils, anaemia and other mild illnesses are in different rooms. They will all have specific meal and medical and activity routines.

Franek is separated from his older brother, Tadeusz, as he is moved to the 'hospital room' for anaemia and septic tonsils. He settles down quickly in the bed next to the window overlooking the sea. It is a soft comfortable bed where he has to sleep by himself. Nurse Kasia gives him a hot cup of milk and pulls the sheets over him.

As the warmth of the hot milk seeps through him, he cuddles up under the sheets. Lying alone in the soft bed, Franek's mind drifts to the last time he felt so comfortable. It was in his mother's arms in their home in

Lubaczow in Poland at least three years ago. He remembered his mothers' arms around him in Kazakhstan, but then they were sleeping in a make-shift cot and it was bitterly cold. In fact, he was sleeping cuddled around her on the night she died in Kazakhstan.

My name is Franciszek Herzog. I am the third son of Major Franciszek and Ludwika Herzog, born in Krolewska Huta or Chorzow, on April 28th 1931. My parents had wanted a girl and had chosen the name Krysia, but since I was a boy they called me Franciszek, after my Father. Mother called me Niusiek and the name has remained in the family till date. So I am called Franciszek, Franus, Franiusiek, Niusiek and Franek interchangeably.

In the spring of 1923, my parents got married in the small church of St Nicholas in Wilno. Uncle Jozek, Father's brother, described the wedding as: The marriage was sanctified by the former chaplain of the PacPomarnacki family. Tension filled the air as the guests gathered in the church. On one side sat the aristocratic clan of Pac-Pomarnacki, with the bride's weeping mother at the head. On the other side stood a group of three young officers—Pilsudski's Socialists. The only thing that united the wedding guests, beside the young couple, was their love for Poland.

Father was transferred to the 75th Infantry Regiment, at that time stationed in Wilno. The young couple rented a small apart-ment on Gimnazjalna Street, and there on 15th March 1924, Wacek (Waclaw) was born. Tadeusz (Tadek), named after Apostle Jude Thaddeus, was also born in Wilno on 28th July 1926.

In 1928, Father was promoted to the rank of Major and at the same time transferred with his regimert to Krolewska Huta, now Chorzow, in Silesia. Besides the duties of a Battalion Commander, he was also in charge of the paramilitary organization of Strzelec (Riflemen Association).

According to my second brother Tadeusz (Tadek), in Chorzow we lived in a big officer's tenement building. We remember a boy, Zbyszek Sobol, the son of a major, who was a year younger than my older brother Waclaw (Wacek). They occupied an apartment just below ours. Zbyszek used to look down on me because I was the younger, and I didn't like that attitude. At that age I could not properly pronounce the letter 'r'. All of Wacek, and Zbyszek's les-sons did not produce any results. Frustrated, Zbyszek suggested to Wacek that they should do something his parents had done to their parrot when they wanted to teach the bird to talk. One day when there was nobody in Sobol apartment, they lured me there and announced that for my good they would undercut my tongue with scissors. I don't remember how I managed to escape from them, but from that day onwards I did not trust Wacek for a very long time.

Towards the end of 1931, Father was transferred to the H.Q. of the Strzelec (Rifleman Ass.) in Warsaw. The Strzelec was part of the Army and Father had the rank of Lieutenant Colonel. His office was on the second floor of the huge building in the Aleje Ujazdowskie, where all departments of the Polish Armed Forces were located. In the same building, Marshall Pilsudski had his office. As head of the Programs and Procedures in the Strzelec, Father visited Latvia, Estonia and Finland to help them in establishing similar organizations in their countries. He must have done a good job, as each country awarded him with high decorations for services rendered.

For the summer of 1933, our parents rented a nice house in the country in Jozefow, not far from Warsaw. Tadek remembered it was the most memorable summer vacation he ever had in his life. Lots of free time, many picnics, running barefoot in the rain, various escapades and any thing else the imagination of a 7-year-old could devise, especially without the restraints of Father's hand, as he only spent weekends with us.

In 1934, Father was transferred to the 38th Infantry regiment located at Przemysl. From there, I have much more vivid recollections, not just still pictures. We lived on the northern side of the town in the area called Winna Gora (Grapevine Mountain). The climate in southeast Poland is milder than in the rest of the country, and actually grapevine could be grown there. The house was situated on top of the hill from which we had a beautiful view of the town below. On a clear day, far to the south, you could see the Carpathian Mountains. The two storey house with columns on both sides of the entrance was quite large and was located in a two and a half acre parcel developed as a beautiful garden. There were 80 fruit trees, rows of bushes of gooseberries and currants, strawberries, and of course, vegetables and flowerbeds. I have no idea who kept it all cultivated. There were the three of us boys, Mother,

Father, a maid and Father's batman. Father was a knowledgeable gardener and liked that type of work (really, I don't know whether there were things that Father couldn't do). Most of the fruit was for direct sale, meaning that somebody would come and pick them from the trees. At home we would make jams, preserves, pickled cucumbers and cabbage. From red and black currants, Father made large quantities of wine. I remember, once Father wanted to pour wine from one carboy to another. As he rested one bottle on his knee, the glass broke and the whole kitchen floor was covered with red wine.

From that time, I remember one episode very vividly. Mother and Wacek went to town. Tadek and his friend wanted to frighten me. They said that there was a ghost and they were running away from it. I followed them, as I did not want to stay behind and let the ghost catch me, but they were too fast for me. I was really frightened and started to cry. The more I cried, the faster they would run, up to the attic, through various rooms, down to the cellar and up again. Eventually, I hid under a bed and covered myself with some blankets. Now Tadek and his friend started looking for me and became afraid that somet ing could have happened to me. They went outside to look for me. A draught closed the front doors and now they could not get inside, as they did not have a key. They were calling and calling me but I didn't hear them; exhausted from crying, I fell asleep. When Mother and Wacek returned and asked about me, Tadek could not give a satisfactory answer and now all of them were a bit worried. Eventually, I woke up and hearing Mother's voice crawled from under the bed.

Wacek and I ate almost anything, whereas Tadek was very fussy about his food; we called him *francuski piesek* (French dog). You had to see him eating sardines. He would take one fish at a time, put it on the plate and the 'operation' would start. First he would cut off the tail, then scrape off the scales from both sides of the sardine and eventually remove the backbone. After that when there was hardly anything left, he would eat it. At the sight of seafood, his face would turn green.

Tadek didn't eat tomatoes, but Wacek and I we loved them to the extent that as soon as they turned pink, we would pick them off the vine and eat them. To curb our appetite, Father told us that by eating tomatoes that are not quite ripe we could get cancer. That was soon after Pilsudski died in 1935 of that dreaded disease and everybody was talking about cancer.

Financially we were well above the average. Father's salary as a Major was 600 zlotys per month and when he was promoted to Lieutenant Colonel, it was over 800 zlotys. On top of that, once a year he had an extra few hundred zlotys for his military decorations. Also he and the family could travel by train at a reduced fare. Father used to say that if he could use all the discounts for his military decorations, every time that he travelled by train, the railway system should pay him. For the Virtuti Militari alone, a 50 per cent discount applied. In those days, a maid would get 30 zlotys per month plus food and board. The starting salary for a teacher in the elementary school was 120 zlotys per month and a principal in the high school would get 450 zlotys per month.

Towards the end of our stay in Przemysl, Wacek finished the 1st grade of *gimnazjum* (once he had failed on account of Latin and had to repeat the whole year). Tadek finished elementary school and passed the entrance examination to the *gimnazjum*. I finished the 1st grade of elementary school.

In 1938, Father was promoted to the rank of Lieutenant Colonel. At that time, he was 44 years old. He had a choice of moving to Krokow, Jaroslaw or Lubaczow. He chose Lubaczow. Here he was a commander of an independent 1st Battalion of the 39th Infantry Regiment. Other battalions of that regiment were stationed in Jaroslaw. In Lubaczow, he had more independence, both in the military field as well as in community work which he loved.

Lubaczow compared to Przemysl was really damp. A small town of about 7,000 inhabitants, about 5,000 Jews and the remainder equally divided between Poles and Ukrainians. Electricity was only available in the evening hours. We rented a house on the periphery of the town by the road leading to Mlodow village. The centre of the town, where there was an elementary school, a *gimnazjum*, a church and a few shops, was about 1 kilometre away. The house we rented, probably one of the best in town had two stories, with nice enclosed and glazed verandas on the front of the first and second floors. In the back of the house, there was a fair size garden with some fruit trees and another small building with three rooms. Our maid lived in one of them during summer months. The other two rooms were used for storage, and later when Father bought a motorcycle, as a garage. Compared to the house in Przemysl, this was primitive. There was no running water in the house. Water was taken from the well in the backyard. The toilet consisted of two outhouses behind the outer building. Naturally in winter and at nights we had to use the night commode or just a potty. I think Tadek wrote an 'Ode' to that important vessel:

You beautiful vessel in gold and red
Peacefully standing under my bed.
In depth of night in that and this,
In need, you bring such comfort and bliss.

Lubaczow I remember well. I was in the 2nd grade. School was located in the centre of the town by the market place. Frequently, Father's batman would take me home after school. There were two reasons for that. Sometimes after school I would play with friends or we would go to do some mischief to the Jewish boys and in consequence, I would be late for dinner. The second reason was for security. Father was on the 'war path' with the Jewish community and he was afraid that they might harm me.

And so, the batman would escort me home, but not on Thursdays. On that day, they had an early dinner in the barracks. I hurried there. With my mess kit I would stand in line to the kettle. In one part of the kit I would take soup and in the other the main course. I loved the soldier's food.

They liked me in the barracks. Frequently, I would go to the guardhouse. There in small cells, they would hold soldiers for mis-behaviour or infringement of the rules and discipline. Five days of *scislego* (rigorous) was the maximum penalty. In that case, the delinquent would get a slice of bread with tea for breakfast, some soup with bread for dinner and bread and water for supper. So, if I managed to sneak in past the guards, I would bring them some fruit or pieces of chocolate. In general, the guardsmen overlooked my doings.

Father didn't like me loitering in the barracks as I learned some 'nice, juicy' vocabulary, the meaning of which I did not under-stand. Then at home, I would show off with my newly acquired knowledge. One day, Father went to Jaroslaw to a staff meeting and was supposed to come home late that evening. In the afternoon, I went to the barracks. Suddenly, I saw Father coming through the gate on his motorcycle. I tried to hide behind a building but Father's quick eye noticed me. With his hand, he signalled me to approach and asked:

'What are you doing here?'

'Mother sent me to the canteen to buy something', I replied.

'Show me the money', Father said.

Naturally, I didn't have any and my lie was obvious.

'You know you are not supposed to come here and on top of that you lie.'

To a passing soldier, Father gave an order to bring guardsmen. Two guardsmen came, saluted and Father said to them:

'Take him in, two days of solitary confinement.'

Well, the Colonel had given an order, so they took me in, locked me in a cell and brought a slice of bread and some water. I loved the dark soldier's bread, but this time I didn't eat any. I was just sobbing. After an hour or so, which seemed like ages to me, Father's aide-de-camp came and said to me:

'The meeting will last a long time tonight, better go to your Father and apologise.'

I remember in Przemysl and Lubaczow, we had an Alsatian dog, Rex. Normally, he was on a chain. The chain was attached to a long wire stretched between two places. The chain could slide on the wire and the dog had a lot of space for running. If it was raining, he could hide in his doghouse. As long as the dog was on its chain, he would not let anyone enter the yard without barking and making a lot of noise. Once the dog was off the chain, he would be the friendliest animal in the world. We used to say that he was like a soldier, when on duty, strict, off duty, friendly.

Once when the dog was on the chain, a mailman came in. Rex jumped on him, knocked him down and started tearing at his leggings. Naturally, the mailman started yelling. We ran out of the house and pulled the dog to the side. Father gave the mailman a pair of brand new military trousers and some money to wipe off his tears.

For some reason, Father was not very keen on scouting, but both Wacek and Tadek belonged to the organisation. Once at a ceremony to which Father had been invited, Wacek was in the honour guard standing with the flag. Naturally, Father spotted him, but said nothing. Even I joined the cub scouts and attended two meetings. At one of these meetings, we went to the woods. I was told to hide in a certain place and watch that nobody would pass me. If I spotted anybody, I was supposed to shout—'Stop!' Nobody came my way and after half an hour the game was over. Our pack leader was Mietek Zathey.

For Christmas of 1938, we were going to Wilno to visit Grandmother. It happened that Grandmother had broken her arm, so Mother decided to go a bit earlier, and the rest of us, with Father, were supposed to come when school break started. However, the morning Mother was to go, our parents decided that I would go with her. Wacek and Tadek were already in school. When they came home, our maid told them that I hadn't returned from school yet. After an hour or so, they decided to go to town to look for me. At friend's homes, they were told that I had not been to school that day. Now they got worried speculating about what might have happened to me. After searching a bit longer, they returned home and then they were told that I was on the way to Wilno.

The trip lasted some 24 hours. In Warsaw, we had to change trains. It was midnight, I was tired and sleepy and we had to climb up a very long stairs and then go down to get to another platform. We boarded the train and after some time it started moving. Though exhausted, I was glued to the window. Never in my life did I see so many lights and many of them coloured. Eventually, I fell asleep and woke in the morning. We were in Wilno.

I did not know Grandmother. There she was an old woman in a darkened room, with a red night lamp glowing, lying in bed on a heap of pillows with her hand in plaster. To be honest, I was afraid of her. Probably I thought that she might hit me on the head with that hand in plaster. I do not remember if she ever hugged me or talked to me in a friendly fashion. There was never any fondness between us. Yet, for Easter that year, we received from her a huge parcel with all sorts of goodies and presents. And later on, I received a big wooden horse on rockers. I am sure, that in her way, Grandmother loved us but somehow she could not show that outwardly.

That Christmas, in 1938, was the most memorable. All that time in Wilno was one great ball. A big bustling city, riding horse drawn sleds through its snow-covered streets, fabulously illuminated with coloured neon lights and many big shops with beautiful displays.

Add to that lots of visits to various relatives I never heard of. Everywhere we were very welcomed. Right after Christmas Father had to go back to his unit, Mother and Wacek got flu so Tadek and I we were 'exploring' Wilno. For Christmas, I got a toy rifle. After lunch, Grandmother liked to take a nap, so I would go outside her bedroom door, load my rifle with caps and fire them. Grandmother would then call me, give 2 zlotys and say, 'Go to the movies, or somewhere else. I want to have peace and quiet.'

Two zlotys was enough to buy two cinema tickets and still have some left over for candy or a ride home in a sled. I saw Disney's *Snow White* and for the first time in my life went to a real theatre. That Christmas was the last one when we were all together.

In Lubaczow, Father was a very much respected and liked person. I recollect seeing a few times that in the morning some peasants would stand outside the gate waiting for Father to come out. They wanted Father to settle their disputes or claims. They preferred to go to him rather than to a judge, as they expected fair judgment and it would cost them nothing. They felt that Father was their man.

According to Tadek, when it came to his military service, Father was beyond reproach. Father never used military transport (horse and buggy, no automobiles) for his or his families' private use. He would say, 'What would Poland look like if all military families were allowed to do that. There would be no transportation left for the Army.' He would often go to the kitchen and check that soldiers were receiving correct amount of meat for their nourishment.

The summer of 1939 has been the last happy summer of my childhood. All three of us were promoted to the next grade. Father went to the war games and the military barracks were empty. The political situation was tense. All the time there was talk of the possibility of war with Germany over a territorial dispute. But the military pact between Poland, France and Great Britain bolstered Polish spirits. The chance of war diminished.

That summer was exceptionally hot and dry. To cool down, we frequently went to the river for a swim. In the middle of August, soldiers suddenly returned to their barracks. Around the town trenches were dug and machine guns placed there as anti-aircraft protection. A paramilitary youth organization was activated.

Wacek, who was by then 15, with Father's permission and approval, joined them. They were supposed to guard bridges, railway stations and other strategic objects against sabotage or other hostile activities. Summer was coming to an end. On Monday, 4th September, schools were to reopen. And then....

War and Siberia—1939–42

The Second World War started on Friday, 1 September 1939, when Germany attacked Poland. Wacek, as part of his duties in 'Przysposobienie Wojskowe', the paramilitary youth organization, was busy digging foxholes in which clusters of machine guns were installed as protection against aircraft attacks. A few days later, came the moment when we had to say goodbye to our Father, since he was going to the warfront. Everybody was crying except him. He allowed Wacek to join the Army if the situation required. To Tadek he said that he would have to stay with Mother and me no matter what happened and 'watch over us like the pupil of his eye' (Polish proverb). When we hung on his neck and kissed his face for the last time, he whispered, 'Even if you have to go selling newspapers to earn a living, do that. Remember.' And then, a moment later, hiding from the people that gathered to bid him farewell, wet eyes and emotions on his face, he climbed into waiting car and was gone ... forever. It took us some time to calm down.

A few days later, German bombardments of Lubaczow started. Main objectives were railway station, army barracks and Jewish district. Lieutenant Colonel Kaczala, who came to replace Father, ordered removal of all the machine guns because firing the planes 'would make Germans angry'. During raids, we usually hid in the cornfield just behind our house. Mother thought this would be safer than staying in the house, which if hit by a bomb could bury us in the ruins. German planes, after dropping their bombs, would fly at low ceiling strafing with their machine guns, people running in panic on streets or open fields. Once Tadek, who was sick at that time, ran out of the house a bit late was fired upon from the plane. Luckily, he managed to reach the cornfield in time and hide.

The German offensive was moving swiftly and the Polish resistance started to crumble. Lubaczow's army garrison left their barracks and Wacek also marched into the unknown. It must have been the 14th of September when in the middle of the night an officer, with remnants of his company, brought a word from our Father to leave the town ahead of the approaching Germans.

After leaving Lubaczow, Father was transferred to command a battalion in the 154th Reserve Inf. Reg. This was in line with the policy that in the event of war, active duty officers, as more experienced, be assigned to the reserve units just being mobilised. Officers from the reserve would go to fully established units. Father did not like this procedure, saying,

> In my battalion, I knew my officers; I knew their good and bad points and in consequence, knew what responsibilities I could entrust them in difficult situations. Then you get a bunch of people that do not know each other and I am supposed to organise them into a fighting battalion within a week.

Father's regiment and his battalion were shattered, but he and the remnants of his unit fought his way to the besieged Lwow. The Officer who came for us was from Father's battalion.

In a hurry, we loaded some belongings on a horse-driven cart and with the company that had about 100 soldiers, departed Lubaczow, going eastward. The house was left wide open. Tadek was still ill and had high temperature. With the approach of the day, we stopped in a forest. In the afternoon, we heard motors of tanks. Patrols were sent out to explore the situation. One of them come back and informed us that along a sandy road, three German tanks were slowly moving into the forest. The first plan was to attack them with grenades, but when another patrol come back and informed us that on the edge of the forest what looked like a battalion of German soldiers was stationed, the idea was abandoned. After some time, the German tanks withdrew.

With the onset of night, again we started moving eastward. However, in the morning Mother decided that there was no point going any further with the detachment. We stopped in Radruz at the estate of a family known to Mother.

Next day on 17th September, news came that Russia had attacked Poland from the east. For Poland that meant the end of the War, at least on the Polish territory. A few days later, we returned to our house in Lubaczow. To our surprise, no looting had occurred, but German soldiers who stayed there for a few days drank most of Father's wine. We did not stay in that house very long. Being afraid of the Ukrainian bands that were terrorizing Poles, we moved closer to town and rented a house opposite army barracks, now occupied by German soldiers.

Another incident from that time sticks in my mind. Being brought up, so to say, in the Army, on occasions I watched German soldiers being drilled in the barracks' square. I still remembered some German language and tried to strike up a conversation with them. At that time Germans, and in particular, regular army officers were quite polite. Once an officer gave me some chocolate. I thanked him and with that chocolate in hand ran home to show it to Mother. When I told her who gave it to me, she scolded me and said, 'How could you take that chocolate from a German, he could have killed your Father or another Pole'. I threw that piece of chocolate on the floor and started crying. It took me a long time to calm down.

Towards the end of September, Wacek returned home. He was well but tired and a bit wan. He had many stories to tell us, some of them probably a little exaggerated; he was always a good storyteller. His unit had been disbanded and he returned home.

In the middle of October, the Germans had withdrawn from Lubaczow to a line on the river San. This was the new border between Germany and Russia agreed upon by Hitler and Stalin, even before the War had started. For 24 hours, Lubaczow was 'free'. Next day at 7 a.m. Russian tanks started rolling into Lubaczow and behind them marched the Red Army. They looked terrible by comparison to the German or even the Polish Army.

At about 8 o'clock that morning, a Jewish militiaman, with a red band on his arm, brought an NKVD officer to our house. The officer turned to Mother and asked:

'Are you the wife of the commander of the Polish battalion from Lubaczow? Where is your husband?'

'Yes. But I do not know where he is,' Mother replied, which of course was true.

Constant harassment by the NKVD and frequent searches of our home forced us to leave Lubaczow and move to the nearby village of Mlodow. There, we rented a room in a small hut.

Gradually, we were selling our furniture, bit by bit, and with the money raised that way, we were buying food and paying rent. We had no other income. Mother had an idea that when spring would come, she would sell the rest of our belongings, buy a cart and two horses and we would try to get to Wilno, which at that time was occupied by Lithuanians. After all, in Wilno, were her mother and other members of her family, and there, we would have better a chance of existence.

It must have been February 1940 that we received the first postcard from Father. He was alive.

He had been trying to locate us by writing to some people in Lubaczow. It was a difficult task, as they were not allowed correspondence until December 1939, and even then, they were allowed only one postcard a month. Later on, I learned that Father was trying to communicate with us before he was sent to Starobielsk. When still on Polish territory, behind wires in the POW camp near Tarnopol, he begged a young boy, who used to come to the wires to pass food and cigarettes to the prisoners, to contact us and tell us about his whereabouts. He tried, but we never received any communication. Father, with the remainder of his unit, had fought his way into the besieged Lwow. There, he took part in the final days of the War until the city capitulated. He was captured by the Russians and sent to the POW camp in Starobielsk.

[Author's note: In Ukraine, after the post-War borders of Poland.]

The third postcard and the first written to us.

Starobielsk 16/2/40

Beloved,
Today I received from you the first sign of life—a postcard dated 4/2.
I wrote to Lubaczow a few times. I was looking for you with your Mother and Witus (1).

There is not much I can write about myself. I am alive and there is no imminent danger at the moment. My kidneys are troubling me a little because of the lack of warm clothing, and my shoes are in pieces, but that's not important as spring will be coming soon. I will be allowed to write to you again in March. You write to me as frequently as possible, but be careful what you write, then there will be a better chance that I will receive it. Postcards are the best. Write to me in detail—where you live, how you manage financially, what happened to our house and belongings. The main thing is to survive and keep on living. Where are the children? What are they doing? Describe in detail. I wrote to your Mother and asked her to take you in, I would feel better if you were with your Mother—it would be easier among your own family though even there it might not be peaceful (2). Have you heard anything of my family? Any news about Wacek (3), Jozek (4), Stefan (5) and the aunts? With me are Wollersdorfer and Schwarcenberg-Czerny (6). Don't worry about me. Think about yourself and how you'll manage. Maybe it won't last long. Look after your health and the children's. I think that people might help you; I always helped them and did them so many good deeds. I do not think that anybody can blame me for anything. Is Kasia (7)with you? Who of our friends is in Lubaczow and how are they managing? Wylegala was wounded, so was Bieniek and Malek (8). Here, days are very dreary, most frequently I think of you; what you are doing, how you are managing—do not despair, somehow everything will slowly pass, everything will be well and we will be together again. Always write very legibly.

Now I have to end, I am enclosing my tenderest kisses for you all. Write frequently,

Your loving, Franek.

(1) Mother's stepbrother.
(2) Meaning Lithuania, Father was right. By June 1940, Lithuania and the other two Baltic states were occupied by Russia.
(3) Wacek left Lubaczow with his voluntary army unit.
(4) Major Jozek, Father's brother, who lived in Krakow.
(5) Captain Stefan, the other brother, was captured behind enemy lines in Russia, sent to Kozielsk POW camp and killed in Katyn in the spring of 1940.
(6) Lieutenant Colonel Wollersdorfer was the divisional doctor, Colonel Schwarcenberg-Czerny was Father's divisional commander.
(7) Kasia, our maid left us when the War started. Of course, we could not afford to pay her.
(8) Wylegala, Bieniek, Malek officers from Father's battalion.

The fourth postcard:

Starobielsk 9/3/1940

Dear, Beloved,
Your postcard, dated 4/2 and 14/2 arrived. To your postcard from 14
/ 2, I replied immediately. No other news from you. I could not get in
touch with you for so long. I wrote to a few people in Lubaczow for
information regarding your whereabouts, and then your first postcard
arrived on 16/2. From the postcards so far received, I do not know
where you are living, how you are managing and what you are doing
in Mlodow, what are the boys doing and are they attending school.
There is not much I can write about myself, my health is fine and
there is no danger for the time being. You write to me as frequently
as possible, postcards are the best, do not send money or parcels, but
think about your own wellbeing. If it is possible move to your mother,
it will be easier for you to survive. All the time I wonder how you are
managing and what you are doing. Please write to me Lala [Mother's
pet name], of our friends in Lubaczow and give them my best regards,
especially Dr Tr. Write about everything concerning your lives but be
careful what you write. I will write again in April if nothing interferes.
Do you have any news about my family and what about Wacek?
I have to end now, kiss you very, very tenderly.

Franek. Let the boys sign the postcard.

We never managed to start our trip to Wilno. On 13 April 1940,
with thousands of other Polish citizens, we were deported to
Kazakhstan in Russia. An NKVD officer, with four soldiers, came
for us in the middle of the night. We were allowed to take certain
amount of things such as clothing, bed linen, bedspreads, blankets,
kitchen utensils, some food and other odds and ends, in reality not
more than what we could pack in an hour into a few suitcases and
hastily made bundles. Another limiting factor was how much we
could carry and how much would fit into a small cart. On the way to
the railway station, passing through the town, we saw lights in various houses. It meant that these families were also being deported.

They loaded us into goods carriages specially adopted for long
distance transportation of people. Each carriage held about 30

people. Inside were bunk beds made from wooden boards. In the middle, stood a metal stove for heating and cooking and on one side, by the wall, there was a hole in the floor serving as a toilet.

I do not remember much of the journey, but a few episodes stuck in my mind. When the train stopped at the last station on the Polish side of the border, many hands stretched out through the iron bars in the windows asking people on the outside for a handful of Polish soil. Even the Russian guards did not object to that. And then, a few minutes later, when we were crossing the actual frontier, everybody started singing the Polish patriotic song; 'We will not abandon Polish Land'. And that song carried from carriage to carriage and everybody was crying.

When we were crossing river Dnieper in Kiev, I could see through the window a seemingly unending stretch of water with no banks. It was springtime now, with snow melting, and the river overflowing its banks and low-lying land.

All the time we were going eastward, we crossed the Ural Mountains and were in Asia. On many stations, we were put in the sidings where trains like ours, full of Polish people, would be standing. Then we would try to pass scraps of information between the carriages.

On the 13th day of our journey, we were disembarked on a station in Alga, near Aktjubinsk in western Kazakhstan. From there we were taken, together with our belongings, to various villages. With about 30 Polish families, we were brought to the village called Lugavoj that encompassed a collective farm or *kolkhoz* named Czerwonyj Sierp (Red Sickle). Our escort, the NKVD, literally dumped us in the middle of the village and checked the list of all present, then left. Tadek got separated from us. He was taken to another village; however, after a few days, he arrived at where we were. Everybody was very happy, not so much that he returned, but because he also brought the belongings of a few other families, guarded diligently.

The curious inhabitants surrounded us. As we found out later, most of them were the Ukrainians and Moldavians deported here during the thirties (during the forced collectivization of their homeland) and of course local inhabitants—Kazakhs. There were only two Russian families in the village. As most Poles knew the Russian or Ukrainian language, there was no difficulty speaking with the locals.

Then started, so well known to thousands of other Polish families, endless days of frustration, misery and hard work. The only hope people had was in God and in France. However, under the onslaught of the German Army, even faster than Poland, France collapsed. The spirit of many people was broken. We, I must admit with pride, were one of the very few that never, even for a moment, lost hope. Mother believed in England.

First of all we had to find some accommodation. With another Polish family, we rented a small, one-room hut. We lived there for a few months. Towards the autumn, we moved to another house which had two rooms. The owners occupied one of them and the other room was for us. A big stove formed a part of the wall separating the two rooms. The important factor was heating. When the owners had fire in the stove, our room was also heated. Unfortunately, just before winter, we had to move out. Some other Polish family offered extra money for the rent and we could not afford that. We found a room in a hut of Kazakh, on the outskirts of the village. That was the harshest period of our existence in Russia.

Soon after our arrival in Kazakhstan, to our great surprise, we received the fifth postcard from Father (see Photograph 1). We have not heard from him since then.

Starobielsk 6/4/40

Dear Lala and Children,
I have received your postcards as well as from Dr L. and your Mother. Thank Mother for good wishes and for remembering me. All my allowed correspondence I send, to you. Wicherkiewicz was with me, he is still looking for Irena—pity that in these difficult times you cannot forgive Lena (1). Maybe your Mother knows something about my brothers. After you receive this postcard do not write to me for the time being. As soon as I am able, I will give you my new address. What am I doing— the same as your Father did, the same fate. The main thing is do not despair—though personally you have to be prepared for everything.

Try to move with your Mother. When I write to you again next time, reply immediately; for me your postcards are the only news from the outside world. Later, I will also write to your Mother, maybe you will be with her by then. Drozdowski is here—son of sister Szczepanowa—every week he receives parcels from Lithuania. Tell

Czyrowa about this card. Why have you written so little so far? When I am at my new location I will write to you immediately. And for the time being, I kiss you all very tenderly; do not worry if there is a longer period of silence from me.

Once again my love,
Yours Franek.

(1) Lena was Uncle Stefan's wife. She and Mother were not the best of friends.

In our village, schooling for Polish children was not compulsory; so I did not attend any school in Russia. Mother described going to local schools as going 'to be soaked in communist doctrine and atheism'. Besides, I did not have warm clothing and shoes for the winter, and winter in that part of Russia lasted for about five months. So Mother tried to teach me herself, mainly by reading Polish books.

Like everybody else, Tadek worked wherever there was any job available, except probably a little more and a little harder. He had to because for a period of time he was, so to say, the only breadwinner in the family. Wacek strained his back carrying sacks with grain and then developed pneumonia. That was the end of his working days for the year. In the winter, there were no jobs available at all. During harvest time, his 'specialty' was delivering water. He had a cart pulled by two oxen. On the cart, there were two huge barrels that had to be filled with water from a spring and the load delivered to the workers in the fields. It was hard, very responsible and not a very pleasant job. But it was well paid. He was not very persistent in his work. After two or three weeks of hard work, he had to rest a bit, especially as Mother was sorry and afraid that he might be wasted. He changed jobs frequently depending on what was available. He planted trees, demolished old buildings and recovered bricks, made new bricks, helped with harvesting and carted crops to the granary. He even worked for one day in a quarry and that cost him a few days of sickness. There was no monetary remuneration for work. Payment was in a form of farm produces and that was done at the end of the season. In the meantime, as we needed money, we had to sell some of our meagre possessions to buy bread, flour and other things and to pay rent. And so our life went on.

Before start of the winter, we rented a room from a Kazakh whose dilapidated house stood on the fringe of the village. Our room had a malfunctioning stove and windows that you could not close tight and through which snow would blew in. The owner lived in the other part of the house so we had to heat the place ourselves and we had very little *kiziak*, no money to buy some, even if any was obtainable in the market. *Kiziak* was the main fuel in this part of Siberia. It is cow's manure mixed with chopped straw, formed into small bricks and dried in the sun. Not too far from our village, there was a small coal mine, but no coal was available for people. We were also very short on food. It was the time when to get a bowl of flour or a few potatoes, Mother's fur coat, pillows, eiderdown, watch and everything else of any value and that was not considered as 'a bare necessity' to survive the winter, was sold.

Tadek remembered that winter thus. It was also the time when I had a foretaste of death from starvation. I felt very weak, slept longer and longer and did not even feel hungry. Luckily I woke up from that 'lethargy' that lasted a few days. I started to live again, started to think of the future. I made myself a pair of boots from a piece of thick felt, started going to the village for water (there was no well near our house) and other supplies and on the way back pilfered some *kiziak* or anything else that I could put my hands on.

I remember from that Kazakh's hut another incident. Mother and Wacek went to the village to see *predsedatel* (chairman of the *kolkhoz*) to get a permit to grind some grain in the communal mill. On the way back, they were caught by *buran* (blinding snowstorm) and Wacek dragged our half-conscious Mother. When Tadek heard his desperate yelling, he jumped out of bed and ran barefooted (Wacek had his boots), through huge snowdrifts, higher than me, to Wacek and helped bring Mother indoors. A few days later, we found her shoes in the snow half way between our hut and the village.

For Christmas, we were still in that miserable place. Oh! How sad that Christmas was! For Christmas Eve, we had piece of *oplatek* (wafer) that was sent to us from Poland, which we broke and wished each other a better future, with a few bitter tears to help us swallow it, some beetroot soup and one potato pancake each and that's all. On Christmas Day, we were hungry.

But somehow, with God's mercy and some good people's help, we left that terrible place where in the morning hoar frost covered the inside walls of our room. Thanks to Mrs Krauzowa, a friend, we moved to the hut of a decent Ukrainian widow with three children. Her name was Paraska Olejnik and she was the collective farm's swineherd keeper. Her hut consisted of one large room divided, as customary, by a big, centrally located, floor to ceiling stove. At least it was warm here and we had somewhere to cook our meals. Somehow, though it cost us a lot for the *kwatira z tiopkoj* (room with heat), we managed till spring. When spring came, we started working again.

In June of 1941, Germany attacked Russia. Amnesty was declared for all Polish people. Tadek and Wacek volunteered for the Polish Army, but that did not change our situation a bit. Wacek had seen some action as a volunteer during the early days of the War, but Tadek was joining the *junak*s or the boys division to train as a soldier. Our second winter in Siberia was approaching. We had no news of our Father's whereabouts, but we had moral and some financial help from Uncle Strumillo, Mother's cousin, who come to Russia from London with the Polish Embassy.

The year 1942 arrived. Polish people in our village, especially the weaker ones, started to die. Deep down inside we were all worried about Mother. Unfortunately, she did not survive the winter. She died around the midnight on 17th January. She was not sick longer than a week.

As mentioned before, most of the jobs available were seasonal and associated with the collective farm. The only full time jobs, such as work with cows, horses, swains in the office, maintenance or shop, were few and not attainable for Polish people. Pay was calculated in the following way. Every job in the *kolkhoz* was appraised for a certain amount of units, called *trudodien* (workday) which split into 100 *sotki* (100 *sotki* = 1 *trudodien*). Payments were in produces only. Let's say that the harvest yielded 10,000 kilogrammes of wheat. From that, *kolkhoz* had to give to the state 8,000 kilogrammes (based on the acreage designated by the state for growing wheat). The remaining 2,000 kilogrammes of wheat were divided by the number of trudodiens earned by all workers on the farm. That established the amount of wheat per trudodien.

Multiply that by the number of trudodiens earned by individual and that was the amount of wheat he would get. Good and just system. But if the harvest was poor and they collected only 7,000 kilogrammes of wheat, they still had to give to the state 8,000 kilogrammes; hence, there was nothing left for the people. And so it was with every product: ray, millet, potatoes, vegetables, milk, butter, etc. *Panimajesz!*[1]

I remember, in the year of 1941, our family earned over 400 trudodiens (I earned over 30 of them). It was a very good harvest that year and they paid 5 kilogrammes of corn per trudodien. Surplus of the grain you could sell for money or exchange for something else. A certain amount of money was needed to buy such things as salt, sugar, paraffin for the lamp, matches, etc. Of course, if they were available in the store, then a long line would form outside the shop.

My main job was catching prairie dogs. I had a few traps, but mostly caught them with my bare hands. On the steppe there were hundreds if not thousands of holes dug by these animals. Most holes were no longer than 2 feet. When I saw a prairie dog standing on its hind legs and looking around, I would chase it. The animal would try to hide in the nearest hole. I had to put my hand into the hole very quickly and with luck, if the hole was short, I would catch the animal by its hind legs. Then, very slowly I would drag the prairie dog out of the hole. As soon as its head appeared, I would catch it by the neck, place the neck between the index and the middle finger and squeeze it tight, thus chocking the animal to death. Then I had to skin the animal and stretch its fur with sticks and let it dry. For the pelt, depending how good it was and how big, I could get in the store up to one rouble. In addition, as prairie dogs were regarded as pests, the *kolkhoz* would give me 10 sotkas for each tail (evidence that I killed the animal). During the spring and summer of 1941, I caught about 250 prairie dogs.

Another of my chores was collecting *kiziak* in the steppe, where cows were grazing. Sometimes it took good half day to collect a barrowfull of that fuel. Stealing from the collective farm whenever and whatever was possible was regarded as a sport, though a bit risky, because if you were caught, the penalty could be harsh. We did not consider stealing as a sin; after all we were taking what belonged to us, as everything was 'a common wealth'.

Mother, not being strong and rather of poor health, worked only occasionally if some light work was available. Wacek, like Tadek, took various jobs. Once a group of men had to build 12 small bridges over streams and small ravines in the steppe, so carts could pass over them. Wacek was telling that they built 11 such bridges, but could not find place to build one more. So they built it over an imaginary stream in the steppe, just to fulfil the plan 100 per cent.

There is another incident that has stuck in my mind. It must have been the beginning of the winter of 1941. Wacek was working that day in the *kolkhoz* and they let him have a pair of oxen and a big cart for the night, to get some straw from the fields. On occasions we would burn straw in the stove. It did not give much heat, but you could cook a meal. Besides, in the bundle of straw, you could find some ears full of grain. From that grain, when ground, Mother could make some cereals or soup.

Well, Tadek decided that he would go for the straw and let Wacek rest. I volunteered to go with him to keep company. We left the village at 9 o'clock in the evening. After journeying about 1 kilometre (oxen travel rather slowly), we heard wolves howling in a distance. It seemed that the howling was getting closer and closer. We had to make a decision whether to return or to carry on. We decided to continue. Eventually the howling stopped. After about two hours, we reached the place where the straw was stacked in the field on both sides of the dirt road. In the meantime, it started snowing.

We moved from one pile of straw to another, parted them and from the middle would take dry bundles and with forks loaded them on the cart. Snow started piling by now. We decided it was time to start going home. The road was recognizable only by a slight hollow in the snow. But when we were loading the straw, we crisscrossed the road a few times. Now we did not know which way to turn, left or right? We turned left. Luckily it stopped snowing. The whole countryside was covered with a fresh, white blanket of the fluffy stuff which somewhat moderated the darkness of the night. After a time, at a distance, we saw some buildings, but it was the neighbouring village, about 6 kilometres from ours. We turned back. I buried myself in the straw and fell asleep. When I woke up, it was already morning and in the distance we saw the familiar buildings of our village. Mother and Wacek were very happy to see us as well as the full cart of straw. For a few days, we had the precious fuel. (When our landlady had fire in the stove for cooking we had heat in our room, but generally for our cooking, we had to provide our own fuel.)

The few days after that, one evening as we tried to speak of 'happy and pleasant' things, to cheat those unpleasant sensations which wrenched our hearts and constricted our throats, Mother suddenly said, 'Do you hear how the night hawk cries?'

These words, louder now and strange sounding, struck at our hearts, causing them to beat harder. Wacek declared that he heard nothing, but he had always been considered the 'deaf' one. Tadek and I listened and heard no sound save the howling of the wind. How, indeed, could a night hawk have been found in treeless wilderness? Tadek answered, however, not knowing why, that he heard it and naturally I too said I heard it, and Wacek after a moment, also confirmed this. But the easy mood did not return to us. Somehow, the talk turned to things metaphysical. Then something rapped at the window. Once, twice, three times. At first we froze, then leapt up as if in answer to a command which each of us had long subconsciously awaited. I imagined it to be a ghost. But Tadek went out and recognised some Poles from the nearby hut. They told us that Mr Bawol, popularly known among us as the 'Apostle', had just died.

A few days after we buried Mr Bawol, Mother become ill. At first we thought it was only the flu which would pass easily and did not fear for her. Only one thing worried us, Mother lost her appetite. At the time, as it happened, the first packages arrived from the Red Cross, and we were able to offer her things which she might be dreaming of in her delirium.

Physically Mother was not worn out. If we had been able to get medical help, we should certainly have saved her. True, the food was not too good or abundant, but Mother did not physically work hard. We could not understand her 'lack of appetite' when we would return from work and the four of us would sit down to a meagre supper. Though she strove valiantly to hide them, her eyes would fill up to our unthinking appeals for more, as 'work takes it all out of us', she would answer that there was no more.

A few days into her illness, we began to realise that things were going badly. At moments, Mother's memory would lapse. She would forget where she was, drift into delirium. Then there would be times of apparent well being (we assumed her temperature must have gone down, but we had no thermometer) and Mother would return to the living. She would try to eat, to converse. Once I remember, we were reading aloud from the Russian newspaper and happened upon a reference to the fact that India had agreed to accept 250 Polish orphans.

'You see boys', said Mother, 'when I die, Tadek and Niusiek can go to India and Wacek will join the Polish Army'.

We felt most awkward, knowing she was serious. We tried to dissuade her, as one does in these situations but I supposed that by then, Mother had found the courage to look truth in the eye.

After this, things grew steadily worse. Wacek strove to have the doctor sent, knowing it was futile as he resided some 28 kilometres away over the roads banked with high snow and had nothing to ride on. Wait. The answer always came. Wait. In February, the doctor is due to make the rounds of your area, then he will see what ails your mother. To wait with what—death?

The death came ever closer to possessing Mother. We gathered what we could. Some medicines and prayers—ardent even into tears—were on our side, but this was all we had at our disposal in the battle against death. Mother recognised us seldom now. Her mind wandered back to Wilno, to the days of her youth. From what we could understand of her delirious mutterings, she spoke with her great-grandparents. We could only look on, bewildered. After this, Mother completely lost consciousness, only starting convulsively when some attack of the heart seized her. Then we would run for Valerian drops which we had been able to obtain from some 'good people'. Sometimes, we had visitors—neighbouring Poles. Each helped in his own way. Each gravely nodded, pondered deeply, gave advice and left.

On the evening of 17th January 1942, we lay, as usual, Wacek and Tadek on the floor and me, as usual, next to Mother on the bed. We kept watch by the light of a small oil lamp made from a bottle with a piece of wick, which Mother called 'Cinderella'. We lay, half asleep, half watchful. Every rustle woke us. I remember holding my breath to ascertain better whether Mother was still breathing. We feared that she would leave us, though we never spoke of it.

Suddenly Mother moved and let out a kind of moan or whimper. I crept out of bed. Tadek and Wacek rushed to her side, immediately pressing a spoonful of water with Valerian to her lips. We clumsy, dim boys found in those moments the most tender phrases springing from us unashamed. We knew or rather felt that a great moment had arrived. Our state of nervous tension, intensified through so many sleepless nights came to a peak upon hearing the liquid we poured down Mother's throat, flow down as if to an empty well to the bottom. Her lips never closed. We understood. Mother lived no more. Yet our minds couldn't fathom what we were seeing, and in our hearts there was no room for the feeling.

Tadek grabbed the night lamp and brought it closer. On Mother's forehead, white as alabaster, sweat shone like a light frost. He cried, 'No—it can't be!' and put his ear to her breast and heard— clear and loud—the beating of a heart; boom-boom-boom! He later said that he felt that the wave of joy which washed over him, a hundred times greater than the fear and uncertainty which had previously held him in its grip, would tear him apart. He had often in the past laid his ear against her chest to hear the faint beating, like the fluttering of caged bird, of her heart. Tadek said that all those memories crossed his mind like lightning, but it was his own heart which he heard. Then he had no more illusions.

I sat by the stove, but seemed not to understand what was happening. Then Tadek told me 'Mommy died'. How strange the words sounded from his mouth for the first time and how terrible.

Wacek wept. Tadek knelt beside the bed and prayed. Later he told me that he felt a strange desire fill his heart. A stronger and stronger desire for revenge—a desire to run somewhere, to tear someone apart, to snatch Mother back from him. He did not cry, but the pain ripped at him, as did the consciousness of the unfathomable wrong which had been done to Mother and to us.

Wacek and Tadek followed Mother's ·casket (a wooden box made from rough boards) to the cemetery. I stayed at home as I did not have any shoes.

Wacek notified Uncle Strumillo about Mother's death. He also sent a postcard to the Polish Embassy in Kujbyshev asking them to transmit that information to Major Jozef Herzog who most probably was in a German POW camp. Soon afterwards, Wacek was supposed to leave with other young Poles from the collective farm to join the Polish Army. In Aktjubinsk, they stopped at the Polish

Mission to get tickets and travel permits. As they were leaving, one of the officials turned to Wacek and said, 'Mr Herzog, I have here a telegram for you from the Polish Embassy'.

It was a telegram from Uncle Strumillo advising us to come to Aktjubinsk as soon as possible, as a friend of his from the Polish Embassy would be going to Tashkent and would have railway tickets for us. In Tashkent, a Polish orphanage was being assembled which would be evacuated to India.

We packed our meagre belongings, paid off as many debts as we could and with good wishes from other Polish families, we got a ride to Aktjubinsk. There, after a few days, Mr K Gostkowski, a colleague of Uncle Strumillo from Kuibishyev, arrived and after some more difficulties with the Russian officials, we left for Tashkent. We travelled, so to speak, 'in style' compared with how people in Russia had to travel. We had so called *plackarty* compartments with sleeping facilities for six people. At night you could lie down and stretch your legs. The journey to Tashkent lasted a few days.

In Tashkent, we stayed only for a few days. We were 'deloused', had a good scrub in a Turkish bath and received some clean clothing. We stayed in the 'Polish Hotel' whose manager was an old ex-officer who knew our Father from Krolewska Huta days. He was very hospitable to us when he learned that we were the son of Mr Herzog for whom he had a great respect.

The next day, after the orphans arrived, we boarded a train that was supposed to take us all the way to Ashkabad. Wacek was still travelling with us, but after a few days, he left us at the railway station of Kermine. Kermine was the assembly point for the candidates for the Polish Navy and Air Force being shipped to England. In Samarkand and Wrevsk, more children from local orphanages joined us, so that by the time we reached Ashkabad, our compartment resembled a barrel of herrings, us being herrings.

At that time, Wacek was nearly a young man. He had some War experience from the September of 1939. He shaved, smoked cigarettes and was dating. His interests were physics and chemistry, and he loved pottering around. He was very strong for his age but his health was not the greatest.

In Ashkabad, the capital of Turkmenistan, we were housed in four buildings with a big courtyard in the middle. One building was for boys, one for girls and one was designated as a sickbay, as many children were sick. Those with typhoid fever were sent to the local hospital in town. Many of them never come back. The fourth building was for staff and kitchens. We slept on mattresses laid on the floor. Luckily it was already spring in Turkmenistan. Beds were reserved only for the sick. I also ended up in that sickbay as I had an attack of malaria.

Gradually we were getting acquainted. We had good and dedicated guardians. One of them was Hanka Ordonowna, a well-known opera singer from Warsaw. She tried to cheer us up and return the smiles on our faces by teaching and singing with us many songs. Fr Franciszek (Francis) Pluta was in charge of the orphanage.

The Journey from Persia to India

The first group of children to leave Russia for Persia [today Iran] was being assembled and left in the middle of March. As I had not fully recovered from malaria, I stayed behind and so did Tadek, not wanting to leave me. When the trucks returned from Meshed, the second group was getting ready to leave. We left Ashkabad at about noon on 19th March 1942. By early evening, we were at the border. They did not keep us long. After some checking of documents, the barrier was slowly raised. We entered Persia which was partially controlled by the Russian and British troops but nevertheless an independent country without the dreaded NKVD and the *kolhozes*.

The convoy of our trucks was slowly climbing the treacherous, narrow roads (serpentines) in the mountains and then going downhill into the valley. Here spring was in full blast, the greenery was splendid and the mountains magnificent. For the night, we stopped at a small town where we got a hot meal. We were hungry and tired, but above all very excited, children and adults alike, that we had left Russia behind. We lay down, side by side on the wooden floor of a shelter and covered ourselves with blankets, but for a long time we could not get to sleep.

Next day, after a Thanksgiving mass by Fr Pluta, we continued on the trucks to Meshed. We had to stay for a few weeks in Meshed as quarantine to make sure that we did not take some infectious diseases to India. We stayed in some buildings which were a part of a Persian orphanage. We were fed well, gained some weight, received new clothing suitable for hotter climate and started to look like 'real people'. Many children were sick, but luckily with nothing as serious as typhoid fever. Many of us, including me, had mumps, but the fever and discomfort lasted only about a week. One big room was converted into a sickbay where everybody, boys and girls were treated. We slept on mattresses laid on the floor.

Hanka Ordonowna was still with us and continued to teach us many songs. One evening we had a big bonfire and many people from Meshed town were invited. We entertained them with Polish songs and Ordonowna, dressed in the Polish national costume, sang and then danced with great vigor and received a thunderous applause.

At the beginning of April we left Meshed for our journey onward to India. We were about 170 children, plus our guardians. The whole convoy must have been 15 or more trucks. It was led by four men—Vice-consul T Lisiecki, Dr St Konarski, H Hadala and Dajek. In each truck there were 14 or so people. Inside the truck, on its sides and in the back, wooden benches were constructed to facilitate sitting. The roof and sides were covered with canvas and the back also had a canvas sheet that could be rolled up. We had very little baggage, just some bundles that were stashed under benches.

As soon as we left Meshed we were in the desert. We had never seen anything like it. A vast plane, as far as one could see, covered with very fine white/yellowish sand. From time to time far on the horizon we could see some trees and water, but in reality it was a mirage. Never could we reach those trees or get to the water. I have no idea how our drivers knew where to drive as there were no visibly marked roads. I am sure they had to drive by compass.

Inside the trucks it was very hot but as soon as we would roll up the back canvas, sand would get in, and then it was more difficult to breath. We stopped frequently to get some fresh air and some water that we carried in big metal canisters. But before we would get out of the truck we had to wait for the sand churned by the moving trucks to settle down. For food we had sandwiches washed down with water and some fruit. We did not pass any towns or even settlements and for the night we usually stopped by some rest houses or big garages and were lucky if they let us sleep on the floor wrapped in blankets. Otherwise we had to sleep in the trucks. Sometimes at those night stops if it was prearranged, they would cook some meals for us.

I remember that Easter Sunday we spent in the desert and Fr Pluta celebrated Mass on the back of the truck.

After a few days of driving through the desert big mountains were in front of us and we started climbing. These mountains were in complete contrast to the one we drove through on the way to Meshed. They were hostile looking, with no greenery, just barren rocks and, once again, hairpin bends with deep ravines on the side. The drivers had to be extremely skilled to negotiate them. A few times, at the more dangerous bends, for safety's sake, we would get off the trucks. Luckily, there were no accidents.

I believe that part of the journey took us through Afghanistan. Apparently bandits were hiding in the mountains and sometimes they attacked convoys. For our safety, one truck with soldiers accompanied us for a day and every driver was issued a gun.

The whole journey from Meshed to the Indian border lasted six days. On 10th April, we entered India at the border town of Nok-Kundi. From here, a special train that would take us to Bombay was waiting for us. Next day, in Quetta, Mrs Kira Banasinska, wife of the Polish Consul General, and at the same time chairperson of the Polish Red Cross, welcomed us. On the platform, a large crowd of people (Europeans and Indians) gathered as they also wanted to greet us on Indian soil. They gave us sweets (candies), fruits and refreshing drinks. I do not know why our train went to Bombay via Delhi. At many stations, the train would stop for a few hours and we would have warm receptions similar to the one in Delhi.

Well, we had to give something from ourselves, so we gave the only thing that we had—singing. It might have been in Delhi where we had to sing the English national anthem. We learned the words without understanding them and on top of that our pronunciation left much to be desired. I am sure we sang 'God shave the King' for 'God save the King'—the British national anthem. No wonder that on the faces of the crowd there were smiles.

At one of the stations a Polish missionary, Brother Eustachy—a Silesian, joined us. He knew English and a few Indian languages. The whole train consisted of a few carriages. The carriages were not divided into compartments, so we had plenty of room, even to run around. There were wooden benches, but much wider than the ones in the trucks, and therefore, so much more comfortable. There were windows to look through and above all no dust and sand. The scenery was ever changing. At night we stretched out on the bench, covering ourselves with a blanket with a small pillow to rest our heads on. During the day, two big ice blocks covered in sawdust were put in each carriage to cool us off. Many people were bringing us sweets and fruits.

On 15th April, we arrived in Bombay. From the station they took us by buses (not trucks!) to the suburb of Bandra. Here, a big house (about 20 rooms) waited for us. The house stood just across the street from the sea. The first thing we did after coming to the house was to have a good meal. One big hall was designated as a dining room, with tables covered with tablecloths and chairs! Unbelievable luxury since leaving Poland.

After the meal, we went to the bathroom to take showers. There was plenty of hot and cold water. What a luxury! Bedrooms had real beds with soft mattresses and clean sheets. Each of us had his own bed. And for a 'good night', on each bed there was a big, juicy orange. There was none on my bed. Probably somebody took it. Tears came to my eyes. Luckily Tadek shared his orange with me.

After a few days, a second building was rented for us. It was situated a bit further from the sea, but higher up, with a splendid view of a fishing pier and the sea. All the boys were transferred to that second building. The girls stayed in the original big building. We had to go there for meals and for classes. Among our guardians there were a few teachers. However, there was a shortage of pens, pencils, exercise books, text books and above all programmes. They had to improvise. I was assigned to 4th grade. Classes were held in the morning. After dinner, there was a compulsory two-hour rest period. We had to lie on our beds and pretend that we were asleep. In the afternoon, we had sports, choir practice and swimming in the nice warm sea.

We were all checked by doctors. I was diagnosed with anaemia, so here I am in the hospital in Bombay. Probably all I need is a good diet and rest and to improve my blood with extra vitamins and iron.

After two weeks, I rejoined the other kids. Tadek and I slowly got accustomed to our new quarters and a new 'normal life' at a Polish school. Tadek has described this period thus, 'straight away I realised how much behind I am in my education and how much I had to make up'. All of us, older boys, live on a veranda. Bobis Tyszkiewicz and I have started publishing a hand-written newsletter *Voice from the Verandah*.

In the middle of July, we left Bandra regretfully and moved to a camp specially built for us near the village of Balachadi, about 20 miles from Jamnagar, which was the capital of Nawanagar state on the Kathiavar peninsula in the province of Gujarat in India. I will write about life in the camp later.

NOTE

1. In Russian, meaning 'do you understand?'

Arrival in India

❦

*T*he arrival of the Polish children in India started initially as a British-sponsored scheme. The Viceroy accepted the idea of taking in 500 orphaned children out of the USSR and hosting them in India. One of the most favoured locations was Kalimpong in the eastern Himalayas where there were several missionary schools. The move had to be thwarted at the very last moment due to the threat of the War spreading to that region with the Japanese advance, well after a group of Polish children were on their way there. No definitive material has been located so far to suggest when the offer was first made and why it had been kept pending.

India had been a transit point for the Jews escaping Nazi persecution in Germany occupied Poland and other regions by 1940. About 40,000 Jewish people escaped to Lithuania, Romania and Hungary from Poland, escaping both the Nazi and the Soviet atrocities. All western escape routes were blocked by the German invasion of Western Europe. The refugees were forced to look elsewhere and had to be creative in seeking routes and permissions to emigrate abroad. Two men, the acting Dutch Consul in Lithuania, Jan Zwartendijk, and the Japanese Consul in Lithuania, Chiune Sugihara, issued more than 4,400 transit visas that paved the way for an escape route from the east. Restrictive immigration policies prevented most refugees from obtaining visas for the USA and Palestine, the two most desired destinations. Zwartendijk issued visas for Curacao and other islands of the Dutch West Indies. On his own initiative, Sugihara issued more than 2,000 transit visas through Japan to people who had the dubious 'Curacao visa' or even nothing that served as final destination visa. 'The Communists' power in this country is rapidly expanding. Under the influence of the N.K.V.D. many acts of terrorism are occurring ... Jews throng our building looking for visas to go to the U.S.

via Japan', Sugihara cabled to the Japanese Foreign Ministry, Tokyo, on 28 July 1940.[1]

The overland trans-Siberian route was permitted by the Soviets for the refugees to reach Japan. While the Jews in Warsaw and other cities were getting confined to ghettos, those who had been able to procure these visas from Lithuania and had applied for exit visas to leave the USSR, were granted permission to travel overland. The Soviet travel agency Intourist booked their passage on the trans-Siberian express. They often stayed at Moscow from where the train left twice a week. The journey took an average of nine days and ended at the eastern Soviet port city of Vladivostok, from where they took a ship to Japan. The transit visas that Sugihara had issued were good for only 8 to 14 days, so a scramble for their extension and availing visas for permanent destinations ensued. By the spring of 1941, policies regarding transit visas were tightened, and they were much harder to obtain in Europe. By the fall of 1941, more than 1,000 had succeeded in their search for visas and had left the country for permanent destinations. About half had gone to the USA.

The British consuls at Kovno in Lithuania and Kobe, Japan, issued visas for Palestine and other British dominions of South Africa, Australia and India.[2] Bombay became a major transit point, where many Jewish people often had to wait for months for onward visas to Palestine, South Africa and Brazil amongst other places. In between, Iraq and Egypt declined transit facilities to these people owing to Arab sentiments. Matters came to a head when six Jewish refugees with visas for Palestine were refused permission to land at Basra and had to return to Bombay in the same vessel in December 1940.[3] About 30 Polish Jews reached Calcutta after the ship they had boarded at Singapore docked for emergency repairs.[4]

The Polish Consulate in Bombay, functional since 1933, quickly constituted the Polish Red Cross and became active in extending relief to these people, in association with the JRA, a worldwide body, which was 'preventing them from starving'.[5] Several Indian industrialists and charitable institutions, including the Tatas, contributed generously to this fund.[6] People arrived with little or no money for onward journey and became destitute.[7] While some took up whatever employment was available, the rest became the responsibility of the Polish Consulate for relief. The Bombay government granted visas for 330 people to be evacuated out of Romania and Yugoslavia. The Iraqi and Egyptian governments declined transit facilities and the Bombay government kept a strict vigil on the state of the finances of the Polish refugees coming into India. The Bombay government wanted the cost of maintaining these refugees to be borne by the central government, who could recover it from HMG and who, in turn, could bill it to the Polish government in England.[8] The foreign office informed the Polish government about their 'embarrassment' by the presence of the destitute amongst these people in June 1941, when the Polish Red Cross was short of funds.[9] The presence of the Jews in Bombay, who were escaping the conditions in Europe, has been extensively dealt with by Bhatti et al.[10] There are unconfirmed reports about certain ships laden with these people being declined landing permission in Bombay and other British Indian ports.

Soon news about the starvation and other inhuman conditions of the Polish people in the USSR started coming in to London. Associating it with the state of the people escaping Nazi Germany, Jam Saheb Digvijaysinghji extended Nawanagar as a wartime destination for the hapless Poles caught in the circumstances in Europe. It must be mentioned here that pre-War Poland was a composite society of Roman Catholics, Jews, Ukrainians, Byelorussians and White Ruthenians, without prejudice to their denomination.

The Polish Red Cross raised relief material to be transported to its citizens in the USSR, within the existing rules. In an initiative spearheaded by Kira Banasinska, wife of the PCG to India, who was nominated as a delegate of the Polish Red Cross, Kira and Wanda Dynowska, a Gandhian who was already in India, lectured about Poland at several places. Contributions and relief material poured in. A flurry of telegrams from 21 May 1941, from the Polish Consul at Bombay and Polish Foreign Office in London were exchanged discussing various routes to reach medicines and supplies to civilian Polish population in the USSR. Routes via Afghanistan and China needed diplomatic arrangements between Poland and those countries. Finally, the Ashkabad-Meshed-Quetta route was accepted as the most feasible to carry comforts for the Polish population in the USSR and bring back children on the return route. The Consulate suggested that six lorries of their own would help very much. A Polish delegation was proposed to be set up in China as many Poles had escaped into China from Mongolia. Discussions with the GOI over bringing in children had been underway since 10 December 1941. It was proposed that the untried semi-built road route to the USSR be used to reach relief material and bring out the children on the return route.[11] They also started exploring hospitality for the Polish population in the various states.[12]

Jan Siedlecki, President of the API, London, argued[13] that the whole arrangement was worked out by Kira Banasinska in Bombay, with the GOI promising to raise charitable funds in India to support 500 Polish children. The arrangement was underwritten by the Polish government-in-exile. But Banasinska could have only worked on this plan of India as a destination for the Polish children only on a firm promise from some official agency while awaiting solely procedural clearances.

The first file on the subject, housed in the India Office Library, London, begins with a letter from Barbara Vere Hodges of the Women's Voluntary Auxiliary Services, and wife of an IMS[14] officer, addressed to 'K' which says, 'Lord Tweedale had a reply from the Polish Ambassador in which he said he was definitely interested in the scheme, and was putting it in the hands of people competent to deal with it'.[15] In her communication dated 1 November 1941,[16] she outlines a fairly detailed plan to evacuate and house in India the Polish refugees. However, the Interdepartmental Conference on Polish Relief held at the foreign office on 29 October 1941 refers to Major Cazalet having put forward a scheme suggested by Vere Hodges for the evacuation of Polish children from the south of the Soviet Union to India, but it was not known whether any further progress had been made in the matter.[17] In fact, the gleaning of subsequent documents, including Captain AWT Webb's exhaustive reports, show that Ms Vere Hodges' suggestions formed the backbone of the methods and administration of the evacuation and camp facilities for the Poles. Hodges mentions that Sir Alan Parsons is about to work with the Red Cross in the section that was sending comforts to Russia; if the evacuation plan was possible he might be able to help a good deal, which he possibly must have for the first batch of 272 children and adults to have come out of the USSR and reached India. In later communications, it began to be known as the 'Tashkent Scheme'.

The PCG at Bombay had organised, with the knowledge of the British authorities in India, an expedition of six motor lorries to take medical supplies to the Poles in the neighbourhood of Tashkent by October 1941. Permission, however, for this expedition to enter the Soviet Union had yet not been granted.[18] Three hundred visas had been granted for Polish refugees to go to India, but there had not been any reply to the application for five hundred visas for children to be evacuated from Tashkent to India as observed by Miss Rolfe of India Office at the Interdepartmental Conference of 29 October 1941.[19]

In his memo dated 9 October 1941, AWG Randall of the foreign office wrote to Mr Clauson of the India Office that Vere Hodges' scheme sent by the India Office had also been received by the Foreign Office directly.[20] The FO had consulted the Poles[21] and they said that they were prepared to back it officially. Randall to Clauson,

> This means that they would be grateful for an approach to the Government of India for permission to transfer to India, in addition to the 300 odd visas promised and not exhausted, a further group of 500, mainly Polish children; if the Government of India agreed the Polish Government would be responsible for organising, paying for the transport and securing exit permits from the Soviet authorities….[22]

It can be surmised that the Polish people were promised some visas by HMG at the beginning of the War to evacuate some of their citizenry from the war zone.

It must be clarified here that several files at the National Archives of India (NAI), New Delhi, reveal that India was a transit point for several hundred Polish Jews, and the Polish Consulate in Bombay was quite busy organising accommodation, relief and onward transportation for them. In his telegram of September 1941, AWG Randall, seeking approval for the 'Tashkent Scheme' from Sir Stafford Cripps, mentions that the Polish government asked for moral support from HMG for the PCG in Bombay to go to Tashkent via Afghanistan and organise a relief centre for Polish refugees in Kazakhstan, 'said to number many thousands and to be in deplorable condition'.[23] On 12 September 1941, the Polish government had informed the British government that Ambassador Kot had reported that there were a million and a half Poles released from internment or deportation by the Moscow government, spread in all parts of the Soviet Union and in desperate need of medicines, clothing, etc.[24] The British Red Cross organised a scheme for relief for the Polish and Czech soldiers, including those capable of joining the Polish Army. But the extent of the problem for civilians was so vast that the organisation of supplies would have to be done on an international scale, such that American and Indian participation should be secured.[25]

Major Victor Cazalet, of the British Army, posted at Moscow, was pushing for the reception of 500 Polish children in India, though the difficulties of transport were formidable.[26]

A minute sheet entry dated 22 September[27] says that the Polish government expects that the general release of Polish prisoners from the Russian camps may result in these people turning up in countries bordering the USSR, such as Manchukuo, China, Afghanistan, etc. A report was received that some of these refugees had already arrived in Iraq, Afghanistan and

Persia and were interned there.[28] The minute sheet continues that the GOI had been getting rather nervous about an influx of Poles from the USSR through Afghanistan and had been making urgent enquiries about the numbers involved and their ultimate destination.[29] The same document continues that there was a proposal on hand for a relief expedition, organised by the PCG in Bombay and his wife, to take emergency relief supplies to Kazakhstan and to institute a special base in Afghanistan. The Poles were making varied and complicated arrangements to send supplies to the Polish refugees by the northern route,[30] Persia and the Caucasus. In his handwritten entry, Millard, an official whose designation could not be established, notes that the Polish Embassy had sent a list of 100 tons of supplies for Russia, including food, for which they require transport. A consignment consisting of every conceivable kind of supply including food had left a fortnight ago, all purchased by the treasury department and out of the Polish-credit[31] with HMG.

The minutes state that it was clearly impossible to evacuate a population of one-and-a-half million people and find accommodation for them in other countries. So the Poles had to confine themselves to bringing out nationals who were likely to be really useful from the point of view of the war effort. There was no doubt that the GOI would look very unfavourably on any scheme for large-scale evacuation of Poles to India.

The GOI was reluctant to receive these additional Polish children on several counts:

- Weather conditions not conducive for European children
- Increasing liabilities due to threat of war reaching India
- Potential of espionage agents coming with these children
- Diversion of scarce resources away from the war effort for civilian consumption
- Increased governmental expenditure

The condition of the Poles in the USSR and their subsequent evacuation leading to a sizeable portion of the civilians reaching India are discussed later.

The Acceptance

According to the Report of the Delegate of Poland in Bombay, dated July 1944, the case of the Polish children being hosted in India started with the official letter of the HMG, 15 October 1941, to the Viceroy of India which suggested taking 500 Polish children from the USSR and putting them in foster British and later Indian families to avoid financial problems. This suggestion was not accepted by the officials and HMG was informed accordingly. They suggested that the children could be placed in convents and schools in the central region. That was for about 300 children, and the rest of them could be sent to Ooty in Anandagiri in South India. But this project was not accepted by the Polish side, because the children would get separated and that would break the cultural links.

Another proposed location was Kalimpong, which has several good boarding schools. This idea was supported for a long time till the group of 160 children who were on the way, had to be stopped midway due to the advance of the Japanese forces. The advance was rapid and the GOI felt that the roads to Kalimpong could get closed. This project had then to be abandoned. So the GOI accepted the offer of Jam Saheb of Nawanagar to build the campsite in Balachadi.[32]

After his unofficial 'offer' to host Polish refugees in Nawanagar, it is possible that Jam Saheb wrote a letter of invitation for the first batch of children because there is reference to a letter of invitation for a subsequent batch of children.[33] Since the Indian Princely States could not deal with foreign countries or their representatives officially,[34] it had to be moved through the GOI who clearly wanted specific instructions from HMG, London. The Polish weekly news magazine *Polska* carried an interview with Jam Saheb Digvijaysinghji in its 25 November 1942 issue,[35] where he spoke about his acquaintance with Ignacy Padrewski.

Reluctantly Lord Linlithgow, the Viceroy of India, replied to Sir Leo Amery, the British Foreign Minister, from Calcutta on 23 December 1941, stating that the consensus of opinion rules out private hospitality as a solution of the lodging problem as well as the following:

> We understand from the wife of the Polish Consul General that there are over a million Polish refugees in Russia and that they are comparatively well to do middle class families. I feel, therefore, that I must endorse the majority view that if Polish children come to India they must be accommodated in camps, either specially constructed or formed by requisitioning existing buildings, in which schools would be set up. My conclusions are therefore that we could, subject to the disadvantages described above, accept and arrange for the education of 500 Polish children without great difficulty, that it would be preferable to keep them in largish parties in hostels to be specially arranged.... Finally, while a special appeal under the auspices of the Polish Relief Fund may be expected to raise sufficient to meet part of the cost of maintenance, it could not be relied on to cover

all expenditure, and I am not aware whether the Polish Government could guarantee to meet any deficiency. My conclusions are of course necessarily formed in ignorance of the conditions of the Polish refugees in Russia and in the absence of information.[36]

The Polish government obviously agreed to be responsible for any difference between the expenditure and the receipts from charity,[37] paving the way for them to be evacuated to India by February 1942. Evacuation began before the camp in Balachadi was constructed. Linlithgow sent an appeal to the Princes for donations for the Polish children (see Appendices 3 and 8 for details).

The Polish Children's Fund was set up with an initial contribution of ₹50,000 from the Viceroy's War Purposes Fund. Since it was to be a charitable fund, letters of appeal went out accordingly.[38] A committee was established to administer the finances of the camp. Home Secretary, E Conran-Smith, invited OK Caroe, Secretary External Affairs Department, to serve on the committee, along with the Archbishop of Delhi; the Mother Superior of the Convent of Jesus and Mary; the representatives of Political and Finance Departments, the Indian Red Cross and Madame Banasinska as the delegate in India of the Polish Ministry of Social Welfare.[39] Captain AWT Webb, Principal Refugee Officer, was appointed the secretary of this committee who initiated the most detailed reports of the matters concerning this committee. He prepared the budgets, maintained the accounts and initiated the reports of immense historical value, which have been referred to regularly in this study. Money was advanced to Madame Banasinska to make the purchases for the various items required in the camps, including personal effects for adults and children alike and communal kit requirements of a large group of people.

Charitable funds began to be raised for the Polish children in India and the Indian Red Cross Society raised ₹8,424, 9 *annas* and 2 paise by November 1942 (₹18,08,708 in 2010 [£621.34 in 1942 = £24,200 in 2010]). More organised appeals for funds were underway. However, the finance department was requested to advance funds as and when required, with the understanding that these would be repaid later either from charitable subscriptions received or by debit to the Polish government, who had agreed to be responsible for any difference between expenditure and receipts from charity.

It was decided that the main source of money to defray expenditure at the camp must remain with the GOI who will act as agents for the Polish government. Funds for the Polish children's camp were advanced by the

GOI for the other evacuee camps in the charge of the home department. All estimates for construction or recurring expenditure would require the concurrence of the finance department. Donations received from the public at large would be credited to the Polish Children's Fund. The committee would act as an advisory body with special reference to the appropriate use of funds donated by the public. For that purpose, it would meet from time to time, have access to budgets and approve the transfer of sums standing to the credit of the Polish Children's Account to the Accountant General, Central Revenues or other suitable authority towards the redemption of the debit being raised by the GOI against the Polish government on account of the maintenance of Polish children in India.

The Journey

Kira Banasinska arranged that the trucks taking relief goods to the USSR would bring the children on the return route. The expedition was to be led by Mr Tadeusz Lisiescki, Deputy Consul at Bombay, and Dr Stanislaus Konarski, a physician, was to accompany the entourage. A collective visa for the children was issued at Meshed and visa was obtained for one of their minor ministers, Henryk Hadala, to accompany the group. An experienced driver, Dajek, was chosen for the assignment, who was ably assisted by six Sikh drivers to drive on a hitherto untried route.

The children were brought out of the orphanage at Ashkabad in batches and quarantined at Meshed for a few weeks, as the lorries went back and forth between Meshed and Ashkabad reaching relief goods and ferrying back children. Finally, in mid-March, 173 people started the journey for India. The party consisted of 90 girls, 71 boys, 11 adults and one priest,[40] Fr Franciszek Pluta, and the four Polish adults mentioned earlier. The journey was difficult and frightening on a half-constructed road and is described by Franek Herzog. They travelled on the Meshed-Birjand-Zahidan route being constructed by the Indian Army as one of the lend-lease supply route (see Map 4).

The party crossed over to the then Indian border at Nok-Kundi on the present Pakistan–Afghanistan border off Quetta on the afternoon of 9 April 1942, where a train was waiting to take them to Bombay. Banasinska had rented two bungalows in Bandra to house the children till Balachadi could be made ready. The party was met in Quetta by Banasinska and

Map 4: Routes taken by Polish evacuees to reach India*

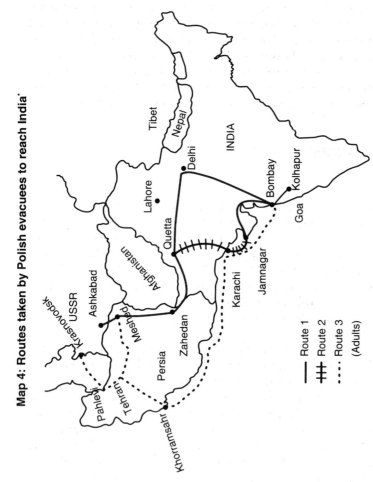

Legend:
— Route 1
‡‡ Route 2
···· Route 3
(Adults)

Notes: 1. The map has been developed by the author and has not been drawn to scale. It does not represent authentic international boundaries.
2. Evacuation route prepared by the author based on various accounts of survivors.

Captain AWT Webb, where the children even gave an impromptu concert.[41] Quetta served as a transit camp for all batches of children evacuated through this route. At Delhi, the party was met by British military
and civilian officials, including Mr E Conran-Smith, Secretary to the GOI
Home Department, where too the concert was repeated. They also sang
the English anthem, though with bad pronunciations.

The catering at the stations was done by M/s Spencers, according to
Captain AWT Webb's report dated 3 November 1942. He also remarks
that the bearing of the children was cheerful in spite of the hardships
they had endured and they were mostly a disciplined lot. He notes two
cases, one where some children were found by their relations and another where a 7-year-old boy carried his 18-month-old sister on his back
for miles to reach the orphanage where children were being collected to
be transported to India.

The Camp at Bandra

During the journey, frequent halts were made and local organisations met
the children with food, drinks and toys. After their arrival in Bombay, a
careful medical check-up disclosed that there were among the children:

20 cases of suspected tuberculosis
11 cases of whooping cough
41 cases of septic tonsils
44 cases of scabies and other skin diseases

A large number of children required dental treatment due to ravages
of scurvy. The services of Dr Tendulkar and Dr Patel were obtained as the
medical officer of the camp at Bandra. Three children and one adult with
tuberculosis were sent to a sanatorium at Panchgani. The children were
visited by several dignitaries including Lady Lumley, wife of the Governor of Bombay and the Archbishop of Bombay. Since Poles did not speak
English, to overcome the language barrier, colloquial English classes were
started for the children.

Initially one big bungalow was rented for the children in Bandra. Soon
that proved inadequate and a second bungalow was also rented. With
regular healthy diet and rest, the children's health started picking up. To
fill up empty hours, some kinds of lessons were begun, possibly some

conversational English to be able to exchange pleasantries with visitors, etiquettes and songs (see Photograph 2).

The expenses incurred at Bandra, as given by Captain AWT Webb, is given in the following:[42]

Table 1: The expenses incurred at Bandra

	₹
Cost of equipping 500 children on arrival at ₹64	32,000
Cost of feeding the first batch of children at the Bandra camp	18,337
Special treatment for ailing children	992
Medicine	3,352
Rent, electricity and water for the Bandra camp	3,687
Total	**58,368**

It must be recalled here that the children had been through severe hunger and depravation and being orphans, they also had to rely on animal instincts, steal and scavenge for food most of the times to survive. So as Captain Webb notes, it was expected that the children, who had been running wild for so long and being driven to extremes by hunger, would be in a deplorable condition of health and indiscipline,[43] but they were not as bad as expected, possibly due to their basic breeding or submission arising out of a sense of security. As Stefan Klosowski described,

> We were grateful to have someone give us food at regular hours after months of having to beg, steal or toil for it ourselves. The quality did not matter because at least we were not hungry anymore. It was enough to have someone put some clothes over us—it did not matter what or whose they were—we were not cold anymore. So, for that much, we did whatever we were told to do.[44]

Franek Herzog writes that he was thrilled to see a real clean bed, complete with mattress and clean bedsheets, all to himself. It was an unbelievable luxury after years of sleeping on makeshift lice-infested bed and bedding in the USSR.

At Bandra, to fill the long lazy afternoons, when the children were not allowed to go outdoors, the older boys started bringing out a newsletter *Voice from the Verandah* filled with news, jokes and write-ups. According to Franek Herzog, in all, six issues of the magazine were brought out.

In his note, Major Geoffrey Clarke, personal assistant to Maharaja Jam Saheb Digvijaysinghji, wrote that there was long lull on the subject of evacuee children after an initial discussion. His Highness Jam Saheb was informed that the first batch of children were likely to arrive within six weeks, with a request that arrangements might be completed to receive them. Despite the site chosen for the camp—by the representative of the Home Department of the GOI—being some 17 miles from Jamnagar town, an equal distance from the nearest railway station, posed severe logistical problems, the camp was made ready to receive the children in great earnest.[45]

On 16 July 1942, the camp at Bandra was broken up and the children were moved to Balachadi.

NOTES AND REFERENCES

1. United States Holocaust Memorial Museum, *Flight and Rescue* (United States: United States Holocaust Memorial Museum, 2001), 10–11.
2. United States Holocaust Memorial Museum, *Flight and Rescue*, 16–17.
3. NAI, EAD, 186-X/40 (Secret), Letter No. 230, GFS Collins to Secy, dated 15 January 1941.
4. S Solomon, *Hooghly Tales* (London: David Ashley Publishing, 1997), 129.
5. NAI, 186/-X/40 (Secret), Thomas Cook & Son to Captain RKM Saker, dated 22 February 1941.
6. TCA, DTT Collection, Minutes of 65th, 67th and 80th Meetings.
7. NAI, EAD 186/-X/40 (Secret).
8. NAI, EAD 186/-X/40 (Secret), Folio 29–31, RKM Saker.
9. AAN, S 38-39 (File number cannot be given but scanned copy of letter is with the author).
10. A Bhatti and V Johannes, *Jewish Exiles in India* (New Delhi: Manohar, 1999).
11. PIGSM, Banasinski Collection, KOL 129/2. Also BNA, CAB/111/310.
12. BNA, CAB/111/310, Letter dated 23 January 1942, Eugenisuz Banasinski to Wanda Dynowska.
13. Jan Seidlecki, President, API (1942–48), London, interview to author, London, 16 March 2004.
14. Possibly Indian Military Service.
15. BL-I&OC, L/P&J/110-N/19-1/412, Folio 298.
16. Ibid.
17. BNA, CAB/111/310.
18. Ibid.
19. Ibid.
20. BNA, FO 371/29214, AWG Randall to Clauson.
21. Possibly the Polish Ambassador to London, Count Edward Raczynski.
22. BNA, CAB/111/310.

23. BNA, FO 371.29214, AWG Randall to Sir S Cripps, September 1941.
24. BNA, CAB/ 111/310, Aide-memoire, Walker to Gorell Barnes, 24 October 1941.
25. Ibid.
26. Ibid.
27. Year assumed to be 1941.
28. Angora telegram 2192 in C lO275, cited in BNA, FO 371.29214.
29. BNA, CAB/111/310.
30. Northern route here could be meaning the land route from India through erstwhile North-west Frontier Provinces (NWFP), now in Pakistan and parts of Afghanistan.
31. BNA, FO 371.29214.
32. PIGSM, C811d/, Report of the Delegate of Poland in Bombay, dated July 1944.
33. BNA, FO 371/ 32630, Notes dated 10 August.
34. BL-I&OC, R2/952/76 C-70/43, Appendix Notes, dated 10 January 1943, indicative communication regarding Kolhapur Durbar (The Prime Minister mentioned the PCG as coming here. We must draw attention at once to the rules debarring States from corresponding directly with foreign countries or inviting foreign consuls to the state without the PD's approval. Sd. JB).
35. Interview to weekly magazine *Polska* (17), dated 25 November 1942, cited in Notes of Chapter on Balachadi Camp, *Poles in India 1942–48, In view of Reminiscences and Documents* (Also referred to as API Book).
36. BL-I&OC, L/ P&J/110-N 19-1/412, folio 254, Linlithgow to Amery, dated 23 December 1941.
37. NAI, 276(8)-X/42, Captain AWT Webb's Reports (hereafter WR), 9.
38. NAI, 276-X/42/Secret, Viceroy's Office.
39. NAI, 276-X/42/Secret, Folio 24 and NAI, 276(8)-X/42, DO 126/142/41- Poll (Evn).
40. NAI, 276(8)-X/42, Captain AWT Webb's Reports, 9, dated 3 November 1942.
41. NAI, 276(8)-X/42, Captain AWT Webb's Reports and archival official pictures courtesy Tadeusz Dobrostanski.
42. NAI, 276(8)-X/42, Captain AWT Webb's Reports, 28.
43. NAI, 276(8)-X/42, Captain AWT Webb's Reports, 15.
44. S Klosowski, a former Balachadi boy and now a retired engineer in Canada visiting Balachadi, interview to author, Balachadi, October 2002.
45. BL-I&OC, POL 9244, Major Geoffrey Clarke's 'Note on Polish Evacuee Children received by HH the Maharaja Jam Saheb of Nawanagar in Nawanagar State', dated 17 October 1942.

India Years

৵৲৵

Franek and Tadek in Balachadi

◌⚮◌

North of Bombay, in the Kathiwar peninsula, about 15 miles from the capital city, Jamnagar, was the village Balachadi. On a cliff rising from the seabed stood the beautiful summer residence of the maharaja Jam Saheb. On the east side of the palace there was a park-like garden and on the west side, facing the sea, there was a big swimming pool. Water in the pool was refreshed at every high tide. In southerly direction from the palace stretched a long sandy beach. A bit inland from the sandy beach on the dunes there was a narrow strip of grass shaded by acacia trees, tall agaves plants and cacti. On that grassy strip there was a well-kept golf course.

Further away from the seashore stretched semi-desert scenery with numerous rocky hills sparsely covered with grass, thorny bushes and swirls of cacti. In some places, especially near wells or reservoirs with fresh water, huge banyan trees with long lianas, palms and other trees were growing.

Our camp was built on one of the hills, about a mile from the palace and approximately the same distance from the village of Balachadi. It was a complex of over 60 very simple barracks covered with red, clay tiles. The basic building material consisted of stone, cement and some lumber and the complex could house 700–800 people.

Barracks for children were 130 feet by 17 feet, with no partitions inside, no ceiling and with an earthen floor. There were two doors and a number of windows on both sides. The windows had no glass panes, only a few wooden bars to which nets were attached as a protection against mosquitoes and other insects.

Each child had his/her own wooden bed with a mattress, pillow, bed linen and a blanket. Above each bed, there was a wooden shelf. By each bed, there was a small table on which a metal trunk stood. In addition to that, in each barrack there were a few benches and two large tables on which we could do our homework or write letters. There was no electricity in the camp so barracks were illuminated with paraffin lamps. Barracks for personnel were smaller and subdivided, each 'apartment' consisting of two small rooms. Toilets and bathrooms were in separate buildings, designated for boys, girls and adults. Kitchens, sickbay and bathrooms had concrete floors.

For the entire duration of our existence in the orphanage at Balachadi, Fr Pluta was its commandant and Mrs Z Rozwadowska his deputy. At its maximum, the orphanage had well over 600 children from the ages of 2 to 17 years, plus teachers, guardians and auxiliary staff. All together, there were some 700 people. And what a cross section both in mentality and morality we represented! Some adults and older children were somewhat corrupted after two years of living in the communist system where the only thing that mattered was survival, no matter at what cost and how. Some children had complexes. As an example, we had among us two Jewish boys. Somebody wanted to drown them. When Fr Pluta asked him why, he replied, 'Why? Because when I was in the Russian orphanage that was run by a Russian Jew, he hated Poles and made my stay there really miserable.'

Several Jewish children came with other transports but within a few months, all of them sponsored by Jewish organizations left for Palestine.

But overall we were lucky. We had good and dedicated guardians. Some of them wanted to substitute for our lost parents. Nobody in the camp, including Fr Pluta, was a professional pedagogue. To inject discipline and to regulate day-to-day life in the camp was his first priority. He was a semi-military man and he wanted to run the camp in that fashion.

Reveille was at 7 a.m., followed by some physical exercises and then washing up. Before breakfast, we marched to the main square for the ceremony of raising the flag. After breakfast, we had classes till lunch, followed by a one-hour compulsory rest period.

In the afternoon, we had a variety of activities depending on the day, for example, going for a swim, scout meetings, choir and orchestra practice, drama lessons, games in the clubroom or sport. Before supper, especially after monsoon, when there were many mosquitoes, we had to put on long pants and shirts with long sleeves. During the hours of most intense sun, we had to wear tropical helmets of cork.

In Bandra, we had had a sort of an improvised schooling and so it continued, to start with in Balachadi. But after more children arrived at the camp in September and again in December, a number of professional teachers came with them. A proper school was organised. We were assigned to classes not so much by age, but by knowledge and ability. Frequently in one grade there were children with a four-year age difference. The problem was with older children that were already at a secondary-school level. There were no qualified teachers to teach them. In 1943, 15 boys, among them Tadek, were placed at St Mary's High School in Mount Abu, Rajputana. About the same number of girls were sent to St Joseph's Convent school in Karachi and Panchgani.

Mrs J Tarnogorska was responsible for running the kitchen. Kitchen staff was recruited from the Portuguese colony of Goa. She had a difficult task of preparing menus from Indian produce that would be palatable to us. Luckily we ate everything that was put in front of us; we had good appetites. Sometimes at night we would raid the kitchen for some leftover food, not so much that we were hungry, but just for the sport.

The period right after monsoons (September/October) was the biggest problem in the camp. Shallow pools and puddles of fresh water were the breeding ground for mosquitoes. During the first year of our stay in Balachadi, 80 per cent of the camp inhabitants developed malaria. The following year, two anti-malaria specialists came to the camp to teach the people in the nearby villages and us how to eliminate breeding places and also showed some other preventive methods. Dr Rubinsztain joined Dr Ashani and then when sufficient supplies of quinine, atabrine, plasmoquine and other medicines arrived to the dispensary run by Dr Joshi, the epidemic of malaria was controlled. Only a small number of children, I among them, developed the so-called tropical malaria with recurring attacks. In the last year of our stay in Balachadi, there were only a few new cases of malaria.

The camp hospital dealt mainly with malaria and anaemia, which frequently developed as a result of malaria, snakebites (we had only one), scorpion poisoning, scratches and cuts. More serious injuries requiring surgeries were sent to the hospitals in Jamnagar or Rajkot. Over the period of two years, there were two deaths. One small boy whose organism was completely ruined by malnutrition and illnesses that he had suffered in Russia, died soon after coming to Balachadi. The other death was due to drowning when a boy went by himself for a swim in the lake.

There were 600 children in the camp and we did some crazy things. To name a few, sneaking out at night for a swim in the sea, jumping headfirst from 25 feet into deep water wells hewed in rock, running barefoot across fields chasing peacocks, where stepping on a cobra or a scorpion was possible, or climbing trees and swinging on lianas pretending we were Tarzan. I have to admit that it was not due to our guardian's supervision, but God Himself must have protected us from crippling injuries or even death.

Monsoons lasting from mid-July to mid-September were very burdensome. Usually it started with a violent storm with thunder and a downpour. Then sunshine would come for a few days and then steady rain would come, not very heavy but lasting for a stretch. Tiles, not of the best quality, were cracked in many places due to our climbing roofs to retrieve balls or other objects thrown there. As a consequence, roofs started leaking. To find a dry spot in the barrack, we would move our beds from place and finally put one on top of the other to form a sort of bunk bed. Then with a blanket we would construct imitation of a tent.

Scouting had a great influence in shaping our young characters and teaching us resourcefulness. Already in Bandra, with the initiative of Heniek Bobotek, a scout patrol, *Orly* (Eagles), was organised. Once we moved to Balachadi, scouting expanded rapidly. But it was with the arrival in the camp of a young, energetic, demanding but understanding teacher, who was also very pretty, scout mistress Janina Ptakowa that the scouting movement was put on the right track and it flourished.

We had two troops of Boy Scouts, two troops of Girl Guides and two of each Cub Scouts and Brownie Packs. All together, there were about 250 children in the organisation. From the very beginning, I liked scouting and working with kids. Bivouacs, camps and campfires broke the otherwise monotonous everyday life in the orphanage.

Thanks to Mr A Maniak, an all-round athlete and an excellent football player from the well-known pre-War club Pogon in Lwow, sport in the camp flourished. For us boys, he was a role model. Our football and volleyball teams competed on equal terms with some Indian Navy teams and most of the times we were victorious. Sport competitions were very frequent and popular.

We all enjoyed going to the beach and swimming. Usually we went twice a week and during holidays even twice a day. The distance from the camp to the beach was less than a mile, so running downhill took us about 10 minutes. About three-fourths of a mile from the shore, there were some trees growing in the shallow water. During high tide only the tops were sticking above water. It was challenging to swim to the trees and after a short rest between branches to swim back. On the way back to the camp, for a snack, we would help ourselves to sugar cane or peanuts from fields. The local Hindu farmers complained to Fr Pluta about this, he compensated them somewhat and then told us to be more careful and not to do any damage to the crop.

Mrs J Dobrostanska and then Mrs C Ciazynska were responsible for cultural and recreational activities. Two barracks were designated as clubrooms where we had a variety of games, including table tennis. There was a battery-operated radio, some newspapers, periodicals and a library. But by far the biggest attraction was a spring-operated gramophone with a big tube and a collection of records with some pre-War hits. We learned some ballroom dancing and from time to time on Saturday evening we would have social dance.

By the end of September 1942, all of the Polish Army left Russia for the Middle East. We had not heard from our Father since that last postcard in Kazakhstan, had lost our mother in the wilderness of Kazakhstan and now we had no news from Wacek. We were bracing for the worst.

By the end of 1942, two more transports of children arrived. Gradually we were getting used to each other and to know each other better and some lasting friendships developed.

Tadek was one of the older boys in the orphanage. He was big, strong and a good sportsman, though once, while pole-vaulting (and showing off) Tadek missed the mattress on which he was supposed to land, hit the ground and broke his arm. He had a good reputation with the elders and respect from his peers. He had a nickname *Slon* (Elephant). I had a good protector in him, but on the other hand, I always had to live in his shadow. The difference of five years at that young age was difficult to bridge. He had his own circle of friends and I had mine.

Christmas of 1942 came. It was supposed to be a festive season, but in our hearts there was sadness, nostalgia and grief. We had the special Christmas Play (Jaselka). Tadek, with great success, played King Herod in the Jaselka. I only got a part of one of the shepherds without even having to say one word.

During the year we also had some other shows or special productions of Polish national dances. Maharaja Jam Saheb attended several of these performances and he would leave ₹501 or ₹1,001. We all found the one rupee very interesting and he said it was for 'good luck' till next time. This money was used for expenses associated with costumes and any surplus would be used for occasional trip to Jamnagar to see a movie. During the last two years we had a band in the camp. Musical instruments were received from America, a gift from National Catholic Women's Conference (NCWC). Maharaja Jam Saheb sent two musicians from his band as instructors. My 'musical talents' were properly recognised, and I was a substitute to a substitute drummer!

And that is basically what our life in the camp looked like. It was difficult, simple but adequate, without any special attractions. We grew together as one family. Photograph 3 shows what I had begun to look like in Balachadi.

From now onwards, I have chronicled events by the year, writing only the high points of an otherwise routine life of school, scouts and friends.

Year 1943

Before Easter, I went for my first confession and received my first communion. I was supposed to have done all that in Lubaczow and even attended preparation instructions, but then it turned out that I was not baptised. Apparently my designated godparents did not talk to each other or could not get together at the same time, so my baptism was postponed. In Silesia where I was born, the civil authorities issued a birth certificate and not the church as was customary in other parts of Poland. So for nine years, I was just a little 'pagan'. In 1939, when bombs started falling on Lubaczow, mother rushed me to the church and I was baptised on the spot.

In May, a group of children with some adults left our camp for Mexico where a camp for Polish refugees was being established. Tadek was very saddened as his two best friends, Heniek Bobotek and Bobis Tyszkiewicz, went with that group. Tadek became the troop leader and that is when I was accepted as a scout.

At the end of April, the school year ended and I was promoted to the 5th grade. We had long vacations that were to last till the middle of July. Our vacation was filled with many activities. There were scout meetings, lot of swimming and trips to the surrounding countryside to familiarise us with it. When Mr Maniak arrived, he soon initiated development of the soccer field, running track, volleyball and basketball courts and other sport facilities. He did not spare himself, so we also worked very hard. I must say, it was hard work but when everything was finished, we were very proud of what we had done.

At long last, we received news from Wacek. He was in England in the Polish Navy. A short while later, we received a long letter describing events since we parted in Russia. Here is what he wrote:

PO Box 293, GPO London
In Place 2-7-44

Dear Brothers;
As soon as I received your letter, I sent Tadek an airmail letter promising to write more details about myself later. Unfortunately due to circumstances beyond my control, I had to postpone writing till today. You have to understand, frequently my time is not my own and sometimes there is nothing to write about or rather you are not allowed to write because of the censorship. Recently we were allowed to write to our families more openly, so here it is.

I don't remember what I wrote regarding myself, so I will start from the beginning. I am sure that you know about my sickness in Russia. I survived it all thanks to the sisters and mother of Przemek Inglot. I left Russia with the last transport in August of '42. For about a week, we stayed in Persia on the shores of the Caspian Sea and then they moved us to Iraq. There we stayed for a couple of months. I used that time to recuperate and to build my strength. As I completely restored my health, I was given category 'A' and they wanted to assign me to the Air Force. Because of the problem with my hearing, I refused and stayed in the Navy.

Towards the end of '42, we left for England. The first stage of our voyage ended in Karachi, India. We stayed there for two months having nothing to do but play tourist. I even wrote to the Polish Consulate in Bombay asking them about your whereabouts, but they told me that they knew nothing. Life otherwise was like paradise. We had plenty of money so I bought myself a watch and a camera. I took more than a hundred pictures that were the greatest memento of our stay there.

Not far from our camp there was an American camp. We visited them frequently as there were many Poles among them. Nearby there was also a camp with Polish children and women who were evacuated from Russia and were now waiting to be resettled in India and Africa. We invited many orphan children to a Christmas Eve dinner. We had a real Christmas tree and plenty of presents for all of them. In return, the children prepared a nice show with singing and Polish National Dances.

Unfortunately, that nice time came to an end and we had to continue our journey. Our next stop was Bombay. It was a very short one, just to change ships and then a long voyage across the Indian Ocean where I experienced my first sea storm. My stomach was a bit upset but otherwise I felt OK. We were all looking forward to the African continent and embarkation, so once again we could have firm ground under our feet.

Durban. We camped just outside the town on the grounds of some sport stadium. Just nearby there were banana plantations and orange groves. It was fantastic. Our trips to town were usually in the evening, as it was too hot to go there during the day and the streets were deserted. The South Africans were very hospitable and we had many invitations to visit them. Because of the language barrier, I only visited one family where they spoke some German.

It was with regret that we left Durban on a big transatlantic ship. When we crossed the equator, an Italian submarine sank us. I survived, but only with my gym pants on. However, it was worth losing everything just for the excitement of being in a shipwreck. If you want I can describe that in more detail in my next letter.

After a few days in a lifeboat, we were 'fished out' and brought to Freeport. Thanks to an excellent English organization, the next day we were able to go to town, clothed and with money in our pockets. We celebrated our survival with some good drinking parties and trips to the jungle. It was like in the H. Sienkiewicz book In Desert and Wilderness. *You could admire wild animals and tropical vegetation as though in some enchanted zoo, and all without a ticket. Again, it did not last for too long and we had to continue our journey.*

The rest of the voyage to England went smoothly and without incident. They sent us to Scotland where I met a few officers from Father's regiment. My heart was bleeding. Not knowing English I could not strike up any conversation and there were so many pretty girls.

I did not stay in the camp too long. I was assigned to the Polish cruiser Dragon. *Now they allowed us to write that we were taking part in the invasion of France.*

I hug you tenderly - Wacek

School vacations ended and the monsoon season arrived. As the broken tiles were never changed as promised, water started dripping on our heads and that meant chaos in the barracks and mud on the floor. On the soccer field there were pools of water and mud, so playing there was out of the question. We had to be satisfied with some indoor games such as marbles, buttons, playing cards and games we just improvised. If it stopped raining for a short time, we would go hunting for parrots with slingshots.

As classes started, a group of older boys including Tadek and some girls left the camp for further education in English schools. The same day Tadek left I broke my right hand just above the wrist while playing ball. It was a compound fracture, so to set it properly, I had to go to hospital in Rajkot. They put on a cast, and I had to have it on for four weeks. In the meantime, I tried to learn to write with my left hand. It was not that difficult as I am a lefthander by nature. When they removed cast there was a visible bend in one of the bones. There was the possibility that they might need to break the bone again and reset it once more. Fortunately with some exercises and time, the bump disappeared.

Tadek, now being away, was writing to me at least once a month. It seemed that he was more concerned about me now than when he was close by. And now, a few fragments from his letters.

St. Mary's High School
Abu, 28-8-43

Dear Niusiek.
I have heard from Sledz (1) that you took me too literally when I told you to carry on in my tradition and not to bring shame to our name. I didn't mean that you have to break your arms and legs. Probably you are happy now that you don't have to go to school, but I will ask your teacher not to go easy on you. Write to me, provided that you can and tell me when you will go back to classes, how many failed grades you got and what mischievous things you did. But please write truly, even if it is something bad. I would rather hear it from you than somebody else. And if you have any problems or do not know what to do in certain situations, then write to me, I might be able to help. I feel very well here. The climate is excellent. We have to study a lot and the only free time is on weekend.

Remember Niusiek, you have to study, especially English. You never know what the future has in store for you and as long as you have the opportunity—study.

Tadek.

(1) Herring, a nickname of Jurek Dobrostanski

Abu, 11-9-43

Dear Niusiek.
Not long ago, I received your last letter and today the second one. I did not know that you broke your right hand otherwise I would not asked you to reply immediately.

Be careful, do not run, jump and most importantly do not bump that hand, as it might not heal properly. I am telling you that from my own experience.

… You asked me to describe our scenery. To do it properly, I do not have enough time and paper, but I will try to do my best. The mountains surrounding us are pretty high. Slopes and valleys are covered with trees and bushes so thick that they form an impenetrable jungle. Only here and there you can see bare rocks. Some of the trees are mangoes, figs and date palms. Apparently when ripe they are delicious. We will see.

There are many streams with crystal clear cold water cascading down over the rocks. A pretty sight. At this time, you can hardly see the mountain tops as they are covered with clouds. Sometime they come all the way down to us (clouds, not mountains).

Our school is located on one of the slopes at 1,400 meters (4,200 feet) about a mile from the town Abu. There are many palaces of various maharajahs from different parts of India. Some of the palaces are very pretty. Abu itself is nothing to talk about. If it was not for the palaces, there would be nothing to look at and admire.

Before I finish, please accept my sincere and best wishes for your namesday. Well, what can I wish you ... first of all that we could celebrate your next one in Wilno. All of us, as it used to be in the days gone ... God Willing! Do not forget that it's also our Father's namesday. I don't think I have to write any more and you will know what to do.

I hug you tenderly—best of everything, Tadek.

At the beginning of December, all the boys from Mount Abu came to the camp for a long holiday. For Christmas I was with Tadek.

And what was going on in the political arena this year? In late April, the Germans announced that in Katyn Forest, not far from Smolensk in Russia, they discovered the mass graves of Polish officers. As it turned out, they were all from the Kozielsk POW camp. Germany accused Russia of the murder. Naturally Russia blamed the Germans. Polish government in London asked the International Red Cross in Switzerland to investigate. Russia refused to participate in such an investigation, accused the Polish government of siding with the Germans and broke diplomatic relationship with Poland. England and America, being afraid to antagonise Russia, also refused to participate in the investigation. Hence, Germany organised its own investigating team comprising forensic medicine experts from occupied countries, but also including some from Switzerland and Sweden and the Polish Red Cross. The commission concluded that the bodies had been in the ground for about three years since 1940. Hence, the Russians must have committed the massacre as at the time the POWs were in their hands. The worst of our presumption became reality. Our Father also had also been executed and thrown into some common mass grave. But where?

Soon after the discovery of the mass graves of Polish officers at Katyn, General Sikorski, Premier and Commander-in-Chief of the

Polish Army, was killed in an air crash at Gibraltar. The entire Polish nation went into grief. It was thanks to General Sikorski that we had been able to leave Russia. General W Anders had also wanted to remove the army from Russian territory. It was also convenient for the British to have additional army in the Middle East, protecting oil fields. The Polish Army that left Russia, numbered some 90,000 men and about 50,000 civilians left Russia.

The German offensive in Russia was halted. Leningrad and Moscow were not taken. British and American troops pushed the German Army out of Africa.

Year 1944

For me Christmas school break was short. In the middle of January we had to go back to classes. For some reason, boys from Mount Abu School stayed in the camp till the middle of March. At this time, Tadek had his first 'serious' love affair. The object of his affection was Marysia Skarzenska, daughter of our principal matron. It seems that he had noticed her the moment she arrived in our camp in September 1942. At that time, we all had crushes on girls, but we admired them from a distance and kept all our tender feelings secret. No dating and no going out, principally because there was nowhere to go to.

Tadek was almost 18 years old and Marysia was two or three years younger. During New Year and the so-called 'carnival season', when we had social dances every Saturday night, Tadek conquered his shyness and started attending these socials and actually dancing there. He also noticed that Marysia looked at him in a different way than she looked at other boys and when she was dancing with him she was closer than when dancing with other. But still Tadek did not have enough courage to tell her that she was a special one. It happened on the day he was leaving for Mount Abu. Tadek went to the quarters where Mrs Skarzenska lived to say goodbye to Marysia. He described the moment as,

> We stood close to each other. I put my arm round her neck and she put her head on my shoulder. After a moment she also put her arm around my neck and shyly kissed my cheek. We looked at each

other and at that moment our lips met briefly. I do not remember what we were saying, but I knew that in a few words we unfolded our feelings for each other. After a time I said, 'Marysia, its time to say goodbye'. We clasped our hands, looked into each other eyes and our lips met again, but this time in a long passionate kiss. I thought that we could stay like that for ever, close to each other and with her lips on mine.

After Tadek left the camp for school, he missed his Marysia very much. He wrote in his memoirs, which I managed to spy occasionally:

I will try to write something about memories and yearning. Only now I can fully see the difference between the two of them. I wrote to Wacek and mentioned things from the past, but they were only memories. Balinski [Polish essayist] was right when he wrote that a person will forsake everything in the world, except memories of happiness, love ... And how I yearn now for Marysia, for her looks, her smile and conversations with her ... Only a week has gone since I saw her and talked to her. Every little thing that reminds me of her wrings my heart with sense of longing and loneliness and I feel like crying.

And now a letter from Tadek that brought us news.

Mount Abu – 14-3-44

Dear Niusiek.

It's been a week since we arrived here, I feel perfectly well. But what about you? Did you by any chance break another bone or something? With you anything is possible, especially now that I am away.

Yesterday A. Plucinski and H. Baczek went to the jungle to get some lemons. And guess what? Instead of lemons they saw a tiger. Nice neighborhood we have here.

Together with this letter I enclose a postcard that I received from the Polish Consulate in Bombay. The card is from uncle Jozek; you might remember him. He stayed with us in Warsaw when he was doing some military studies and later visited us in Przemysl with his wife aunt Maria. I sent him some news about the three of us....

Please let me know whether you were promoted to the 6-th grade and what you are doing now that you have vacation? I am very busy as it's less than two months to exams and it will be all in English.

Study as much as you can. Uncle Jozek writes that he hopes that when we return to Poland we will bring more than just ourselves. 'Study! Study!' that's what he writes.

I hug you tenderly—best of everything, Tadek.

The card was from Uncle Jozek in Woldenberg POW camp in Germany. He had received the postcard that Wacek sent to him via the Polish Embassy in Kujbyshev after our mother died. That postcard was sent to the Polish Embassy in Turkey and then through the Red Cross to the POW camp. The Red Cross also supplied a list of children evacuated from Russia to India. When Uncle Jozek found our names on the list, he sent us this postcard via the Polish embassy in Turkey.

8-XI-p1943. Beloved! I have received your card informing of the death of your mother in Siberia. Of your father and Uncle Stefan, I have no news. Is Wacek alright? I am well. Auntie Bozena and Grandmother are in Poland. Be diligent in studies. Tadek, take care of Niusiek and listen to your elders. May God continue to protect you. Love, your uncle. Jozek

We had another surprise. Uncle Strumillo, who now was with the Polish Mission in Cairo, Egypt, sent us some money. As Tadek was older and needed more, he took ₹200 and I received ₹75. That was a fortune. Now I could buy a few things like clothing, airmail letters, peanuts, or other tidbits at the bazaar and also have some decent pictures taken.

In the meantime, in the middle of 1943, they started building the Valivade camp, south of Bombay, near the town of Kolhapur in the Marathi province. It was supposed to house some 6,000 Polish evacuees from Russia, mainly old people, invalids, women and children. This camp which in time became a little town had a few elementary schools, trade schools and a high school (*gimnazjum* and *liceum*). Also an orphanage was there, but smaller than the one in Balachadi. In our camp, due to lack of qualified teachers, no high school could be opened, so in May all 6th graders, boys and girls, were sent to Valivade for further education in grammar or trade schools. Our camp became smaller and we, the 6th graders, became the senior class, the elite.

In May of 1944, the Polish 2nd Corp. under General Anders fought a bloody battle against the Germans at Monte Casino, a monastery turned into a fortress. The British, American, French and Indian forces could not take it in three attempts, and finally it was the Polish Army which was successful but it cost them dearly. Our camp was once again grieving. A father of five children (Czenczyk family) from our camp was killed and also the husband of our math teacher, Mrs Tyszkiewicz.

In June, all our boys from Mount Abu were moved to Valivade and Tadek was amongst them. Photograph 4 was taken at this time. He was now in the 4th grade of *gimnazjum* and in September passed the lower level matriculation exams. Although he was complaining a lot about schoolwork, he found time to be in the amateur theatre where he performed with great success and was also involved with scouts. There he met Marysia (Janiszewska) and fell in love with her!

Franek in Balachadi

From now on we had some extra privileges, for example, at lights-out time, we could stay up for another hour and from time to time could go to Jamnagar and rent bicycle or go to the movies. But then we also had some extra responsibilities. First of all, we had to behave ourselves and be an example to the younger kids. Some of us were moved for the duration of a few months to barracks with younger boys as 'councilors' to help with discipline, homework and general upkeep of dormitories. Twice I had such duties.

Our scouting was developing well and by now we had two each of Boy Scout and Girl Guide troops and four Cub Scout and a few Brownie Packs. All the leaders were from our senior class. I become a Cub Scout Pack leader.

I do not really know what prompted Tadek to opt to go to England at that time and join the merchant marine school. Was it a 'call for adventure' or just a desire to expand his horizons? I do not know. To start with, a group of some 40 older boys were supposed to go in

November, but then the trip was postponed. They went to Bombay a few times only to return to Valivade again. That of course was disrupting his studies. Eventually they sailed to England in February of 1945.

And what was Wacek doing at that time? He was in the Navy on the Polish cruiser *Dragon* as a radar operator and took part in the invasion of France. Later he told us that the view from the ship was spectacular. Furthest from the French coast were battleships, then cruisers, then destroyers and eventually transporters and landing crafts from which soldiers went ashore followed by equipment. Guns from all the ships were firing and you could hear shells flying and even see them overhead. And high above were, hundreds of bombers flying towards France. In the far distance, you could see beaches covered in smoke.

A few days into invasion, *Dragon* was hit just below water level by a so-called 'human torpedo'. Forty six sailors that were under the deck were killed. The ship did not sink but was hauled towards the French coast and settled on the bottom to form with other damaged ships, an artificial harbour. The crew was taken to England to some camp in Devon and there they waited for a new ship. Towards the end of the year, they were on board another cruiser—*Conrad*.

A few letters from Tadek:

Valivade - 25-6-44

...It's been two days since our arrival here in Valivade. This noon we had an interview with the gimnazjum principal and were placed in various classes. Tomorrow I will start in 4-th grade. I will have plenty of work even more than I thought at the beginning. Hopefully I will manage.

At the moment there is not much I can tell you about this camp. It looks more or less what I expected. It's huge. Our group that came from Abu lives in the orphanage in barracks similar to the one we have in Balachadi. Our group occupies one end of the building. We have a table, benches, lamp etc. We will be able to study well into the night and that's what I like.

Valivade
10-10-44

...I am very happy with all my examinations. Now we have a month vacation and I am going to a training camp for scoutmasters. I am sure I will learn a lot and it will not be a waste of time. And how is it with your scouting? You don't mention it in your letters? During your vacations have a good rest but don't get lazy. Being an altar boy is also good, do not neglect it.

Valivade
November, 44

Thank you for your letter. I didn't write, as I was too busy. Now everything is finished. Tomorrow we are off to England. From now on write to Wacek and I will get all the news about you from him. As soon as possible I will give you my permanent address. I have no idea how it will be with the navy school, but at least I will be in England and hopefully it will be easier there to do all the things I want to do....

With me everything is fine. I passed all my exams as well as the scoutmaster course. Don't forget that in January is the 3rd anniversary of mother's death.

That's all for now. Time permitting I will write from Bombay before sailing.

– Tadzik

And now a few of Wacek's letters.

At location
23-8-44

Dear Niusiek.
Many thanks for your letter dated 8-4-44, which I received today. You say that you might be promoted to the 6th grade. Congratulations. Soon you will bypass me in studies.

...You are asking about my English. I have to admit that it's not too good. All the time I am on the Polish ship, in Polish environment, so I don't have many opportunities to practice English. It's only during leave that I can improve it somewhat. Most of that time I spend in Scotland with two very nice old ladies. Both of them are determined to teach me English and Scottish. With the first one it's not so bad, but

the other one is out of the question. During my stay with these two ladies, I feel as though I am home and hate returning to ship.

On the ship we also have some excitement. Recently it was invasion. What a pity I did not have camera as I could have brought a lot of interesting pictures back to Poland. At the moment we are in a camp in Devon waiting for a new ship. To kill time I am sunbathing in a meadow instead on a beach.

Wacek was not sure whether Tadek had left for England; so the next letter he wrote to both of us.

P. O. Box 293
GPO London
5-12-44

Dear Brothers.
...It's useless to explain why I did not write sooner. I think I wrote something before going on the new ship. Now my conscience is bothering me so I will write again. I think all your letters arrived, but not necessarily in the order they were sent. What a pity you do not have a picture of mother or Niusiek. With the next letter I will try to send a decent picture of myself. Uncle Strumillo also is asking for one. By the way, recently I received L5 that he sent for me from Kujbyshev on 27-3-42. What do you make of that? Expeditious! If you have his new address, please send it to me. So far I did not make contact with uncle Piotr. Always, when I have some free time I don't know where he is.

Dear Brothers.
I am very pleased with your achievements at school. To tell the truth I am envious. Somehow I cannot understand you Tadek why you are so eager to go to war? Is it not enough that I am sitting here getting dumber and dumber day by day? What for? If Father's words are dogmas for you, as you say, then remember what he told you about studying as he was leaving for war. However, if you come here then do what I told you before. In the first place, finish high school and then think about higher education. At your age you are not eligible for the military service unless you volunteer.

With me everything is normal, meaning that terrible boredom is usually on the ship. When in port I usually go to a movie, for a walk, or a dance (recently I learned to dance). I am so used to a hammock that I

*regard sleeping in bed as a treat. To improve my English, just for fun, I
write letters to various girlfriends inventing some ridiculous stories....*

—Wacek

And what was happening in the world at that time? Germany
was losing the War, that's for sure. In Italy, with the taking of the
Monte Casino and after the Gustav Line was broken, the Allies and
Polish 2nd Corp. were pushing northward, liberating all major cities
including Rome, Ancona and Bologna. In France, the invasion was
successful, and Allied forces were approaching Germany itself. In
that offensive, the Polish Panzer Division under General S Maczek
and the Parachute Brigade of General S Sosabowski (of Arnheim
fame) was involved.

The Russian Army was already on Polish territory; not as libera-
tors but rather as an occupying force. Now it became known that
at the Tehran Conference in 1943, Churchill and Roosevelt capitulated to Stalin's demand that eastern Poland be given to Russia.

On 1 August, the Warsaw Uprising against the Germans started.
It lasted 63 days. Hundreds of thousands of civilians were killed
and the city was 80 per cent destroyed. At the time, the Russian
Army stood on the other side of Vistula River but would not give
any help. Even when Allied aircraft flew with supplies from Italy,
they were not allowed to land on the Russian side for refueling and
had to make their way back to Italy. Many of them were shot down
and many airmen lost their lives. In spite of all that and knowing
that Poland was 'sold out', Polish forces in the west were still fighting Germans, side by side with the Allies.

Yet the only discussions that were ranging around us were school
grades, the approaching monsoons, the next trip to Jamnagar for a
movie or what we thought about a particular girl and vice versa.

Year 1945

After some more trouble with transport, a group of boys, including
Tadek, left for England to join the Polish Maritime Institute, in the
middle of February (see Appendix 6). From now on, Wacek and Tadek
were close to each other and I was in far away India. Disregarding

distance, Tadek was still trying to guide me and in his letters was telling me what to do and tried to mould me in his image. What he was forgetting was that there was five years' difference between us. When he was 14, he was very religious and had idealistic outlook on life. Now, at 19, he thought that by thinking independently all the obstacles could be conquered with intellect. In the group going to England there were many scouts and Tadek was put in charge. He felt sort of responsible for them. But that soon changed. In the new school, in a new environment, after meeting new people there and later in Scotland in the *liceum* (the last two years of high school) and seeing life from a different and more brutal perspective, his outlook on life changed dramatically. In Russia, life was also brutal but at that time he was still a child and had his mother.

By the end of May, school year ended and we had entrance examinations to the *gimnazjum*. Everything went smoothly for me, and I was getting ready for my transfer to the Valivade camp. But then it was decided that the 1st grade of *gimnazjum* will be opened in Balachadi. Probably specific programmes and required textbooks were supplied. Fr Pluta was to teach us Latin. A few boys that did not pass entrance exams were sent to Jamnagar and there in a garage learnt trade of car repair.

Even before school ended, war in Europe also ended with unconditional surrender of Germany. Hitler committed suicide. War with Japan continued till the end of the summer when America dropped atomic bombs (a new, nuclear type of weapon) on Hiroshima and Nagasaki. At that point Japan also surrendered.

In Poland was the Polish Communist government and in reality Russia ruled there. We did not bother much about the future. We left worrying to the adults. We had more important thing to think about. We had to organise our first scout camp in tents, prepare the programme and had to run our own kitchen. Everything went well to everybody's satisfaction. I took the scout oath and received scout cross, something I had dreamt about for a long time. I also moved up on the scout ladder and gained the rank of an 'explorer'.

School year started in mid-July. I was in the *gimnazjum* now but had no problems except with Latin. Throughout my school years and then in college, I never put too much emphasis on learning, only on passing examinations. I am fairly intelligent and that helped me to move along. However, I always knew that I must get higher education.

Towards the end of the year, a possibility transpired for some boys to go to America to a Polish High School attached to a college and seminary. Anybody who thought that they might have the vocation could apply. I too applied though not quite sure what the vocation meant, but the idea of going to America was appealing. A group of some 25 boys left. I was a year too young to go.

Christmas was approaching and we had to produce Jaselka. This time I got an important part of the chief shepherd. This was the first Christmas that I was on my own, but I did not feel depressed. By now, after two years of being together, we started forming 'a family'.

And what were Wacek and Tadek doing at this time? Tadek soon after getting into the Navy school realised that it was not for him. After a few months, he decided to join the army, not to fight but to get to a high school (run by the military) in Scotland and get his matriculation there. The formalities dragged on and it was September before he got there. At the same time, Wacek also was accepted to that school by virtue of some existing arrangement. (During the War years, many young people lost on schooling. Polish military ran special accelerated courses to give people a chance to finish high school and then with matriculation in hand get to colleges and universities.) Tadek was in the 1st grade of *liceum* and Wacek in the 3rd grade of *gimnazjum*.

And now some letters. The first one is from Wacek.

Somewhere in England,
January '45

…Just as I started writing this, your letter arrived with photographs from your volleyball match with some Indian team. For the photographs included in the previous letter also many thanks. Even if you did not put a dot over your head I would still recognize you. Do you know how? By your smile which I still remember so well. Nobody in the whole world has such a smile.

At the moment I am on our new cruiser. I cannot write a lot about it, because of the censorship. But one thing is for sure; before the Germans got us we gave them hell. You know the saying: 'at war soldiers are firing, God directs the bullets'. Germans must have been surprised to see the Polish cruiser 'rearranging their furniture'. One of our sailors who escaped from the German Army, to which he was forcibly drafted, was telling us this story.

I was stationed with my artillery unit on the French coast one day. We noticed a British convoy sneaking close to the shore within range of our artillery. I was an observer and through my binocular saw the famous Polish destroyer Blyskawica leading the convoy. So I called an officer and showed him that. He swore badly and said something to that effect: 'What is she doing there; she should have been at the bottom with the rest of the Polish Navy'. He was even madder when I told him that the destroyer escaped from Poland at the beginning of the war. For 5 years she has been afloat and still is in perfect shape.

We in here, time permitting have football matches with the British sailors. Once we won 8:0 and they had to bring a truck to take all the goals home. I don't play football, sicknesses in Russia left mark on my health. But I love playing volleyball or throw discus, but of course only when we are in port.

At the moment I am very depressed as I worry about the future of Poland so wrongfully treated by the Allies. Think about this, Poland was the oldest and most loyal British Allay. To tell the truth it was England that joined Poland in the defense of the free world. And now they abandoned us so dishonorably. I think we will never see our beloved Wilno again. It gives me shivers to think that these Asiatic barbarians might desecrate Our Lady of Ostrabrama, that Wilno might become den of bandits and that in our grandmother's house they might establish headquarters for NKVD. NO! I can't believe that.

I hug you lovingly as never before—Wacek

And now three letters from Tadek:

Landywood
30-7-45

Why didn't you write to me for such a long time? Before I left for England I asked you to write to me regularly. The only news about you I have from Wacek.

I sent you two letters but somebody informed me that you never received them. Your letter I just received confirms this. But don't worry about me, even devil wouldn't have me.

But still, why didn't you write to me sooner? Remember, if we do not stick together nobody will help us. Beside, in this world you cannot count on others. Today you can be a nice, likable Niusiek, but that does not obligate them to be nice to you in the future. Life is hard and you must have moral and physical support. And where can you find it if not in your older brothers. Today you have possibilities to make something of yourself but you need guidance and love that would substitute in part for guidance and love that only mother could have given you. For sure we will not grudge that for you.

Recently Wacek visited me but only for a very short time. At present I have a lot of work preparing for exams.

Landywood
10-8-45

...As promised I am not waiting for reply to my letter and write to you again. In the near future I will be going to Glasgow to take additional exams. Exams from the navy school, being more of a trade school do not qualify me to enter the liceum.

Nothing of interest is going here. Before I was studying a lot and now I just sit around, read a lot of books, play football and dabble in our school theatre. The enclosed photos in some way might show what life looks in here.

Shortly Wacek will come to visit me again. At that time we will take some pictures. Enclosed please find Pound 1 so you can buy some airmail stamps and some peanuts at the bazaar.

I am sure that you know what is going on in the world and in politics. Don't worry about it, don't panic and don't let anybody influence you to do something you don't believe in. Now we have two governments; the communist one in Poland and the other here in London. But above all you are a Pole and don't forget that. Study and develop your identity. You, from the three of us have the best chance to make something of yourself. I have to push and shove to get higher. Wacek's situation is really critical. But let's not lose hope.

Landywood, 17-9-45

Your two letters arrived nearly together. Thanks a lot and for the photos as well. You have grown a lot, but otherwise you did not change that much. Do you have a good eye now? Congratulation for taking the scout's oath and gaining the rank of explorer. I am glad that you still work with cub scouts.

There is only one thing I am not happy about (apart your malaria) is the fact that my advises don't leave any marks on you, it seems they wash away with the monsoon rain. I would like to see you write a bit more than 'rain stopped, and started again and we are not sure whether monsoon is over or not'. Yes, you can write about this, but surely there must be things more important than these and you don't even mention them. Remember, it's time to stop being a child; you have to start thinking independently and don't repeat everything you were told like a tape recorder. First digest all the information and then draw your own conclusions.

I hope that scouting gives you a lot of satisfaction. It should be that way. Give yourself completely to the movement and you can be sure you will not go astray. Better thinkers and more experienced people than you and I opened for us that road and it is paved with life itself. All we have to do is to follow that road; it is wide enough to caper on it to the heart delight.

Now I am pretty sure that by the end of October I will be in that liceum in Glasgow. The school year will last six months so in a year's time I should have my matriculation. In Glasgow I will be with Wacek. He is being sent to that school as well.

Did you receive that one Pound sterling that I enclosed in my previous letter? From Glasgow I might be able to send you a little more as I will be on the army payroll. Is it still the same that you don't get any pocket money?

Hug you tenderly, Tadek

PS. On your namesday accept from me all the best wishes of luck and happiness. Don't forget that with you father also celebrated his namesday.

We had started getting ₹3 per month when we moved to Valivade. One pound sterling was equal to ₹13.

The next letters from Wacek and Tadek were in the same envelope.

Polish College, Hydro Hotel
Pertshire, Scotland
20-10-45

Wacek writes, ... You might be surprised to receive my letter together with Tadek's in the same envelope. At long last we are together in the same school. What terrible times arrived when in school younger brother is two years ahead of the older one. A bit longer and even you would be ahead of me. No wonder; it's a long time since I had a pen in my hand. The only thing I used my hands for was to hold a broom while washing deck or a brush painting ship's side. Never mind I will survive.

Tadek writes ... *I am very happy indeed that I am with Wacek and we will be together for at least a year. What a pity that Wacek at 21 will have to stay at school for a few years more. Imagine, he has to start studying again after six years of being away from the school. I am a bit worried that Russia and sea duties damaged his health as well.*

Scenery here in Scotland is beautiful, mountains around us with many forests, meadows and fields. It looks a bit like in Southern Poland in the mountain region (Podkarpacie). The town nearby is small and with minimal attractions. That's good, so we can devote more time to studying. Weather so far is not too bad, so before Wacek arrived I hiked a bit through the mountains. There were plenty of blackberries in the woods and that made hiking more pleasant.

Location of the school must have been changed as the next letter was written from:

Bridge of Allen,
23-12-45

... First of all I want to write to you about your idea of going to America. I assume that you haven't left yet so you will have time to think seriously about your future. With your 14 years it's difficult to talk about vocation to the priesthood. But if decision is based on your inner feelings then our advice to the contrary is out of the question and would be wrong. But on the other hand if you are using this as means of going to America, then you should consider all the consequences. I think that Fr Pluta is trying to send you somewhere where you will have chance for further education.

However, if Maharaja does not throw you out and for the next few years you will be able to stay in Balachadi (without risk to your health due to malaria) then I don't see any reason for hurry in leaving the camp. But if you stay try to avoid developing a one-track mind out-look on life. Read as much as possible, all the classical literature: Prus, Zeromski, Sienkiewicz, Slowacki, periodicals, newspapers etc. etc. And try to thing independently.

Remember, in America it will be similar to what it was in Lubaczow under Russians. To get something you will have to stand in line. However, in Lubaczow you moved forward over the heads of others. Remember, in America you will not have that advantage as a son 'of our colonel'*.

Re-think everything I wrote and until you are 19 you can refer to this letter. I am sure that at that point you will understand me 100 per cent. – Tadek

Franek's Note: *In 1939, when Russians came to Lubaczow, shops, especially groceries, were empty. As news came that something was delivered, a long line would formed in front of the shop. When I joined the line, people would lift me up and pass me over their head to the front of the line, next to the door.

Year 1946

Although life in the camp was going normally, we could feel changes coming. With the end of the War, the Polish government in London lost accreditation with most of the countries, in particular with England and the US. Responsibility for our upkeep and thousands, if not millions of refugees all over the world, was taken over by an international organization the United Nations Relief and Rehabilitation Administration (UNRRA). This organization was pressuring people to return to their homeland. In the Valivade camp, panic erupted. Hardly anybody wanted to go back to Poland that was under the Russian domination. In Balachadi, it was fairly quiet. However, the problem was with complete orphans. Fr Pluta described the situation as such:

> The war has ended and a problem has emerged with no visible solution regarding return to Poland. I have received a copy of a letter by Capt. Webb to the British Government where he writes 'by no means Polish children can return to communistic Poland'.
> Mrs Buraczkiewicz, an emissary of the communist government in Poland is trying to establish a list of all orphans. We have prepared two lists. One with children that have father, mother or at least a grown brother or sister or some other relative in the Polish

Army in Italy, England or anywhere in the 'free world'. The second list is of children who think that they are orphans, as they do not know what happened to their parents and other immediate family members. That second list has over 200 names. The Polish Government in Warsaw demands that all orphans be returned to Poland and they will take care of them.

And that is our dilemma. What shall we do?

There was ferment in the camp till the next meeting by Fr Pluta, when he said,

We had a meeting with Maharaja, in his office, that included Lieutenant Colonel Geoffrey Clark and me. An idea of adoption has emerged. I as the commandant and chaplain would be responsible for the children's morale, Maharaja Jam Saheb would support financially and Lieutenant Colonel Clark is supposed to get an approval for the idea from the British India Government. An attorney has been brought from Bombay to draft the act of adoption that could be approved by the court of the Nawanagar State. The document states that the Maharaja Jam Saheb, Lieutenant Colonel Geoeffrey Clark and Reverend Francis Pluta legally substitute for parents of children in the Balachadi camp.

I was probably on the list but I have never seen the document. I do not know if there was a note in small print about entitlement to inheritance!

After that was settled, Fr Pluta went to America where he was born and where his brother lived in Cleveland, Ohio, in search of sponsors for the children. He was partially successful. A group of 50 girls went to the Bernadine Sisters convent in Reading, Pennsylvania. A group of boys went to a catholic school in Wisconsin. As mentioned earlier, I was too young and my plans to go to the US fizzled out.

By the end of May, school year finished, and I passed to the next grade. About that time, news had come that the Balachadi camp will be closed and everybody will be transferred to Valivade. But still we would have our last vacations, our last scout and cub scout camps. See Photograph 5 taken about this time.

On Monday, 1st July 1946, school started. I was depressed for not being able to attend classes as I was in hospital with another bout of tropical malaria. I had to stay there till Thursday. Not to waste time, I decided to catch up on some reading. I read the novel by Kassak—*Szczucka Beatum Scelis* (Blessed Transgression). In the afternoon, I got another book by the same author, *Golden Freedom*. I stayed in bed all day, though I had no temperature. I was weak and in general didn't feel well.

That's how it was with the tropical malaria. I had it in my blood all the time. When I had my first attack of malaria in Ashkabad in 1942, I had a high temperature and the shivers. Now the symptoms were slightly above normal temperature, headache and general weakness. Normal cure consisted of five days' stay in hospital and taking quinine, then for five days you had to take atabrine and finally for five days plasmoquine. After a few weeks, malaria would re-occur. Not until we moved to Valivade and I had a series of injections, that I was completely cured.

Now that the move to the Valivade camp was inevitable, everything, including schoolwork, started falling apart. We knew that in Valivade we will go to different classes, will have different teachers, new friends and new environment. We had to start packing and at the same time throwing away some of the junk that accumulated over the period of the last four years. Our departure was scheduled for the end of November. We had to bid farewell to that place which for over four years was our home in the literal sense. We had to bid farewell to Maharaja Jam Saheb and scores of other wonderful people who will stay in our memories and in our hearts forever. So when the time came to lower the white and red Polish flag that we received back in 1942 from the Polish sailors from *Kosciuszko* ship, there were tears in many eyes. Successive stage in our lives was coming to an end and a new one started unfolding.

Home for the Next Few Years

⊂⊗⊃

They were a bunch of miserable-looking sad lot, slightly afraid of what was there, not knowing what awaited them. We, that is, my brother, about four years old then and I, were there with my governess AnnieBa, Colonel Geoffrey Clarke, my father's liaison officer and Cathy, his wife when they arrived. I don't know how much my brother remembers about that day, but the most I remember is them scrambling out of their train looking totally terrified coming into this land where everything was so different. Soon they were quite happy as they received the warmth, and knowing those days and the traditions, they would have been given something to nibble at. So, that must have cheered them up a bit because they really looked underfed when they came. They were very emaciated. We were told that they had been cared for for some weeks now and I wondered how they had been before that, for they were such a sad and miserable looking bunch. The youngest, I think, when this lot came, must have been two or three years old or less. There were a few children who were being carried— not walking yet.

We received them, saw them go off to Balachadi, which had been quickly built temporary huts at that time. Most of it was still unfinished. We just saw them as a batch and wondered who they were why they were there till we started going to the camps and meeting with them, and till they started learning some [English] language and had some people to translate to gradually understand what they had undergone.

—Hershad Kumariji[1]

*B*alachadi is a small spur, 17 miles from Jamnagar in the Kathiawar peninsula of India. In 1942, it was the summer residence of the royal family of the Princely State of Nawanagar. Nawanagar had a long and chequered history as a Jadeja Rajput kingdom of Kathiawar, retaining its independence and identity till 1857. Subsequently, it swore allegiance to the British Crown and came within the framework of Princely States of India under the British Crown. Its then ruler Digvijaysinghji was the Chancellor of the Indian Chamber of Princes and a member of the Imperial War Cabinet in London, in the footsteps of his predecessor Ranjit Singhji, popularly known as 'Ranji', the cricketer, who had held the same positions during the First World War.

The Balachadi camp was sited adjoining His Highness Jam Saheb's own small seaside resort. It enjoyed markedly lower temperatures than the city. It was close to the sea and had a good supply of water from a well.

Within six weeks from the receipt of the information of the children's arrival, the state authorities built a camp of *pukka* masonry, complete with furniture, ready for the reception of the children. The preparation of the camp entailed not only clearing the ground but also making of a road, about a mile in length, extension and installation of telephone communication, installation and erection of necessary machinery to ensure adequate water supply and laying in of necessary stores, arranging for and completing of various contracts between local merchants and the camp authorities, and various other formalities. All this was done by the state authorities concerned in spite of the considerable working difficulties.[2]

The camp was constructed under the supervision of the chief engineer of the Jamnagar state. It consisted of 30 large barracks, two dining rooms with attached kitchens, staff quarters, hospital, dispensary, operating theatre, servants quarters, bath houses and latrines and was built at a cost of ₹156,605 averaging ₹315 per child (see Map 5). This was markedly lower than the prevailing rate of ₹1,000 per evacuee for housing and furnishing allowed by HMG for Balkan–Maltese and Anglo-Burmese evacuees. At the camps for Maltese evacuees in Satara and Coimbatore, the cost had been ₹1,000 per evacuee. In Balachadi, the per child allowance of ₹315 per year covered, in addition to housing and furnishing, the hospital, staff quarters, sanitary arrangements and servants quarters. None of these heads of expenses were included in the ceiling of ₹1,000 per person per year for the camps at Satara and Coimbatore.[3] It seems—from various parameters quoted by Captain Webb—that austerity measures in the evacuee camps began with the Polish camp.

The construction was stone in lime mortar roofed with country tiles. The major heads of expenses for the construction and equipping the camp were as follows:

Map 5: Layout of camp, Balachadi

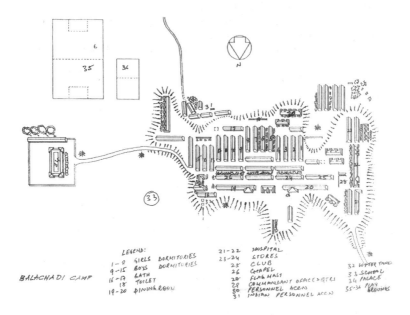

Source: Franek Herzog.

Table 2: Major expenses

Expense	Cost
Cost of construction	108,600
Cost of furniture	16,420
Cost of additional works	28,746
Cost of furnishing and equipping the camp hospital and dispensary	2,839
Total	**156,605**

Source: NAI, 276(8)-X/42, Captain AWT Webb's Reports, 33.[4]

Wieslaw Stypula describes[5] the camp as:

About 15 miles from Jamnagar on a cliff rising from the sea bed stood the beautiful summer residence of the maharaja Jam Saheb. On the east side of the palace there was a park like garden and on the west side facing the sea there was a big swimming pool. Water in the pool was refreshed at every high tide. In southerly direction from the palace stretched a long sandy beach. A bit inland from the sandy beach on the dunes there was a narrow strip of grass shaded by acacia trees, tall agaves plants and cacti. On that grassy strip there was a well-kept golf course. Further away from the seashore stretched semi desert scenery with numerous rocky hills sparsely covered with grass, thorny bushes and swirls of cacti. In some places, especially near wells or reservoirs with fresh water, huge banyan-trees with long lianas, palms and other trees were growing.

Our camp was built on one of the hills, about a mile from the palace and approximately the same distance from the village of Balachadi. It could house 700 to 800 people. There were over 60 very simple barracks covered with red, clay tiles. Basic building material consisted of stone, cement, some lumber and bamboo mats.

Mrs Banasinska accompanied the first batch of children from Bandra to Balachadi and personally oversaw their settling in. The internal administration of the camp was left entirely to Fr Franciszek Pluta and his staff of about 20 ladies, overseen by the GOI. For coordinating with HHG, there was a British liaison officer, Mrs Cathy Clarke, wife of Major Geoffrey Clarke, a trained nurse who had an excellent knowledge of the local conditions and Gujerati [sic] language.[6]

Wieslaw Stypula recalled being welcomed to the camp with 'Do not consider yourselves orphans, you are now Nawanagaris, and I am Bapu, father to all Nawanagaris, including you!' by Jam Saheb when he visited the camp for the first time.[7] With this statement, Jam Saheb endeared himself permanently to the lot of suffering Polish orphaned children on Indian soil. It had a deeply emotive impact on them and every other kind gesture that followed, only reaffirmed that feeling, which makes them nostalgic to this day.

His Highness placed at their disposal his gardens, squash courts and swimming pool and being adjacent to the sea, the older children could bathe directly from the sandy shores. He also gave one of his own buildings adjacent to the camp to be used as school. The camp made its own chapel. Till the resident Polish doctor was posted by the Polish Government, Dr Amrutlal Ashani, of the Nawanagar State Medical Department officiated.[8]

Fr Franciszek Pluta was the camp commandant, assisted by Brother Oskar, a Czech, and Brother Eustachy. There were several ladies who took over different functions. A hospital was arranged and several ladies took over nursing duties. There were several very young children; so older girls assisted the matron (see Photograph 8).

A few villagers from the nearby villages were employed to cook, clean, guard and carry water in the camp for salaries varying from ₹47 per month for a head cook to ₹15 for a water carrier. Among them was Suleiman Khan, who used to light the lamps in the evenings, clean the camp and hospital during the day. He recalls the camp quite accurately and speaks a few words in Polish, reminiscent of that era.[9]

The camp was divided into sections intersected with roads, all named by the inmates, who planted trees and flowering shrubs along them. The main road running through the centre of the camp was named 'Digvijaysinghji Avenue' during the first visit by His Highness Jam Saheb to the camp, a day or two after the children had moved in. The note written by Major Geoffrey Clarke to AWG Randall, and further forwarded to Count E Raczynski, Ambassador of Poland to London, mentions that in the new Warsaw to be rebuilt after the War, one of the principal streets will be renamed with His Highness's name after this avenue in the Balachadi camp.[10] The Polish flag was broken over the camp by Madame Banasinska while the children sang the Polish national anthem.[11]

Some teachers had living quarters made by dividing the barrack into four or five sections, one for each of them. The grounds in front could be fenced and used as a garden.

The second batch of 220 children and 17 guardians reached Quetta on 8 August 1942. After a wait of several weeks, owing to the Indus being in spate, the group travelled in a convoy of military lorries till Dera Ghazi Khan, from where they proceeded by special train to Jamnagar, reaching the camp on 27 September 1942.[12]

While in Quetta, the group was accommodated in the military station and during their long wait, they received visitors and had a cultural extravaganza. Since the Polish were to be maintained out of charitable funds, the long stay in Quetta provided an opportunity for the British to organise publicity. Photographer Malik was asked to take some pictures of the 'suffering but cheerful Poles being received in India'. In the group, was Janina Dobrostanska, an actress with her sons, Jerzy and Tadeusz. Being an adult, she was able to obtain some of the photographs taken then and later. Subsequently, in recent times, Tadeusz has generously shared them all with the researchers on this subject. Most photographs reproduced here, unless indicated otherwise, have been donated by Tadeusz Dobrostanski, a former Balachadi boy and now a resident of Melbourne, Australia.

A list of children at Balachadi in 1942 is reproduced with permission as Appendix 1.

On the whole, the health of the second batch of children was better than that of the first. The incidence of pulmonary tuberculosis, however, was higher and steps to get these children into hill sanatoria were taken and several were sent to Bel Air Sanatoria, Panchgani.[13] Of the 500 children accepted by the GOI, 383 were in Balachadi and the remaining 117 were collected and were ready in Meshed (Iran) for their move to Balachadi. The health of the children steadily improved during their stay in Balachadi. They had a simple but wholesome diet of two full meals a day, with an early morning breakfast and afternoon tea. From Captain Webb's reports it can be made out that the children were often served *suji* for breakfast and *dal–bhat* for lunch to keep costs low, which was objected to by Madame Banasinska in view of the starvation the children had been through. Her demand for better nutrition was met by the advice about the difference between 'good feeding' and 'ample nourishment'.

Webb argues that the cost of feeding the children in the camp was ₹46 and 4 *anna*s per child and ₹90 per adult per month, which was higher than their original estimates of ₹40 per month. While he agreed that there had been a general rise in prices due to the wartime conditions, he insisted that menus had to be adapted to cheap local produce to remain within the allocated budget, possibly regardless of quantities or quality. According to Webb, the British soldier had a ration allocation of ₹22 a month including firewood and the figure of ₹45 per month compared very favourably with the figures in other camps to Madame Banasinska's objections.[14] It can be surmised from the tone and tenor of the report that austerity measures in evacuee camps began with the Polish camps.

In those days ₹40/- per month wouldn't have fed a child. By that time grain and things had gone so much up in price that our domestics etc were all bemoaning the price of bajra (the staple food of our side), terribly upset as that which had been 6 *anna*s a *maund* had become 14 *anna*s a *maund*. [A *maund* is about 40 kilogrammes and an *anna* was four paise or a sixteenth of a rupee before it converted to the metric system.] They lamented, 'how are we going to make 2 ends meet?' And they would have used wheat for their camp which would be more expensive compared to bajra. Veggies were not expensive. Per day, a child's food would have cost ₹3/- [with] milk and all. They used to be given milk and sugar was rationed towards the end of the war. Those facts I can't tell for sure as they wouldn't have interested a child of six. I just remember the bemoaning of all the servants about bajra becoming 14 *anna*s a maund.

—Hershad Kumariji

Most of the Balachadi children contacted during the research do not recall clearly what kind of food was served on a regular basis. As all growing children, they recall being always welcoming of any extra food. Stefan Klosowski recalled one of the guardians, Mrs Ptakowa, as being especially kind, for she would often manage some extra fruit for them, sometimes hiding it under their pillows in the dormitory, obviously in contravention to some orders or rules existing in the camp.

It is surmised from the reports that the children were issued two sets of clothes every year consisting uniform of white shirts or blouses for the boys and girls, respectively, and khaki drill shorts or skirts as applicable, with a set of undergarments and a pair of open sandals. Most pictures show the children in those clothes, except when in costumes for cultural events. The colours were confirmed by Daniela Szydlo and Stefan Klosowski.

To keep costs low, the older children also did their own washing. Stefan Klosowski recalled that he not only had to wash his own clothes but also of his younger sister Halina, who was too young to do it herself. Older children had to help with all kinds of work in the camp. Stypula writes that the boys prepared their own football field, beginning with clearing the stones.

Captain AWT Webb reported[15] that on 1 June 1942, the Governor General (Home Department) received a telegram from the Secretary of State asking the GOI to accept another 500 children, on the condition that the Polish government would defray the cost. Jam Saheb again wrote a letter of invitation for the children to the Polish Ambassador, Raczynski, which was duly submitted to the Foreign Office.[16] The GOI agreed, but on the condition that none should be sent until they had intimated that accommodation was ready. It was estimated that three months would be required to prepare accommodation for the additional 500 children. It was then decided to extend the camp at Balachadi to take in 1,000 children in all, for reasons of economy. The estimates were passed and the work completed. The fresh batch of children was to come from Meshed along with the balance from the first batch. The acceptance was communicated to Count Edward Raczynski, Ambassador of Poland to the UK by the Foreign Office in a letter dated 15 July 1942.[17]

There was, however, a financial technicality. The GOI had accepted the financial responsibility only for the first 500 children. The financial responsibility of the second batch of children would have to rest with the Delegate of the Polish Ministry of Social Welfare, and it was likely to lead to differences of opinion on the policy to pursue in the camp. There is no mention of how the difference was resolved, but Webb's report of November 1942 includes the expenses incurred to expand the Balachadi camp to accommodate 1,000 children. Under the head 'Extensions to Expand Accommodation to take 1000 Children' the expenses are mentioned in the same page listing the amount spent the first time.[18] The heads are as follows:

Cost of extension	₹97,770/00
Furnishing of the extended camp	₹30,412/10
Water pumping engine	₹8,000/10
Operating theatre, equipment and two surgical wards	₹15,769/00
Furnishing of school	₹6,800/00

Total	₹1,58,751/10

Total cost of construction of the Balachadi camp:

Original + Extension = ₹156,605 + 158,751/10 = 315,356/10.

It was estimated that the cost of equipping each child would be ₹64 per head and an adult ₹90. The break-up was given as follows:

For Children:

Clothing	₹24
Linen (mattresses, pillows, blankets, counterpanes and mosquito nets)	₹30
Crockery, cutlery and share of kitchen equipment	₹10

Total	₹64 per child

For Adults:

Clothing	₹50
Linen (mattresses, pillows, blankets, counterpanes and mosquito nets)	₹30
Crockery, cutlery and share of kitchen equipment	₹10

Total	₹90 per adult

A list of items to be bought was prepared, existing surpluses evaluated and accordingly Madame Banasinska was advanced ₹33,843 by the Finance Department to make the purchases.[19]

The Polish people are deeply religious and church played a central role in pre-War Polish society. To have an establishment without a place to pray was unthinkable for the Poles. Since Balachadi was 17 miles from Jamnagar, where the only church existed in the cantonment, it would have been nearly impossible to take all the children there whenever needed. After the atheistic onslaught on the children's psyche during the period spent in the USSR, the need for a church nearby and emotional anchoring through religion was felt by the commandant and Banasinska to be of utmost necessity. With the camp commandant being an army chaplain, who had even celebrated Easter mass during the journey to India from the USSR to Persia using the back of a truck as altar, it was decided to have a place to worship in the camp itself. One of the dormitories, meant to house about 50 children, was converted into the camp chapel.

Hospital

The camp was equipped with a hospital and initially there was no Polish doctor in the group. Jam Saheb arranged for Dr Amrutlal Ashani, a general physician who had been in Burma till the War broke out, to officiate. The camp commander and Madame Banasinska were so impressed with his dedication to the children that they requested to retain his services when the Polish Legation in Tehran posted them a medical officer. Soon he was joined by Anant Joshi, a compounder. Ashani, Joshi and a team of Polish nurses took good care of the children recovering from the ravages of malnutrition and scurvy caused by the starvation in the USSR. A dentist, Mrs Hamburger, was appointed temporarily to attend to the numerous dental problems.

The hospital was fully equipped. Later, an operation theatre was added. A special wing was furnished in Irwin Hospital of Jamnagar to treat difficult cases. According to Dr Kirit Ashani,[20] son of late Dr Amrutlal Ashani, both Jam Saheb and Madame Banasinska ensured that the camp hospital always had all the required medicines, regardless of the prevalent wartime shortages at the time. It is to the credit of all concerned that only one child died of sickness in all the years of the camp's existence. The child, Boleslaw Jarosz, according to Fr Pluta, was frail and had carried the sickness with him from Russia.[21] The only other death of a child in the camp was in a swimming accident.

But the enduring problem was malaria, especially caused by the children's low resistance after suffering the ravages of malnutrition, typhus, dysentery and a host of other diseases. In 1942–43, there was an epidemic of malaria all over India. Combined with the heat, dust and humidity of India, especially in Kathiawar, there was a dissent among the camp staff about the suitability of Indian weather for Polish people. Their misgivings had deep-rooted fears after the number of deaths they had encountered in the USSR and Iran. So, initially, they were extremely sceptic about India as a suitable wartime destination for their precious lives and those of their wards, who they had managed to secure and bring out of the USSR, often losing several members of their family on the way.

School

School, scouting and church were the three institutions around which pre-War Polish national life was built. All the three institutions had to be built up in the 'Little Poland' created in distant India. After nominating a complete barrack as Chapel, much to the chagrin of the British administrators, the next most important institution was school. Since most of the camp buildings had been taken up for various purposes, the difficulty was addressed to His Highness Jam Saheb during one of his visits to the camp, presumably the first or the second. His Highness Jam Saheb promptly gave the use of a building otherwise known as Himmatsinghji's Palace as the school. The British administrators released ₹6,800 as nonrecurring expense towards desks and blackboards and the following recurring monthly expenses:[22]

Monthly grant for books and stationery	₹275
Salaries for 40 Polish teachers at ₹100 per month	₹4,000
Salaries for 5 English teachers at ₹100 per month	₹500
Total	₹4,775 per month

Klosowski, Herzog, Stypula and Roman Gutowski all recalled[23] that initially there were no books; so Polish alphabets, basic numeracy and religion were the initial subjects. Stypula writes that the children were divided into four classes according to what they remembered or knew.[24] Initially, teachers had to teach from memory. Slowly, they began to get a few books from the Polish Legation in Tehran. There were so few books that older children had to help the teachers copy them and several children shared the meagre books. Later, the supply increased, but at no point of time, did anyone recall having a complete set of books to themselves.

They began their school in one of my uncle's premises that was next to the camp. He had a sort of a summer palace which was a pool with some rooms around it. It had a little courtyard and some outhouses. The school began there and towards the end they had a school building inside the camp itself. To begin with they were at Himmatkaka's, what he used to call, his farmhouse.

—Hershad Kumariji[25]

Some of the older children, who had had some regular schooling before the advent of the War or were nearing the age when they would soon have to leave the camp and seek employment, had to be sent to proper schools. At this time, some Catholic institutions stepped in with support and about 11 boys went to St Mary's School, Mt Abu; among them were Henryk Bonshek and late Tadeusz Herzog.[26] About 12 girls were sent to St Joseph's Convent, Karachi. Among them was Daniela Szydlo.[27]

Since I was amongst the older children in Balachadi, nine of my compatriots and I were sent to the Convent School at Karachi after Christmas of 1942. My sister was sent to the school in Panchgani as she had a lung infection and my brother to St. Nary's convent, Mt. Abu.

—Daniela Szydlo[28]

The fact is also confirmed by Sister Margaret Hoogwerf.[29] Initially, all the children had difficulty adjusting to a new English-speaking environment and fared poorly, but later they all managed. One of the Polish girls even got married to an American soldier in Karachi. Hoogwerf recalled that all the Polish girls were extremely beautiful and talented. Little communication took place due to the language barrier.

We could speak no English so it was quite difficult initially. We were placed in a class with much younger children. Slowly we learn't [sic] 'Yes Sister, Thank You Sister' and began to get by, though we essentially kept to ourselves mostly due to the language problem. But two years later, in Valivade, we had a headstart over the other Poles.

—Daniela Szydlo[30]

The number of children in the schools outside Balachadi in the years 1943 and 1944 have been reproduced in the below.

Table 3: The number of children in the schools outside Balachadi, 1943–44

School	No. of children in 1943	No. of children in 1944
St Mary's Convent School, Bombay	07	05
St Joseph's Convent School, Karachi	12	12
St Mary's High School, Mt Abu	15	15
St Joseph's High School, Panchgani	12	12
Total	46	44

Source: AAN, document number not available.

The names of the schools were furnished by those who attended them. Jan Siedlecki attended St Mary's School, Bombay; Daniela Szydlo attended Joseph's Convent School, Karachi; Sr Margaret Hoogwerf was a fellow student in 1943. Henry Bonshek and the late Tadeusz Herzog attended St Mary' High School, Mt Abu. Sr Margaret Hoogwerf was later posted to St Joseph's Convent, Panchgani, and came across more Polish children.

English was introduced in the school at Balachadi once again as the British administrators felt that the children should be equipped with the language for future requirements. In fact, both Henryk Bonshek and Wieslaw Stypula wrote that the only English they learnt was in India, which had a great impact in picking up the pieces of their life blown away by the events of the War. The school in Balachadi was soon holding examinations and issuing certificates to the children according to the standards laid down by the Polish Ministry of Social Welfare as in pre-War Poland. The certificates issued in Balachadi were valid documents of the Polish system of education[31] (see Photographs 6 and 7).

An Appraisal of the System

All these details were conveyed by Major Geoffrey Clarke to Mr RN Gilchrist[32] of the Political Department, when Clarke accompanied His Highness Jam Saheb to London later in 1942, who in turn forwarded the note to AWG Randall of the Foreign Office. Randall found it prudent to forward it to the Ambassador of Poland to the UK, Count Edward Raczynski.

The arrangements in the camp were quite in accordance with the recommendations of Barbara Vere-Hodge, but there is no mention of her anywhere in the files, books or memoirs after her initial letters addressed to 'Paul' and 'K'. That lady surely was the catalyst for the safe childhood of several hundred Polish children.

Count Raczynski, Ambassador of the Polish government in exile in London to HMG, London, mentions that Jam Saheb and he were invited to a Christmas party by Madame Popiel at Belgrave Square, attended by the Polish President Raczkiewicz. His daughter said a few words to His Highness Jam Saheb in 'Hindustani' which she had learnt by heart, which greatly pleased Jam Saheb.[33] The Poles valued the gesture, one would surmise.

A third batch of over 200 children travelled the overland route from Meshed to Zahidan, by train to Karachi and finally by ship to Bedi port in the Nawanagar state. They were from the last 400 children of the 1,000 accepted by the GOI to be hosted in India.

By this time, the camp at Balachadi was fully operational and receiving the Polish children arriving in batches. A list of the children in Balachadi is given in Appendix 1, but it reflects only those who stayed in the camp after arriving in three batches. A usual transport had many more children being evacuated out of the USSR, but many were 'found' by family and relatives and left the transport to join them at different transit points in Meshed and Karachi explained by Wesley Adamczyk[34] and Daniela Szydlo. A censored telegram identifying some children is given in Appendix 2.

The Jewish Question

In fact, the JRA, which had been preparing a mass evacuation of the Jewish people to the promised land of Palestine, was very organised, well endowed and active. They removed several girls from Bombay on arrival.[35] In fact, Dr Kenneth X Robbins, an independent scholar, established in 1998 that there were no Jewish children in Balachadi. In early 2004, Zygmunt Mandel, 76, from Israel contacted Dr Robbins on e-mail after reading the published paper somewhere saying that he had actually reached Balachadi along with 11 other Jewish children and spent a short while there before being taken by the JRA to Palestine. He sent a map to depict his journey, with dates from memory and an extract from the JRA documents with his name on it and that of 11 other children and their ages at the time. He provided the translation from Hebrew to English.[36]

Most archival files in India on the subject are bunched up under the heading of the Jewish movement through India in the NAI, New Delhi. Mr Mandel's testimony goes to prove that since the Jews were an integral part of Polish society, they were being evacuated from the USSR by the Polish Army without prejudice to their denomination; the only rider being that they had to be a part of the Polish Army being formed in the USSR. A little more on this issue is dealt with in 'The Transit Camps and War-duration Domicile'.

The USSR too had its own reservation about accepting the Jews as a part of the Polish Army, as it did about native Ukrainians or Byelorussians. In some quarters, it is believed that during the registration imposed on the Polish population at the beginning of the War, several Jewish people had registered themselves as 'Jews' and not Poles, which later became a tool for the Soviets to segregate people and issue travel or amnesty documents for those needing them to joining the Polish Army being formed in the USSR.

Reverend Zladislaw Peszkovski,[37] a young Polish cavalry officer at the beginning of the War and later a survivor of the Katyn massacre, scoutmaster of the Polish boys in India and later a theologist of fame, opines that there were some behind-the-scenes exchange of the Jews taking place between the USSR and its former ally Germany, for other Polish political undesirables. It may be recalled here that the 'Pogroms' against the Jews had taken place under the aegis of the Russian Czar. So in 1939–45, while the Jews suffered the Holocaust under the German Nazis, the complete Polish population on the Soviet side of the Molotov-Ribbentrop line went through the *Gulags* in Soviet Russia. Those evacuated out of the USSR as a part of the amnesty included the Jews as well as the ethnic Poles, reflective of the unprejudiced Polish population at the time.

Sports

Some more teachers arrived in the camp and notable amongst them was Antoni Maniak, who took over the physical training. 'There were two soldiers from the Second Polish Corps—Wronko a history teacher and Antoni Maniak for physical training. Maniak helped us build a stadium, running track and trained us in gymnastics and soon became our favourite teacher', observes Stypula.[38]

Sports was greatly encouraged by the commandant as he was running the camp in a military style. The regular diet, rest and physical exercises improved the children's health considerably. There were regular physical training classes, and the introduction of physical training and sports found favour with all concerned—including the British administrators and Jam Saheb.

Slowly, the children started training for football (soccer) and basketball. Roman Gutowski recalled[39] that the 'luxury' of a football or some sports equipment came from the impromptu donations of ₹501 or ₹1,001 that Jam Saheb made during his visits. Only the older 'sportsmen' were allowed to practise with a real football, others had to improvise with a bunch of old rags, etc.

Stypula says that the boys became so proficient in the game that they played against and defeated most teams in their league, and finally they played and won against the Naval team.[40]

> We started with the villagers of Hadiyana, who were no match for us. So we decided to compete with the naval officers of Okha port. We were coached in lawn hockey and soccer. We lost the first hockey match 9:1. In the afternoon was the soccer match, which we won 2:1. The Navy team was a mix of British and Indian personnel. A British officer was appointed as referee and although he clearly favoured the Navy team, he was objective in his decisions.
>
> Jam Saheb came to witness the match, albeit a little late. After the official greetings and presentation of players, we sang the three anthems—Jamnagar, British and Polish. Initially the game was slow, till the first goal was scored by Dedena, for the Polish team. Jam Saheb was very happy and clapped often. The second half the referee gave a penalty. Of course they scored a goal, and there were just 15 minutes left for the match. Mr Antoni scored the winning goal minutes before the end of the game. There was no net on the goal post and the ball went way past into the nearby village. We had won!! After this match, soccer became the enduring sport of Balachadi camp.

The Expanding Group

The abominable condition of the Poles in the USSR was now well-known in British political circles. The Polish authorities started pressing the Allies for a larger evacuation of their population. The children needed to be given highest priority. Having accommodated the first batch of children, India became the only dependable destination. Foreign Minister Anthony Eden's letter to Leo Amery, Secretary of State for India, reproduced in Appendix 11, is self-explanatory. India had become the most dependable state in the situation.

On 18 July 1942, Webb reports that the GOI received a request from the PCG for permission to bring into India at least 5,000–7,000 more Polish children. The PCG informed the GOI that both His Highness Jam Saheb of Nawanagar and His Highness Maharaja of Patiala had agreed to provide facilities for building the requisite camps and that all the cost of transport, accommodation and maintenance would be borne entirely by the Polish government.[41] It was projected that of these, 2,000 children would go to Jamnagar and 3,000 to Patiala, in camps that were yet to be built.

By August 1942, the Foreign Office was growing rather impatient with India's reluctance. Aware of the offers of Nawanagar and Patiala, Randall wrote to JP Gibson in the India Office about the children being excellent material and very valuable for the future of Poland. In his letter of 20 August 1942, he wanted 'to inform Kuibyshev (Polish Legation in the USSR) as soon as possible that there was prospect that the boys can be accommodated'. He also suggested that the Polish children could be accommodated in any of the larger Indian states.[42] The letter is reproduced in Appendix 4.

The abominable condition of the Poles in the USSR was now well known in British political circles. Their evacuation was being regularly discussed in Polish–British meetings when General Anders, the Polish Commander, like a latter-day Moses, allowed the families of Polish soldiers being evacuated out of the USSR to join the men. A sizeable number of the civilians reached Persia and the British had to suddenly gear up to receiving and disposing a sizeable number of Polish civilians, since they, unlike the Russians (Soviets) could not let them die.[43] The GOI was also asked to accommodate these people. Karachi, in India, then became a safe place to route the Poles in transit as other locations were being finalised. This event is detailed in 'Transit Camps and War-duration Domicile'.

In his report dated 27 October 1942, Captain AWT Webb mentions that the GOI had accepted to receive 1,000 Polish refugee children, evacuated from South Russia in two batches of 500 each, in addition to the 500 already accepted. By February 1943, the GOI India also accepted receiving 5,000 women, children and men of over military age in India, in war-duration domicile.

Of the first two batches of 500 each, amounting to 1,000 children to be accommodated in India by the then GOI, approximately 600 were at Balachadi camp and the remaining 400 in Meshed awaiting transport to Zahidan and then by sea to Bedi Port in Nawanagar state. Of the third batch of 5,000 children from South USSR, only 45 children had reached Meshed when the Soviet government suddenly placed a ban on the evacuation of further Polish children from Ashkabad in the USSR to Meshed in Iran. While General Sikorski, the Polish Premier, was trying to get this ban lifted, the prospects looked pessimistic. The Polish authorities then requested India to accept 1,000 children from the Istfahan camp in the place of a similar number from South Russia. In fact, the 1,000 children at Istfahan were due to go at an early date to Nyasaland, in British East Africa, but the camp site there was found unhealthy. There was, thus, little prospect of arrival of the remaining 3,955 children of this third batch. It was also unlikely that an equal number of women, children and old men from Tehran would be taken in their place. There was a general murmur about sending the Istfahan children to Balachadi as they had experienced advantageous climate there.

Viceroy Lord Linlithgow sent out a letter to the Indian Princes, seeking charitable funds from them for the upkeep of the Polish refugee children. The letter is reproduced with permission in Appendix 3.

In his report dated 27 October 1942, Captain AWT Webb mentions that the GOI had accepted to receive an additional 5,000 Polish refugee children evacuated from South Russia. By February 1943, the GOI also accepted to receive 5,000 women, children and men of over military age in India, in war-duration domicile. The gesture was not lost on the Poles. Count Edward Raczynski, Ambassador of Poland to the UK, wrote a letter expressing gratitude to Anthony Eden which is reproduced with permission as Appendix 5.

The fourth batch of mixed population was to be housed separately and arrangements for their reception at Karachi (Country Club Camp) from 1 March 1943 were underway. They would be arriving in groups of 1,000 at short intervals. This camp and their eventual settlement in Valivade would be discussed in 'The Transit Camps and War-duration Domicile'.

The arrangements for the various batches were as such:

1. Balachadi camp with slight extension for 1,045 children, partly in India and the rest in Iran, headed for India. Maharaja Jam Saheb had consented to the proposed extensions and steps to that effect had been initiated.

2. The 1,000 children originally headed for Nyasaland and routed to India, were to be accommodated at Chela, off Jamnagar.[44] The camp site at Chela was evaluated at ₹11 lakh and offered to the Polish authorities for half of that price, that is, ₹5.5 lakh.

3. The mixed group of 5,000 women, children and men would be accommodated in a camp in Karachi, lent by the US Army, for whom the site of accommodation had been located near Kolhapur.

4. For the 3,955 children, the GOI had agreed to take from South Russia, if they arrive as and when the ban is lifted or to take in their place another mixed group of people from Tehran, there are prospects of finding suitable sites for a camp at either Lonavla on the Poona Ghats or Igatpuri, reported Webb.[45]

It must be mentioned here that the offer of His Highness, the Maharaja of Patiala to provide a camping site for 3,000 children in his state had to be declined. Located in the Simla Hills, the location was suitable from a climatic point of view, but there was 'insufficiency' of water, said Webb in the same report. This was confirmed by Sardar Hardev S Chhina, an official in the erstwhile Patiala state and later Chief Secretary to the Government of Punjab.[46] But the pertinent point remains that maybe the British felt it would be embarrassing to have an economical Polish Allies camp so close to Simla, the Foreign Office, while the 'enemy' elements camp in Yeol, off Dharamsala, had better facilities and standards. Also, citing 'insufficiency of water' served two additional purposes:

1. Of not having Poles so close to the Foreign Office, when the preparations of betraying them at Tehran and Yalta were already in formative stages

2. Keeping a strong Indian king uninvolved, lest the Poles and the Indians unite against the British, as referred to in a later Webb Report while referring to Gandhian philosophist Wanda Dynowska, aka Umadevi

It must be noted here that HMG was already holding negotiations with the Soviets on post-War boundaries in Europe. According to Professor Norman Davies, the Poles, the Czechs and other smaller European states were more like 'minor clients and hopeful petitioners'[47] of Britain while the partners were the USA and the Soviet Union. By sometime in 1943, the UK had already ceded East Poland to Stalin in secret negotiations, yet unknown to the Poles.

The Polish Minister of Labour and Social Welfare, Mr Jan Stanczyk, visited India in July–August to inspect the conditions of the Polish population in India.[48] He stated that he did not expect more than 4,000 to arrive in India from Tehran. He later revised his estimate to 7,000 in case of a third evacuation from the USSR. By this time General Sikorski, the Polish Premier, holding both political and military charge, had died in a plane crash off Gibraltar and there had been no movement on his request to the Soviets for the evacuation of another 150,000 Poles.

Soon after his return, the Minister condemned India as a destination for Polish children, raising the hackles of the British and several others. In his report dated 20 May 1943 to the Secretary to the GOI, Home Department,[49] Captain AWT Webb wrote:

> The circumstances under which [the site for Chela camp] was selected and the subsequent disapproval expressed by the P.C.G. concerning its unsuitability require comment.... The season was the hottest of the year, the ground had been cut up by lorries and carts of the builders, and a strong wind was blowing. The Consul-General got dust in his ears and shoes which seem to have caused him considerable annoyance. At dinner that night he expressed forcibly to his host, the Jam Saheb, his unqualified disapproval of the site and surroundings of the camp. He also sent a telegram to the same effect to his wife, the Delegate in India of the Polish Minister of Social Welfare.... He was invited to Delhi to explain his objections more clearly, to which he admitted that the only faults he found were the dust and lack of trees.... The next day Madame Banasinska departed to see Chela for herself....
>
> As a damage control exercise, she reported that the site was suitable for Polish women and children, but not for the Istfahan orphans. She wanted some modifications made in the construction already executed, which was declined by Capt. A.W.T. Webb, as it would place considerable extra expenditure. Besides, the Government of India were unable to appreciate the logic which agreed that the camp was suitable for children with mothers, but declared it to be quite unsuitable for children with guardians.[50]

The Minister's visit coincided with a malaria epidemic, raging through the whole country. In the camp hospital, he saw many children down with malaria (see Photograph 29) and was given to understand by the camp officials that the climatic conditions were unhygienic for European children, especially those who had suffered the ravages of starvation in the USSR.

Captain Webb mentions in his report that a certain 'hospital mindedness' among the children was being favoured by the camp staff. He goes into great details about normal children being allowed to report sick in the morning to miss school, who later played rigorous games by afternoon.[51]

An archival picture shows the Minister with tuberculosis-affected children in Panchgani. It can be estimated that he also visited Kolhapur in the Deccan where the camp for the mixed group of women, children and men of over-military age were to be settled. That region of India receives the monsoons by mid to late June, after which the temperatures are considerably lowered and the weather pleasant. So, it can be assumed that he favoured the Deccan region as a destination for the Poles in India. It may be assumed from Webb's suggestion of Igatpuri as a venue for a camp that the Polish Minister must have travelled through the Ghats while going to Panchgani from Bombay, where the Polish Consulate was located, or to Kolhapur and preferred the weather there to the still dry Kathiawar and must have pointed it out to Captain Webb or his representative.

The net result after the Minister's visit was that the Polish Ministry of Social Welfare did not want any more children to be sent to Nawanagar in Balachadi or Chela camps after the adverse reports about the suitability of these camps. Jam Saheb was sufficiently miffed and was not approachable on the subject of a camp for the mixed population.

With the Chela camp rejected, an orphanage was built in the Valivade camp, meant to house truncated families, and the Istfahan camp was scheduled to be moved to Nyasaland. However, the Istfahan camp never moved to Nyasaland and became the biggest and longest running orphanage for Polish children in Iran.

Scouting

The third important pillar of Polish society was scouting, which was initiated with great gusto in the camps, not just to keep the energy harnessed but also to breed the much-needed spirit of patriotism. Stypula writes:

> A scouting team was organized. Scout Janka [Ptakowa] came to Balachadi. Forty years later at the Reunion of the Jamnagar Children in USA she explained her motivation to come to Balachadi. Three days after her child died in Meshed, Bishop Gawlina was visiting. Distraught after the loss of her child, she asked him what she should do. He advised her to go to Teheran where the Polish soldiers were camping. She would find a new life with someone there. One night, while passing by the orphanage in Meshed

she heard a child crying for his mother. She walked in to comfort the child and that was the turning point of her life. She stayed there thereafter. Later she came to Balachadi to establish the Scouting which was an important part of pre-War Polish life and education.

Her first annual report from Balachadi stated that there were three teams of girl scouts and two teams of boy scouts, and three teams each of young boy scouts and young girl scouts. Two teams of girls from Karachi and Panchgani joined us and one team of boys from Mt Abu.

So on September 1, 1943, the whole battalion of Scouts amounted to 239 children. On August 15, 1943 we had the Scouting Oath, attended by the Jam Saheb. I took my oath on October 8, 1943. There was a camp for the scouts at Okha,[52] 50 kilometers from Jamnagar. There were 100 participants divided into two teams—girls and boys. I was to go for this camp too, but fell ill soon after qualifying. I had fever for one week and was in the hospital for the whole duration of the camp and was discharged when it was nearly time for them all to return.

The scouts used to usually go out of the camp and have mock battles every alternate Sunday. All of us were keen to upgrade our scouting skills and earn appropriate tabs. There were practical and theory exams and we had to clear both. I was trying to upgrade to a cook. I was ordered to fry the pancakes in the forest. I didn't pass. We also had to learn Morse Code communication. Swimming, cycling, life guard trapping and first-aid were other activities in which each of us was trying to upgrade ourselves. For each skill acquired we got an emblem to wear with our uniforms. I got the most exotic one for gathering intelligence.

I was called to the office by Janka and told that the scouting movement in the camp had grown and she needed two scout leaders to train the younger children into scouts. Bogdan (Tchaikovsky) and I were selected for this prestigious job of being young scoutmasters. My pride knew no bounds. I could not sleep that night thinking how I was to lead this group. I looked for my own strengths on which to build up my charge. I was especially good in javelin, trumpet and strict discipline.

Once someone who was an expert in oriental martial arts had told us the importance of the hardness of the edge of the palm. We practiced breaking things with the edge of our palm and had hands so sore that we could not often hold our pens in class. But the exercise of hardening the edge of our palms continued for the next three months. Slowly the training of the young scouts began and took off without any hitch.[53]

Reverend Zladiszlaw Peszkovski was a young cavalry officer in the Polish Army when the War broke out. Narrowly missing being executed at Katyn forest when held in captivity by the USSR, he joined the Anders' Army upon formation to leave the USSR for Tehran. He was posted to India as scoutmaster to the children after the formation of the Valivade camp in Kolhapur. He regularly led the scouts into mock battles fighting the Germans, which the boys practiced after his departure.

He was very well received by all the inmates at Balachadi camp, especially the boys because he was a 'real soldier'. He recalled long private interviews with Jam Saheb in the latter's office where Jam Saheb wanted to know the intimate details about the conditions in the USSR. Stypula writes that Jam Saheb was deeply interested in all matters of Polish history, politics, culture, literature, etc.[54]

Jam Saheb Shatrushalayasinghji, son of Jam Saheb Digvijaysinghji, reminisced with Stefan Klosowski during his visit in 2002, that as a young boy, he once stopped to watch two groups of boys from the camp fighting a mock battle. The battle was over when one group was discovered. He recalled[55] being chided by his father that his (Jam Saheb Junior) stopping and looking in the direction of the groups had caused the discovery of group!

The boys practiced guerrilla tactics and learnt to run barefoot over the brambles. In fact, all the former Balachadi boys said that the local villagers from Balachadi and Hadiyana were very surprised to see white boys running around bare feet and with minimal clothes. The camp boys also had a reasonable interaction with the village boys in the neighbourhood.

Camp Life

In spite of the rejection of Chela, off Balachadi, as a location for more Polish children, Jam Saheb continued to shower his attention and affection on the camp. Stypula writes that he was a frequent visitor to the camp and deeply interested in the curriculum being followed for the children's development. As an encouragement, he often invited the children to his palace, which were the 'rewards for good behaviour' doled out by the camp staff.[56]

Slowly, the children gained in strength and started leading as normal a life as possible with mischief thrown in, in good measure. Klosowski and Raba recalled being among the group of boys chasing peacocks around the mudplains and having roughly roasted peacock meat once in a while. The feathers used to serve as trophies. He recalled a dormitory full of boys practicing soccer by moonlight because it was too hot inside to sleep![57]

One of the boys, Ferdinand Burdzy, exchanged some issued soap for a pair of chickens with a local village boy and started a poultry, or animal farm, on the sides of the camp.[58] It grew and thrived and obviously had

the tacit support of the camp officials as Klosowski, Stypula and even
Roman Gutowski, who was seven-year old at the time, remembered the
farm and said that the eggs and chicken from Burdzy's farm gave them
occasional treats. Gutowski said, 'It was an honour to help Burdzy with
his farm and I had the priviledge for almost a year.'[59] As time passed, the
children adopted all kinds of animals and there was a turtle, a roe deer
and a mongoose that most of the erstwhile children recall.

Cultural Life at Balachadi

Cultural upliftment was an important head of expense under the British
administrators, and money was allocated to buy books, periodicals and
indoor games. Slowly, the items were built up and Stypula writes:

> The camp had a slow pace, far from the maddening happenings around
> the world. All the news used to come in only from the mails that would
> come in weeks after they had been dispatched. Some Polish newspapers
> and magazines, printed in the Middle East would come in but the news
> or information they carried were far from what was current. Some pub-
> lications from the U.K. and the U.S.A. were also there but the same. The
> hottest topic of discussion was the Uprising of Warsaw and we discussed
> the heroic acts of our soldiers for hours, often interspersing them with
> our own brushes with them. There were some Polish books in the library
> too, but they soon started disappearing. A register for the books was in-
> troduced as the most precious of the collection were the ones that disap-
> peared. 'Kamienie na szaniec' ('Stones of the rampart') by Kaminski sur-
> vived. (It is a book about the young people in Warsaw laying down their
> lives in defence of their country.) It was amongst our favourite readings.[60]

As mentioned earlier, singing and the choir was encouraged. During the Christmas season of 1942, Captain ACV Elphinston, ADC to the
Viceroy, collected ₹6,525 during a charity concert for the benefit of the
Polish children in Balachadi camp. An amount of ₹6,000 was reserved
as leave travel assistance for the staff and for ₹525 for a piano and some
musical instruments were bought. An orchestra was formed, and several
children became proficient musicians.

Klosowski recalled being invited to the palace to play.[61] Stypula
elucidates that it was during the fifth birthday of Jam Saheb's son,
Shatrushalayasinghji. He writes that Jam Saheb visited the camp on 3
May 1943, the Polish Constitution Day. He was very well read on Polish

history and culture. Most Poles believe that he was a personal friend of Ignacy Padrewski, one of the Polish prime ministers.

Klosowski and Stypula recall[62] the palace as the epitome of luxury, laid out with beautiful carpets and hunting trophies. Both recall that initially they meant nothing to the visiting children, and then, Jam Saheb would start telling them a story or two around one of the items, bringing the whole thing alive. Those who were fortunate to visit repeatedly knew the stories surrounding most of the pieces. These in turn would be communicated in the dormitory on return and soon almost all the boys knew the history of virtually all the items in Jam Saheb's ante-room where he received the children.

Cultural life started picking up in the camp. The teachers wanted Polish culture to remain alive in the inhabitants, especially because of its chequered history and the psychological onslaught they had suffered in the Soviet camps where the Soviet guards usually jeered that there was no Poland anymore. Polish national and regional costumes were created with great enthusiasm. The practice continued and from the number of pictures showing the children in traditional Polish costumes, it can safely be assumed that each child probably had one to be worn during occasions. Janina Dobrostanska was at the forefront of this activity, supported by others. The children practised various items as per their ages and ability. Stypula writes:

> Day by day the cultural life of the camps grew richer. Janina Dobrostanska, Jadwiga Tarnogorska and Czeslawa Ciazynska were at the forefront of the camp's cultural life. But it all started from the Commandant who liked singing very much. He used to teach us Latin, and even singing in between classes often. The idea of a choir came up, but there weren't many volunteers. So it was made compulsory for those of us the guardians thought had some talent. Similar was the situation with the dancing group. The boys definitely were not eager to join it, but many had no choice.
>
> The first concert was scheduled for 12 September 1944. It was to be held in the Main Square. *Zbojnicki* or the Highlanders Dance was to be held. The choir had to practise and practice, as did the dancers. During the dance the dancers have to jump across the campfire, but some one invariably jumped into it!! Jam Saheb was invited to the show, and everybody was nervous. Another piece was a veritable disaster and one of the girls was so afraid that she ran away from the stage. Jam Saheb then went upto the stage and said he wanted to dance with all the girls, and he did!!! Slowly everything fell into place and the rest of the program went through quite smoothly.[63]

Christmas time was a period of great fun and activity for the children, reported Webb.[64]

Christmas 1942 in Balachadi was a grand time for the children and enjoyed all the more since the two previous X'mas seasons had been a grim affair with Father Christmas unmistakably absent. Miss Anne Guthrie of the International Young Women's Christian Association, as a result of an appeal through the Young Women's Christian Association's magazine collected sufficient funds to give every child a present. In addition to this Her Highness the Maharani of Nawanagar donated 50 dozen crackers and a crate of fireworks, Mrs A.G. Ratcliffe of Poona, a crate of toys and cheque amounting to ₹590/- were received for X'mas fare. Over and above all this Mrs Clarke collected locally ₹1,385/- to buy a piano for the camp, Mrs Braithwaite of New Delhi and Mrs Webb of Delhi also deserve mention for their success in raising funds for the children. The happiness of the children on Christmas day, 1942, was well summed up by one who witnessed it in these words: 'It was the kind of thing which will remain fresh in one's memory long after more important things have become dim.'

That year, in 1942, the royal family sent a camel loaded with gifts to the camp for the children. Princess Hershad Kumariji and her siblings were also invited to camp celebrations and she recalled[65] that the Polish children were thrilled to see a real camel. Nativity plays were organised and according to an oblique reference in Dr Kenneth Robbin's paper which established that the children in the camp were only Catholic, the Christmas celebrations in the camp were attended by other European children in Nawanagar state.[66]

My most vivid memories are of the St Niklaus Day and seeing them all dressed up. They had put as many as they could in their Polish costumes, and the three camels coming bearing the incense and other things for the celebrations as described and visualized it from the Bible. There was no Father Christmas, but St Niklaus, followed after Jesus Christ, was born.

There was a Nativity scene and the camels decorated the way they were visualized, from Middle Asian kings coming to see baby Jesus Christ—all bedecked in orange and green—all kinds of things that they visualized; half of it was the local tradition with some extra touches here and there. The image of the Polish children coming up on the inclining slat is still with me. That day we were presented the Polish dolls. For the next festival, both my brother and I, got the dresses.

—Hershad Kumariji

The children from the camp were often invited to the palace and the occasion (see Photographs 11 and 12) is recalled by many, like Alina Baczyk Haus.[67] The staff and other visitors to the camp were also invited to the palace. Usually, the children put up cultural shows whenever any dignitary visited Balachadi, as referred to in the article about Lady Fitzherbert's visit, published in the *Statesman*, dated 17 January 1943.

Entry to the camps was restricted and Jayesh Vara, son of Pachanbhai Vara, the official photographer of Nawanagar state, said that they had taken most of these photographs. He, however, could not produce the negatives because they had been destroyed with time. He recalled in 2002 that they were told to go to the camp on special occasions to take pictures, which they then handed over to Mr ND Marshall, who was the tennis coach and became the Liaison Officer after the death of Mrs Catherine Clarke. Marshall, in turn, usually liaised with Jadwiga Tarnogorska who dealt with all matters related to outside the camp.

Webb's reports indicate that individual pictures of all the children were taken for issuance of individual passports. Children were 'allotted' to various donors. Sabina Kotlinska was allotted to the Cochin state who donated ₹2,200 towards her upkeep in 1944 as a part of their War Purposes Fund[68] (see Photograph 10).

Visits by Dignitaries

Dignitaries often visited the camp, and a few visits are recorded in photographs and other material.[69] Sometimes during its existence, the camp was visited among others by the Archbishop of Poona; Lady Fitzherbert, wife of the Flag Officer Commanding, Royal Indian Navy; and the Deputy Consul of the Consulate at Bombay. The visits and their records were good promotional material for the British administrators to raise charitable funds. In fact, many of these pictures are the official pictures of the camp taken to raise awareness about the children and the ordeals they had suffered before reaching India and how happy they were to be in India. Two reports in newspapers were traced in the files of the British Library—Oriental and India Collection, London. There is also a mention of shooting a newsreel to be shown to the Indian audience, but it could not be traced at the Films Division Archives in Pune or Mumbai.

Making Contact

Letters, though slow to arrive, were very important and everyone waited for one. By this time, the Red Cross had started putting out information about the inhabitants in one camp to other camps in a bid to reunite families. The Polish section of International Red Cross was created on 14 September 1939, and was working in the USSR and Poland. So, usually everyone in the camp wrote down the details of their family and sent it to the Central Tracing Agency, International Committee of the Red Cross (ICRC), to be put up in other camps or scanned the lists sent by them about the inhabitants in the other camps seeking family and friends. Several children were reunited with their families. (See Appendix 2, a telegraphic query illustrating the situation above.)

It was also a routine practice for the children to write letters of encouragement to the soldiers of the Polish Army fighting in Monte Cassino, El Alamien and other places. If anyone had a known relative, then it was to them, or just anyone as a means to nurture relationships. Several children developed 'pen-pals' among the soldiers, and many started receiving money and gifts from them, much to the displeasure of the camp authorities.

The Central Tracing Agency states that 400,000 Polish POW were captured by Germany and more than 200,000 in the USSR.[70] The lists of officers was maintained and the common soldiers were given the status of 'civilian workers' in defiance of the 1929 Convention relative to the treatment of the POWs. While the German authorities gave some information, the Soviet Union did not adhere to the 1929 Convention and did not provide any information concerning Poles deported to the USSR. The database of missing Polish soldiers was created by various methods, but remained grossly incomplete. The Polish section of the Central Tracing Agency remains active to this day due to the scale of the tragedy afflicting the Polish population.

Movement and Closure

It was usual for children and their correspondents to write about the people surrounding them. Roman Gutowski recalled[71] that his friend received a letter from Poland in which the friend's mother mentioned that Mrs Gutowska and her daughters were staying with them in Poland after returning from Russia. This boy promptly sent a picture of Gutowski along with his known details as a joke since he had the same name. Indeed it turned out to be his mother, who had long assumed her son to have perished after leaving him in the orphanage in Kazakhstan. (Read testimony of Roman Gutowski in 'Voices from the Past'.) Wieslaw Stypula writes[72] that his mother located him through the Red Cross. In fact, several children located a parent, sibling or other relative keen to take them on and left the camp to be reunited with their families. Older boys left to join the services,[73] as did Tadeusz Herzog and Henryk Baczyk. The list of boys travelling from Bombay to the UK to join the Polish maritime school is reproduced in Appendix 6. Older girls went to Bombay where they trained as typists or nurses and were given some kind of employment by the Polish Legation office, run under the Consulate.

By 1945, the tide of events took unexpected turns in Poland, which had its reverberations in the settlements in India too.

Tide of Events

The motions for the formation of Union of Polish Patriots (Związek Patriotów Polskich, ZPP) began in late 1941 and was established in Moscow in March 1943 under the leadership of Wanda Wasilewska. They agreed to the Soviet demands for the Polish eastern provinces and conceded that post-War Poland would be a state allied to Moscow. Immediately following the rupturing of diplomatic relations with the Polish government in April 1943, after the discovery of the mass graves in Katyn, Stalin approved the formation of a another Polish Army on Soviet soil, under Lieutenant Colonel Zygmunt Berling, as proposed by Wasilewska, since General Wladyslaw Anders had chosen to align himself with the British forces in the Middle East. This second Polish Army was called the Polish Armed Forces in the east or the Polish People's Army (*Wojsko Ludowe*). Berling was the commander of the temporary Polish camp at Kranowodsk and promoted to the rank of General by Stalin himself and became the deputy commander of the *Wojsko Ludowe* on 22 July 1944. The Polish government-in-exile in London was given no say regarding its formation and use. The ZPP and its nominees formed the 'Lublin Committee' under Soviet patronage.

During Operation Barbarossa, there had been no agreement on the Polish–Soviet border. The cause was lost further after the death of General Sikorski, the Polish Premier on 4 July 1942, in an air crash off Gibraltar. There was little consensus about the policy to follow with the Soviet Union among his successors, Mikolajczyk, the political head, and Sosnkowski, the military head, as General Sikorski had held both portfolios together. At the conference of the Big Three at Tehran in November 1943, they conceded to Stalin most of the large area of eastern Poland that had been seized as a result of the Nazi-Soviet Pact in 1939. It was agreed that Poland would be compensated at the expense of Germany and the restored Polish state would enjoy 'friendly relations' with the USSR.

The Treaty of Versailles, 1919, that had followed the First World War, had never defined a permanent Polish–Soviet boundary, and its recommendations, dated 8 December 1919, that the line of River Bug should form a 'provisional minimum frontier' was never implemented. This frontier was then revived at the Spa conference of July 1920 and agreed to by the Poles, as a potential truce line for terminating the Polish–Soviet war of 1920. It was at Spa that it became known as the Curzon Line, named after the then British foreign secretary.

The Curzon Line had, however, remained undefined in eastern Galicia, and though it was agreed that the truce line should run where the armies stood when the truce came into effect, the telegram explaining this to Moscow contained a glaring ambiguity. It simultaneously proposed two lines in eastern Galicia: one to the east and the other to the west of the city of Lwow.

In any case, the line was never implemented, as the truce was soon broken when the Bolshevik armies advanced across it and eventually it was the events on the battlefield which determined the boundary between the two countries, with the Treaty of Riga, 1921, establishing a frontier considerably east of the Curzon Line. For the Poles, this closed the matter, but the signing of the German-Soviet Treaty of Friendship, Co-operation, and Demarcation (Molotov-Ribbentrop Pact) of 28 September 1939, resulted in a German–Soviet partition of Poland. This established a line mostly to the west of the Curzon Line mentioned in the Spa telegram that ran to the west of Lwow.[74]

At Tehran, Molotov, the Soviet foreign minister 're-discovered' the 'Curzon Line' prepared by the British Foreign Office in 1921. According to Professor Norman Davies, Molotov did not produce the telegram with the two variants of the Curzon Line. The copy of the map where the Curzon Line ran to the west of Lwow was recovered from the British

Foreign Office whose true author was Lewis Namier, a clerk in HMG's Foreign Office,[75] which was used as the final document at the Tehran Conference. Britain, in its inability to produce the full set of documents to counter the Soviet claim, was caught on a back foot. Professor Davies also says that the 'mean-spirited sophistry' of British diplomats[76] ensured that the interpretation of the Treaty of Friendship between Poland and Britain did not include safeguarding pre-War borders. Unable to retain at least Lwow and the Boryslaw oilfield, Premier Mikolajczyk resigned on 24 November 1944. Stalin maintained that the line established by the Treaty of Riga was defunct. At Tehran and Yalta, the Big Three agreed to a revived Curzon Line as the post-War Polish–Soviet frontier that excluded Lwow from Poland. The UK and the USA urged the Polish government-in-exile to accept the Soviet version of the Curzon Line in 1944 and, in the end, the new boundary became a *fait accompli*.[77]

In June 1945, a new Polish government of national unity was formed. The line-up of the new government had been agreed previously in Moscow. The London Poles got five of the 21 ministerial posts, the rest going to the Lublin Committee. At the Potsdam Conference which began on 17 July 1945, the western borders of Poland were agreed upon by the Great Powers or the Big Three. Poland advanced its borders at the expense of Germany, by over 200 kilometres in places, recovering land which belonged to the Polish rulers in the Middle Ages. The German population was expelled from these areas in a massive operation that saw 3.5 million people removed, some under great hardship. With Stalin having refused to re-establish the pre-War Polish–Soviet frontier, a population transfer of a similar scale was carried out in the east, following agreements between the Polish provisional government and communist authorities in the Lithuanian, Byelorussian and Ukrainian republics. Hundreds of thousands of Poles were 'repatriated', a majority leaving their homes in what is now Ukrainian territory. Most of them were taken to the west to colonise the region freshly acquired from the Germans. The cities of Stettin, Oppeln and Breslau became Szczecin, Opole and Wroclaw, respectively.

Not all Poles were willing to return to a homeland under a communist domination. In May 1945, Polish servicemen and women in the west numbered 250,000 and were dispersed in Germany, Italy, the Middle East and the UK and its colonies. Once the western Allies transferred diplomatic recognition to the communist authorities in Warsaw, the troops were faced with a dilemma; should they accept the authority of this new regime and agree to be repatriated. The feelings had its reverberations in the camps in India too. Mrs Buraczkiewicz, a representative of the new Polish government, visited the camps in Balachadi and Valivade and was booed, and some boys even threatened to jump off the ship or whatever means of transportation to avoid being taken back to Poland by force.[78]

Most people had suffered tremendously and had seen their friends and family members die in the Soviet Union. They viewed the communists with hatred and suspicion. Many of those from eastern Poland, also known as the Kresy region, had no homes to return to. They had been absorbed into the USSR. Others preferred to wait until the elections, which, they hoped, would throw the communists out of power.

The hostility of the Polish communist and the Soviet media towards General Anders and other Polish commanders was reflected in the violence of their language and by the later decision to strip him and 75 other senior officers of their Polish citizenship.[79]

The Foreign Office advised the India Office to advise the GOI that the Polish Consul-General should no longer continue to perform consular functions in spite of its causing inconvenience to the local Poles.[80] The Polish Children's Fund was also closed as it was a war-duration subscription. Most of the people in the camp were not willing to be repatriated to post-War Poland with new political affiliation. 'It was a hot potato, nobody wanted to touch it', described Reverend Z Peszkovski in 2004.[81] While the British were still undecided as to how to deal with this situation of several thousand Polish people unwilling to return to Poland, those children who could locate family members in Poland were encouraged to reunite with them. Fr Pluta travelled to the USA and arranged to have 50 girls sponsored by the St Bernadine Sisters of Pennsylvania and 31 boys by the Orchard Lake Seminary, Michigan, for higher education in the USA to prevent them from being taken forcibly to Poland against their wishes.[82]

The facts are borne out by the independent testimony of Alina Baczyk Haus, *Alina's Odyssey* on the Internet and is reproduced in the chapter 'Voices from the Past' with permission. Roman Gutowski said that he was scheduled to go to the USA, when he found his mother in Warsaw through a friend's correspondence mentioned in an earlier section. He then changed his destination and travelled to Poland instead.[83]

It was at this time, with the political conditions a complete confusion and India gearing for her own freedom, that Fr Pluta approached Jam Saheb for help. A plan was worked out where Fr Pluta, Jam Saheb and Lieutenant Colonel Geoffrey Clarke would adopt all the remaining children in the camp whose families had not been located and did not wish to be sent to

Poland.[84] Fr Pluta, as commandant and chaplain, would be responsible for the children's morale, Jam Saheb would support them financially and Lieutenant Colonel Clarke was supposed to get the approval of the British Indian Government. Accordingly, a court order was obtained from the Nawanagar state courts. No official documents have been available, but in his letter to RN Gilchrist of the India Office, His Highness Eggers quoted an extract of Webb's letter of 19 December [1946] that says, 'the best legal advise [had] been taken and that the opinion of an eminent Bombay lawyer, the formal documents are water-tight from a legal point of view'.[85] The letter is reproduced with permission as Appendix 7.

It is probably this 'adoption' procedure that paved the way for 81 children to go to the USA. It may be assumed that Jam Saheb paid for the passage of these children, though no records have been found anywhere. Fr Pluta was later termed an 'international kidnapper'. He spent the rest of his life in the USA, never returning to Poland.

With the closure of the Polish Children's Fund, all the Polish refugees were handed over to the UNRRA and were financially supported by the Interim Treasury Committee (ITC) till the UNRRA took them over. For reasons of economy, the last of the children of Balachadi camp were merged with the camp in Kolhapur in 1946. Stefan Klosowski, Franek Herzog, Wieslaw Stypula and Zbigniew Bartosz all recall[86] spending a year in Valivade camp from where they went on a bicycling trip to Goa as a scouting expedition with Reverend Z Peszkovski. It was possibly the time when all the legalities were being worked out and the children were awaiting passage to their chosen destinations.

Financial Status

In his first report covering the period of March 1942–October 1942, Webb reported credits into the Polish Children's Fund from the Viceroy's War Purposes Fund of ₹50,000 and a contribution of ₹104,000 by the government from Indian revenues and other donations.[87] For the period covering October 1942–February 1943, Webb reported a credit of ₹100,000 into the Polish Children's Fund by the government from Indian Revenues. He also reported that promises amounting to ₹24,413 per month have been received from various Indian rulers and others. He reported that this amount would cover the expenses for 406 children at the rate of ₹60 per month.[88] Subsequently, he stated that promises amounting to ₹300,000 had been received and he believed that they might even go up to ₹500,000.[89] Webb continued that for the period of February 1943 to July 1943, donations amounting to ₹185,079 had been received for the Polish Children's Fund[90] for July 1943 to November 1943 the amount was ₹67,127.[91]

The memorandum attached to Webb's report covering the period of 21 November 1943 to 11 November 1944,[92] states that donations from the public during the financial year 1 January 1943–31 December 1943 amounted to ₹491,660. Against it, ₹360,000 was paid to the Accountant General Central Revenues for transfer to the Polish government's account in London, being the maintenance of 500 orphans for 12 months at ₹720 per head. An amount of ₹131,660 was carried forward into the next financial year.

Webb continued that an excess of approximately ₹25,519 had been incurred initially during transportation of and equipping the children, over the Viceroy's donation of ₹50,000, an expense that should legitimately be billed to the Polish government in London or deducted from the collections in India. He stated that there have been actual collections or promises amounting to ₹250,000 towards the maintenance of the children for 1944. So, the collections together with the balance being carried forward this year totalled to ₹356,141 or just about the ₹360,000 needed to maintain the children through 1944. So, if the Polish government agreed to a transfer of ₹25,000 from their fund account in London, ₹25,000 could be carried over as balance for the year to come.[93]

Though the Balachadi camp remained functional till 1945, the financial records for the period November 1944–November 1945 are not traceable. In his telegram dated 1 July 1947[94] to RN Gilchrist, Captain Webb says that the Indian public have contributed some ₹0.6 million towards the upkeep of Polish refugees in India.

In a communication dated 15 July 1943, Gilchrist informed Sir Walford Selby of the Polish Relief Fund that approximately ₹400,000 amounting to £29,500 had been collected in India.[95] Some of the documents have been reproduced with permission as Appendices 8–10. Some back-of-the-envelope calculations yield that ₹600,000 in 1942–48 amounted to approximately £45,000 then and £300,000 in 2008–09 terms.

In a memorandum, Webb mentioned that India had supported 500 Polish children through 1943 and would continue to do so through 1944. Contributions to the Polish Children's Fund had been somewhat less than in 1944 due to the famine in Bengal and some parts of the Madras Presidency. Several former subscribers to the Fund had expressed their inability to continue their donations. He maintained that and hoped to be able to carry on further, but much depended upon the economic conditions of the country, though several subscribers had pledged their donations indefinitely.

In his telegram dated 1 July 1947 to RN Gilchrist, Captain Webb says that the Indian public have contributed some ₹600,000 towards the up-keep of Polish refugees in India.

A glance through the list of donors from the piecemeal records reveals several Princely States, but Nawanagar does not feature in them. It is possible that Jam Saheb did not subscribe to the Fund as a glance at the expenditure column shows generous sums allocated to adults towards taking holidays, etc. He probably preferred to contribute directly to the camp and the money be used for the children, which tallies with Stypula's and Gutowski's memories of getting a football soon after Jam Saheb's visit to the camp.

In conclusion, at the site of the former camp stands Sainik School Balachadi since 1978, home to about the same number of children, ironically run in the same military style. The only difference is that it is purely a boys school now.

NOTES AND REFERENCES

1. Hershad Kumariji, personal interview to the author, New Delhi, June 2004. Subsequent quotes are from the same interview.
2. BL-I&OC, POL 9244, Major Geoffrey Clarke's 'Note on Polish Evacuee,Children received by HH the Maharaja Jam Saheb of Nawanagar in Nawanagar State', dated 17 October 1942.
3. NAI, 276(8)-X/42, Captain AWT Webb's Reports (hereafter WR), 32.
4. Ibid.
5. W Stypula, *1000 Visitors of the Maharaja* (Warsaw: Orion (22)615 54 01, 2000). The book is in Polish. An abridged verbal translation was provided by Dr K Stronski, Professor of Polish, Department of Slavonic Studies, Delhi University in December 2003. All references to this book are based on the abridged version and actual page numbers cannot be quoted.
6. NAI, 276(8)-X/42, WR, 5.
7. W Stypula, videotaped interview to scholar, Warsaw, 2004.
8. NAI, 276(8)-X/42, WR, 11.
9. Suleiman Khan, interview to author, Balachadi, October 2002.
10. A road could not be named after Jam Saheb at the end of the War owing to the new political situation, but in 1989, a private school was named such. The author visited the school in Warsaw and took pictures (see Photograph 34).
11. F Herzog.

12. NAI, 276(8)-X/42, WR, dated 3 November 1942.
13. Ibid.
14. Ibid., 19.
15. Ibid.., 46.
16. BNA, FO 371/ 32630, Notes referring to Letter No. W10764/87/48, Cheetam to Gibson.
17. AAN, Letter No. W 9800/87/48 dated 15 July 1942, Maurice Peterson to Count E Raczynski.
18. NAI, 276(8)-X/42, WR, 32.
19. Ibid., 33.
20. Kirit Ashani, son of Late Dr A Ashani, interview to author, Jamnagar, October 2002.
21. Fr Pluta, Reunion speech of 18 July 1986, courtesy Franek Herzog.
22. NAI, 276(8)-X/42, WR, 24.
23. A former Balachadi boy, now a retired civil engineer in Warsaw, interview to author, Warsaw, March 2004.
24. W Stypula, *1000 Visitors of the Maharaja*.
25. Hershad Kumariji, personal interview to the author, New Delhi, June 2004.
26. NAI, 210(72)-G/44. List in Appendix, as also a bill.
27. Daniela Szydlo, now a resident of London, videotaped interview to author, London, March 2004.
28. Ibid.
29. Sister Margaret Hoogwerf, now posted at St Joseph's Convent, Bandra, interview to author, March 2003.
30. Daniela Szydlo, videotaped interview.
31. AAN, document number not available.
32. BL-I&OC, Major Geoffrey Clarke's 'Note on Polish Evacuee children'.
33. E Raczynski, *In Allied London* (London: Weidenfeld and Nicholson, 1962), 128 (covering the events of 26 December 1942).
34. W Adamczyk, email to author.
35. KX Robbins, 'The Camp for Polish Refugee Children at Balachadi Nawanagr (India)', *Journal of Indo-Judaic Studies*, Washington, 1998, 105.
36. Z Mandel to Robbins, who then referred him to author.
37. Reverend Z Peszkovski is the sole surviving adult from amongst the Poles who reached India. An excerpt of his interview with the author is given in 'Voices from the Past'.
38. W Stypula, *1000 Visitors of the Maharaja*.
39. R Gutowski, videotaped interview to author, Warsaw, March 2004.
40. W Stypula, *1000 Visitors of the Maharaja*.
41. AAN, Amb. RP Londony, sygn 1812, Maurice Peterson (FO) to Count Edward Raczynski, dated 15 July 1942.
42. BL-I&OC, Letter No. W 11294/87/48, AWG Randall to JP Gibson.
43. BL-I&OC, L/P&J/8/413, Telegram No. 503, from Tehran to Foreign Office, dated 18 April 1942.

44. It was an abandoned RAF station. According to Princess Hershad Kumariji, the runway had been caving in due to the soil conditions, interview to author, New Delhi, June 2002.
45. NAI, 276(8)-X/42, WR, 47.
46. HS Chhina, personal letter to author. He was an official of the Patiala state at that time and was later Chief Secretary of Punjab state.
47. N Davies, *Rising '44* (London: Macmillan, 2003), 29.
48. BNA, FO 371/42882, Captain AWT Webb's report dated 13 September 1943.
49. BNA, FO 371/3.6736.
50. Ibid.
51. NAI, 276(8)-X/42, W.R., 77.
52. Possibly Okha, a place not far from Jamnagar.
53. W Stypula, *1000 Visitors of the Maharaja*.
54. Ibid.
55. Meeting of Jam Saheb Junior, Stefan Klosowski and author, Jamnagar, October 2002.
56. W Stypula, *1000 Visitors of the Maharaja*.
57. S Klosowski, interview to author.
58. F Burdzy, interview in *Polityka*, Warsaw, dated 2 June 2001.
59. Gutowski, videotaped interview to author, Warsaw, March 2004.
60. W Stypula, *1000 Visitors of the Maharaja*.
61. Klosowski, interview to author.
62. W Stypula, *1000 Visitors of the Maharaja*.
63. Ibid.
64. NAI, 276(8)-X/42, WR, 48.
65. Hershad Kumarji, interview to author, June 2002, New Delhi. Excerpts of her interview with the author are given in 'Voices from the Past'.
66. Reference to Mary Bunty Allen, daughter of the Chief Transport Officer, Nawanagar, cited in Robbins, *Journal of Indo-Judaic Studies*, Washington. Subesequent quote by Hershad Kumariji as interviewed by the author.
67. Alina Baczyk Haus, an old girl from Balachadi, now a resident of USA, was thrilled to see these pictures on a website and wrote to the author in an email that it is she on the edge of the picture (Photograph 12) whose face was partially cut off.
68. Rama Varma (Appan) Tampuran, War Publicity officer, 'Cochin' (published under the special authority of His Highness, the Maharaja of Cochin, 1944).
69. Archival pictures in personal collection of Tadeusz Dobrostanski and made available to author; newspaper clippings in BL-I&OC files.
70. G Djurovic, *The Central Tracing Agency of the International Committee of the Red Cross* (Geneva: International Committee of the Red Cross, 1986), 137–42.
71. R Gutowski, videotaped interview to author, Warsaw, March 2004.
72. W Stypula, *1000 Visitors of the Maharaja*.
73. NAI, 210(72)-G/44, Letter No. VR 43555, dated 11 September 1944.

74. P Latawski, *Oxford Companion to WW II*, London, 1995, 707–8.
75. N Davies, *Rising '44*, 144.
76. Ibid., 30.
77. P Latawski, *Oxford Companion to WW II*, 707–8.
78. Reunion speech of Fr Pluta on 18 July 1998. Also, cited in A Neizgoda, '1000 Children of the Maharaja', *Polityka*, Warsaw, 2 June 2001.
79. K Sword, *Oxford Companion to WW II*, 701–2.
80. BL- I&OC, L/P&J/8/414(Coll 110 N3), Folio 446, Hancock to Gilchrist, dated 16 October 1945.
81. Z Peszkovski, videotaped interview to author, 2004, Warsaw. Excerpts of his interview with the author are given in 'Voices from the Past'.
82. Reunion speech of Fr Pluta.
83. R Gutowski, *1000 Visitors of the Maharaja*.
84. Reunion speech of Fr Pluta.
85. BL- I&OC, Letter no. OF 91/4/53, HH Eggers to RN Gilchrist, dated 23 May 1947.
86. In individual interviews to author, S Klosowski, at Balachadi, F Herzog, over email, W Stypula and Z Bartosz, in individual interviews at Warsaw.
87. NAI, 276(8)-X/42, WR, 29.
88. NAI, 276(8)-X/42, WR, 58–59.
89. NAI, 276(8)-X/42, WR, 72.
90. NAI, 276(8)-X/42, WR, 82.
91. NAI, 276(8)-X/42, WR, P 91, ibid.
92. PIGSM, C-811c, Report of the Delegate, Memorandum attached to Webb's report covering the period of 21 November 1943 to 11 November 1944.
93. Ibid., Webb's report.
94. BL-I&OC, L/P&J/8/415, Telegram No. Pol. 8701, GOI to Secretary of State for India, dated 1 July 1947.
95. BL-I&OC, L/P&J/110-N 19-1/412, Folio No. 40, Gilchrist to Selby, dated 15 July 1943.

The Transit Camps and War-duration Domicile

❧

*K*arachi was a major port city and a cantonment in undivided British India on the Arabian Sea. It was the most important port for military supply lines for Lend-Lease supplies and logistical support for troops deployed in Persia, Iraq and the Middle East, especially those originating from India. The most important role for India during the Second World War was as a supply base. There was a major British–Indian military and naval presence there. When the USA joined the War after the bombing of Pearl Harbour, they too established a naval base in Karachi to manage the logistics of the Lend-Lease supplies. In fact, Karachi became the second most important port for the purpose after Basra in Persia. So when the Poles had to be removed from Persia, in transit to other destination, Karachi was the obvious choice as they could be brought in military transport returning from Basra and Ahvaz after delivering the supplies. Karachi was the venue of two Polish transit camps: Country Club from 4 November 1942 to 2 October 1945 and Malir camp from 2 March 1943 to 18 August 1943.[1]

Arrival of the Poles

Following Germany's attack on the USSR, an *Udovestrine* or amnesty was declared for the Polish people in the Soviet territory. The British negotiated the formation of a Polish Army inside the USSR. The Polish Enrolment Commission, formed to locate former Polish soldiers in the Soviet Union, could visit only some labour camps; most people came to know about it accidentally and passed the news around. Zofia Mendonca nee Krawiec, of Pune, recalled noticing a few well-dressed people talking to the camp authorities a few days prior to them finding themselves abandoned by the camp authorities,[2] whereas Danuta Pniewska, of London, showed the clipping of the Russian newspaper by which they came to know about the amnesty. The unlettered man in charge of the *kolhoz* in Kazakhstan heard that his name was in the newspaper (Maisky—the name he shared with the then Soviet Foreign Minister) and gave the paper to Danuta's mother to figure out why. It was the caption of a picture announcing the Sikorski-Maisky Treaty and the resumption of Polish–Soviet relations and the formation of a Polish Army from the people in the Soviet Union.[3] The camps disgorged and a sea of Polish humanity started moving towards the collection centres.

Relations between Poland and the Soviet Union began to falter over rations and the state of preparedness of the recently regrouped Polish Army to wage a war against Germany. General Sikorski, the Polish Premier, preferred the Polish troops to be employed in the Caucasus, closer to the British forces in the Middle East where they could be assured of supplies. From the British point of view, the best solution to the problem would be the withdrawal of the five Soviet divisions from Persia to the Caucasus and their replacement in Persia by the Polish divisions from the USSR.[4] The decision to carry out an evacuation of the troops was finally reached at a key meeting between Sikorski and Stalin in Moscow on 3 December 1941. Citing the problems of supply and the miserable conditions under which the Polish troops were being maintained, the Polish leader proposed, 'the entire army and all the people eligible for military service' should be removed, perhaps to Persia. There, the promised USA and British help would enable the soldiers to recover in due course, to return to the Soviet territory to fight alongside the Red Army. This, Sikorski said, had been settled with Churchill.[5]

Stalin received appeals from Churchill and Harriman (at Polish prompting) to allow the Polish troops to leave the Soviet soil for a region where they could be more easily supplied. Accordingly, he gave his assent, 'one corps, 2 to 3 divisions may leave'. Recruitment was to continue for a further six divisions which would remain in the Soviet Union.[6] Stalin also conceded to a request from General Sikorski that Polish recruitment and training should be conducted in a region with a less severe climate. Accordingly, at the beginning of 1942, the Polish forces were transferred from the Volga region to camps in Central Asia. The move took place over a five-week period during January and February. The Polish Army headquarters was shifted from Buzuluk to Yangi-Yul, near Tashkent.

Polish Army camps now began to be formed over a huge area of Soviet Central Asia, adjoining the Chinese and Afghan borders. Hundreds of miles now separated the various divisional headquarters.[7] Nuclei were set up in the areas allotted to the troops. Soon a flood of men began to arrive. Their health, owing to the lack of food, was still poor and epidemics, particularly typhus, spread rapidly, for there [was] little soap in and an enormous number of parasites.[8] Planning for the evacuation now began in earnest. On the British side, it involved intensive communication among London, the Middle East Command, No. 30 Military Mission in the Soviet Union and even British Military Command in India.[9]

In Central Asia, General Anders, the Polish commander, was supporting a large number of civilians, that is, women and children from the army rations to keep them from starving to death. In March 1942, the Red Army informed Anders that SAWO, the Russian/Uzbek acronym for the Central Asian Military District, upon which the Poles had depended for supplies, would in future be able to supply the Poles with only 26,000 rations.[10] At that time, there were already 70,000 men in the ranks of the Polish Army and a large number of civilian dependents, with 1,000–1,500 new recruits trickling in every day, and the numbers were expected to rise to 100,000. The Poles were told that food was scarce and the Red Army was itself having to cut down ration allocations. In London, a foreign office official noted that, if true, this was an indication of the severe scarcity of food in the USSR, and speculated, 'the Russians may be willing now to get rid of these Polish mouths'.[11]

Stalin agreed that the Poles should receive rations for 44,000 troops— 'three divisions and a reserve regiment'—from 1 April 1942, and the rest of the 30,000 troops and 10,000 supernumerary elements including civilian dependants troops should be evacuated. He personally marked out a land and sea route which led across the Caspian Sea via Krasnovodsk in Soviet Uzbekistan, with an alternative land route via Ashkabad and Meshed pencilled in.[12] Zhukov, the head of the NKVD, was nominated to be in charge of the evacuation.

When General Anders realised that the original British plan provided for only 2,500 Poles per week at Pahlevi, Persia, at 14 days' notice of movement; he stressed that the matter was one of life and death for 40,000 Poles and asked only for bare subsistence for them.[13] Churchill took personal interest in the matter and conveyed the same to Sikorski. It was also proposed that the Polish forces be concentrated in Palestine with the Carpathian Brigade, instead of being sent as detachments to Britain using valuable shipping, which was accepted by Sikorski.[14]

The convoys of Polish troops and civilians were to go by rail to Krasnovodsk, in USSR, and from there, by troops ship to Pahlevi, in Persia, across the Caspian Sea. Till as late as 24 March 1942, the Soviet authorities in Tehran professed continuing ignorance of the date of evacuation. On that day, the first ship *Karamin* left Krasnovodsk and reached Pahlevi the next day. The evacuation staff, expecting the first transport on 27 March 1942, were surprised that the ship was already in harbour waiting. The first Poles were landed the same evening.[15]

The Persia and Iraq Force (PAI Force) Command expecting only the troops was astonished to find civilians travelling with the troops. On 27 March 1942, a cipher telegram from London to Commander Polish Forces the USSR read:

> British authorities are alarmed by the news that families are included in military transports, this not being within the framework of the evacuation scheme. In view of the great food difficulties in Iran it is necessary to stop absolutely transport of families until agreement is reached with British authorities as it may hamper or restrict military evacuation. How many members of families have you already evacuated and how many do you intend to evacuate?
>
> —Chief of General Staff. 2228[16]

Neither governments—British or Polish—were prepared in any way or expected a civilian evacuation. By 31 March 1942, about 13,000 Polish dependants had arrived at Pahlevi and were being conveyed to Tehran. There was a general feeling of being pushed hard in London. Instead of receiving an army, they had inherited a welfare problem.[17] When this news was brought to Churchill, he wrote impatiently on the telegram from Tehran, 'Foreign Secretary. Are we going to get nothing but women and children? We must have the men.'[18]

By this time, the evacuation of the families along with the military had begun and continued. Although instructions were immediately sent by the British and Polish authorities to stop the outflow, it had proved impossible in practice to prevent civilians reaching Pahlevi. 'Once there, we have had to do our best to cope with them', the Foreign Office minute to Churchill said and continued,

> ...although we shall have 10,000–15,000 civilians on our hands, we shall nevertheless get out of Russia 81,000 to 86,000 troops, which is several

thousand more than we had originally expected. The morale of these troops could hardly be good had those with wives and children been compelled to leave them behind in the U.S.S.R....[19]

Anders received orders from the Polish headquarters in London—under pressure from the British—to prevent the further evacuation of civilians. However, like Nelson, he chose to turn a blind eye. All telegrams from the Polish headquarters were relegated to a bottom drawer of his office desk and not acted upon. [20]

About 12,000 civilians, including 3,000 children arrived in Persia.[21] The Polish government discussed the issue of the civilian evacuees at a cabinet meeting on the morning of 31 March 1942. They, it seems, were as much in the dark as the British. They had been in constant communication with General Anders over the preceding few days, but 'it was clear that the military authorities on the spot had been totally unable to stop the movement of their civilians'. There was no doubt, claimed the Polish spokesman, that the Soviet government were putting pressure on them to go, and unfortunately it appeared that the local inhabitants, not unnaturally in view of the food shortage, had adopted a hostile attitude.[22] A flurry of communication followed between the British Foreign Office and their embassies in Tehran and Kuibyshev (the USSR), Foreign office to the India Office and from the India Office to New Delhi. The British Embassy at Kuibyshev observed that the Soviet military authorities had encouraged Anders to slip as many as possible out of the USSR (whether they had visas or not) and not to bring the Polish Ambassador or the Soviet civil authorities into it.[23] The Polish Ambassador was 'somewhat distressed' as he had himself been working on an evacuation scheme with the Soviet authorities which would give priority to children and certain civilian adults.[24] He assured the British Ambassador at Kuibyshev that civilian evacuation had been effectively stopped.[25]

In the first evacuation between 25 March 1942 to 5 April 1942, 43,858 Polish people arrived at Pahlevi, of which 10,789 were civilians, including 3,100 children. The other figures are: 1,603 officers, 28,427 other ranks, 1,159 Women's Voluntary Service (WVS) and 1,880 cadets.[26] To control and direct onward movement of such a large number of people required a major administrative and logistical effort. A variety of military transport was available—up to 100 vehicles—much of which was utilised in bringing supplies up to the Pahlevi area. Indian and Armenian drivers drove round the clock to remove the evacuees from the port.[27] The end of the evacuation was announced by a Soviet officer, Captain Samilov, from

Krasnovodsk, who said that Stalin's orders to have the evacuation from the Soviet territory completed by 2 April 1942, had been carried out, and the frontier was now closed.[28] Lieutenant Colonel Ross, British officer-in-charge of the reception at Pahlevi, reported that 160 civilians who had not managed to get away from Krasnovodsk by ship, had been sent back by the Soviet authorities to Tashkent.[29]

The inward movement of the evacuees to Pahlevi, in the second phase of the operation, continued for a further three weeks. While most of the military evacuees were directed towards Palestine, the civilians were initially more of a problem. As far as the Iranian authorities were concerned, the Poles were merely 'in transit'. Initially, the Persian authorities were worried that the average Persian, already reeling under occupation and wartime shortages, would suffer further with the presence of a large body of additional population. They wanted the Poles to be despatched further. However, they soon started co-operating energetically in the provision of accommodation and medical assistance.[30] It also covertly served as an anti-Soviet propaganda in Persia, though discouraged by the British. In the same communication, Sir R Bullard, the British Ambassador to Tehran, wrote, 'Russians can no longer upset Persian citizens by singing the glories of the Soviet Union, while Tehran is full of Poles who were starving in Russia and who admitted that Russians in the same circumstances were starving too.'[31]

The British Foreign Mission in Tehran, however,

> ...doubted that the outflow of Polish civilians refugees from Soviet Russia would end with the 12,000 odd who had arrived in Persia. They thought the day was not far off when the Soviet Government will either deport Poles wholesale or assist them (unofficially) voluntarily to escape.[32]

Sir R Bullard, the British Ambassador to Persia, continued in the same communication,

> If we are to be faced in the near future with mass exit from Soviet Russia of Polish civilian refugees, the question of finding for them a war-duration domicile will become one of the greatest urgency, seeing that it is extremely doubtful whether Persia would willingly grant asylum to any more.[33]

On 22 June 1942, the British Minister of State in Cairo recommended to the Foreign Office that

1. The Middle East Relief and Refugee Administration (M.E.R.R.A.) must be allowed to coordinate all such action if chaos is to be avoided.

2. Immediate action to be taken through the Soviet Ambassador and the Polish Government in London to avert the exodus of 50,000 children from Russia until

   (i) the existing 10,000 Polish refugees in Persia have been removed;
   (ii) arrangements have been made for the transit of any further numbers that we agree to cope with, through Persia, as quickly as possible to ultimate destination.

3. Immediate steps be taken both in London and Cairo to ensure that no Allied Government takes any unconcerted action in refugee matters without reference to M.E.R.R.A.

4. Commander-in-Chief regards Polish refugees already in Persia as a serious potential operational embarrassment and cannot contemplate further influx unless conditions specified in (3) are rigidly observed.

5. To put matters bluntly, if these Poles die in Russia the war effort will not be affected. If they pass into Persia, we unlike the Russians, will not be able to allow them to die and our war effort will be gravely impaired. Action must be taken to stop these people from leaving the U.S.S.R. before we are ready to receive them (and then only at the rate we are able to receive and ship them away from the head of the Persian Gulf) however many die in consequence.

6. Study is being made of the possibility of utilising United States shipping from the Persian Gulf.[34]

This communication was passed on to the Under Secretary of State, India Office. From 11 April 1942, the GOI, which kept a strict vigil on all developments in Persia, was on tenterhooks about the Polish exodus from Russian Turkestan to India. 'We must watch for any signs of this and try by all means to discourage it, since India is at the moment not a suitable place for the reception of such refugees', wrote WHJ Christie of the Viceroy Staff to ADK Owen of the Overseas Department,[35] as it would create a difficult situation on the frontiers of India, since it would scarcely be possible to refuse them admission.[36] The same communication continued that Captain LAC Fry, who had served in consular posts in East Persia, had been asked to ensure,

> If there are any signs of such an attempt to reach India by parties of Polish women and children, other than those who are being brought under official auspices, the earliest possible warning shall be given, as, undoubtedly, if they were to present themselves at the frontier of British India the position would be an extremely difficult one.[37]

Following the first evacuation of the Polish divisions from Soviet Central Asia, the number of troops remaining in the Soviet Union at the beginning of April 1942 were 40,508, including women soldiers and cadets (*junaks*). It was agreed that three infantry divisions and some ancillary formations would be created within the ceiling of 44,000 troops. The numbers in the Polish units began to grow and the Soviets stepped in to remind the Poles that they had agreed to only 44,000 recruits and further recruitment should stop. At this stage, a major disagreement developed over interpretations of the Polish-Soviet Accord reached between Anders and Stalin. The Poles felt that, while their units in the USSR were limited by the agreement to 44,000 recruits, there was no reason why recruitment could not continue and the surplus elements be evacuated to reinforce the Polish forces in the Middle East, as had happened a month earlier. The idea was firmly rejected by the Soviet leadership.[38]

The Second Evacuation

Anders pressed Sikorski to approve the evacuation of Poles from Russia as quickly as possible—while Soviet Russia was still weak. Sikorski once again turned to Churchill for help in pressing Stalin to agree to the evacuation of some Polish units from the USSR. The Poles asked for

1. maintenance of a Polish recruiting centre in the USSR after the departure of Polish troops and a resumption of recruitment of all Polish citizens able to bear arms.
2. the families of troops leaving the USSR and the auxiliary military services of women and boy scouts were to leave with the troops. This covered about 20,000 civilians.
3. necessary measures were to be taken to begin the evacuation from Russia in collaboration with the Polish Embassy of 50,000 Polish children accompanied by 5,000 mothers or guardians.[39]

There was irritation on the British side about these conditions. It was pointed out that the Polish government had been asked to do all in their power to *prevent* a large-scale exodus of civilians, which was contrary to points (2) and (3) stated above. Churchill, whose attention was drawn to the Foreign Office reservations, pointed out that the evacuation depended upon the military situation in North Africa. He noted,

The above leaves me in doubt whether you want the three Polish divisions or not, if you have to take with them this mass of women and children.

Personally I want them. If we win the Alamein battle we ought to be able to handle them even with their encumbrances.[40] If we don't win—project impracticable.[41]

The Poles appealed,

We ask for nothing. Our 44,000 troops in Central Asia each receive a ration supposedly equivalent to about 60% of British rations—and they do not receive this in full. On this they have to keep themselves and some 16,000 dependants alive. As regards the destination and accommodation, the dependants will go anywhere and sleep on the bare ground if necessary, as some are doing even now. Even if half of them died of hardship outside the U.S.S.R., that is better than all dying inside. Anything is better than leaving them behind.[42]

The British took the decision to proceed and to include the civilians. On 31 July 1942, a Polish–Soviet military protocol was signed in Tashkent, providing for the evacuation of the Polish Army and 'military families' to Persia. The second article of the protocol concerned these military families and included measures designed to prevent 'Soviet citizens' from leaving with the Poles. This included both the Soviet wives of the Polish soldiers and also those residents of the Polish eastern territories who were not of Polish ethnic origin and were deemed to have acquired Soviet citizenship by the decree of November 1939. Family members who came from eastern Poland and were Polish by nationality had to have confirmation from their Polish commander that they were indeed close kin of a soldier. This affected parents, wives, husbands, children and sick brothers and sisters who were being maintained by the army. The NKVD was to check all documentation and General Anders undertook that the Poles would admit to the transports only those whose names were on the lists.[43]

On the basis of the Polish-Soviet Protocol, the army staff issued the order on 1 August 1942 for the second evacuation to be set in motion, using the same route as the first evacuation. The movement began on 9 August 1942 and was completed on 1 September 1942, taking 22 days in all. Of the 69,247 Poles evacuated during this second operation, 25,501 were civilians. Of the civilian evacuees, 9,633 were children.[44] Of these, 568 people, chiefly civilians, died in Pahlevi. The peak figure of sick was reached at the port on 8 September 1942, when there were 868 Poles in hospital and 2,000 in the convalescent camp. Ross reported, 'It was a sad commentary on the conditions under which they had lived in Russia. It was also, as one might add, a vindication of the pressure exerted by the Polish authorities to have them evacuated'.[45]

Several stories of personal heroism and going beyond the call of duty emerge. Zofia Morawska was in charge of one of the orphanages in Kazakhstan. On receiving instructions to prepare the orphanage for evacuation and to collect her daughter from the nearby *kolhoz*, she went around several *kolhozes*, often walking tens of kilometres every evening to inform her fellow Poles about the impending evacuation and their last chance to leave the USSR.[46]

According to R Umiastowsky, there was sea of hopeful Polish civilians to get a place in the troops ship, while the Soviet authorities allowed only those people whose name appears in an 'approved' list. He describes a heart-wrenching scene of a young lad's bid to somehow board the ship by hoisting himself up quietly from one of the gunnel ropes. The NKVD guards shook the ropes violently till the hands of the exhausted boy could not hold him any longer. He crashed on the pier, breaking his skull. The guards then just walked across and casually kicked his body into the water.[47] Other incidents of random shooting by the NKVD at the embarkation areas have also been cited by some survivors.

Conditions on board were beyond description. In a successful effort to get as many Poles away from Krasnovodsk in the shortest possible time, the Soviets had packed the evacuees on board until it was almost impossible to move. Sanitary conditions were pathetically below belief—six lavatories to serve 4,000–5,000 people. 'Only the fact that the Poles were inured to all kinds of hardships by their two and a half years in the Soviet Union enabled them to endure this journey', wrote Ross, in his report.[48]

I was about 12 years old at that time and after being in various places in Kazakhstan since being deported with my mother from the outskirts of L'vov, I found myself at the orphanage at Kang Batash from where we were moved to Guzar. I enrolled in the Army as a junak or cadet. There were about 350 youngsters like me there and it was not far from the place where the Polish Army camp was. There was a school for the cadets where we attended school in the morning, exercised and learnt to use the rifle during the day. The rifle was a rogue Russian one that was taller than I was. I was 1 metre and 32 cms then. The top of the barrel was above my head and much too heavy for me.

There we also started getting malaria. One day at the parade for about the 350 of us, there were only 70 of us standing. The rest were ill. In those months then, I believe I had only one tablet of quinine, which I believe was because the nurse took pity on me. There were no medicines at that time.

Then news came that we were allowed to leave Russia, so once again the transports were organised and we were moved to the Caspian Sea town of Krasnovodsk. We arrived there and were on the bare desert. There were many drums there. I don't know what they were transporting but we used them to make partitions to stop the wind. We waited there for several days. It was hot and one day we were taken for a swim to the sea. The sea was full of oil—floating in levels. So, when you entered and went into the water upto your knees, you had about three layers of oil on you. There was no water to wash with. Now we were also covered in oil. The next day there was a sandstorm and the sand stuck on us. We looked like mummies! And how were we dressed—in oversized Army uniforms. At my height and the fact that we were only skin and bones at that time, my size would have been children's size 3 or 4, and I was issued a battle dress of size 8 for the lack of options. It was almost like a skirt, because it went below my knees. The Angola shirt went right upto my ankles. But never mind, it kept us warm.

Thereafter we were all loaded into the boat to take us from Krasnovodsk to Pahlevi in Persia. The boat was so overcrowded that it was okay if you sat down, but if you stood up, you could not sit down again because the people would get closer to you and there would be no space to bend your knees and sit down. At that time many of us had dysentery. So, just imagine, so many of us in that state packed together like sardines for several hours. All soldiers, cadets, grown ups and children in that state and no toilets. Often there was a shout, '*Junak*s (cadets) use the toilet overboard.' Several boys fell overboard attempting that and nobody could pick them up.

We landed on the sandy beaches of Pahlevi. There were just a few mat roofs—no covers, nothing, just mat roofs. The first thing was delousing us. We were all taken by the Army authorities from the landing area to the showers.

—Karol Huppert, 72, London

Upon landing, the civilian evacuees were registered by the Polish Civil Delegation, who was also responsible for preparing the civilian parties for convoys onwards. As earlier, the military convoys travelled towards Palestine, while the civilians were moved to Tehran area. In addition to the seaborne evacuation, a smaller group of 2,694 Poles made their way in stages overland to Meshed at the end of August.[49] The military commission in Ashkakad brought an additional 2,637 people in November.[50] Ross wrote in his final report to MERRA, in December 1943:

A small Transit Camp has been in existence at Meshed since the summer of 1942. It was originally intended for the reception of Polish orphans released from the Soviet Union and travelling overland to destinations in India via Zahidan, but in fact served as a convenient staging post, not only for the orphans, of whom as many as 675 have travelled with their guardians to India by this route, but for other small groups of Poles who have left the Soviet Union by the eastern route via Ashkabad, capital of Turkmenistan, which is only about 20 miles from the Soviet-Persian frontier at Badgiran.

At intervals, small parties of adults and children have arrived at Meshed even since the rupture of diplomatic relations between the Russians and the Poles and it is interesting that, even though Meshed is in the Russian zone of occupation, the Soviet authorities there have not made any attempt to force the Poles to leave.

Since the Soviets occupied northern Persia, there was a great fear amongst the Polish people in Persia that in case of any political shifts, they would be capable of grabbing the Polish refugees once more.[51] On the shores of the Caspian Sea at Pahlavi, Iran, the Polish evacuees found a hastily constructed camp of tents and open shelters nestled in the sand. Królikowski described the songs and prayers which could be heard throughout the day as Polish refugees gave thanks for their deliverance at altars which had been erected along the beaches.[52] Many people recalled the joy they felt at their first taste of freedom.

Pahlevi looked very nice to us. After two years of starvation in the USSR, we couldn't believe that food was abundantly available, that we could even buy it if we had something to sell or exchange. There were fruits and eggs that the Iranian boys would come along the beaches selling every morning. One day I exchanged a trinket for two dozen eggs. I buried them in the hot sand for some hours and they became hard boiled eggs. I had just eaten the 21st, when Janine found me out and took away the remaining three. I was feeling full after four years and was shouting in delight 'I am feeling good', but Janine insisted on taking away the remaining eggs. I am cross with her to this day. It was such a beautiful feeling after a very very long time—to feel full in the stomach and not have hunger gnawing in the stomach. I went to sleep and awoke in the evening to find my family— father mother, Janine and Jozia all hunched over me trying to wake me up. I was just thirsty.

Janine recalled, 'Zofia had been sleeping for ten hours. We were worried sick because we thought she had become too ill. We were afraid she would die, for eating so many eggs.'

We prayed at the makeshift altar and slept on the sand. The latrines were a meeting place where you could chat because you had to wait at least fifteen to twenty minutes in a queue. The hospitals were full of so many sick and dying people. It was great to be simply alive at that time.

—Zofia Mendonca, 77, India

Makeshift hospitals were constructed to cater to the many people with illnesses such as dysentery, malaria, typhus, eye and skin infections. Królikowksi cites a report entitled *Polish Pastoral Service Abroad* which estimated that around 600 people died in Pahlavi, 'at freedom's doorstep'. Many of those who succumbed to diseases were children. Unaccompanied or sick children, and some whose families were too weak to care for them, were placed in orphanages where the weakest of them received special care. They were all quarantined for lice, heads shaved and given disinfectant baths and issued used clothing and not according to size or gender. It was here that several Poles first encountered Indian soldiers. The stay in Pahlavi varied from a few days to a few weeks, from where they were moved to Tehran. Adults and children alike needed immediate medical attention, and the Polish military hospitals were overflowing (see Photograph 13).

That was also the first time in my life I saw an Indian soldier. Amongst the soldiers sent to take care of us, there were British soldiers, Polish soldiers and some Indian soldiers—I believe the Gurkhas. The Indians often fed us dates. They were kind in their manner of dealing with us. A pat on the shoulder or a ruffle of the hair to egg us on towards the disinfection areas, when we were really dirty and lousy. You can imagine the impression it made because they were the kindest people we came across.

By that time, my malaria was so lovely that I was either shaking from the fever or lying with the high temperatures of 42 degrees. Unknown to me, my mother managed to get out of Russia and by some Providence found me in Pahlavi. She organised my discharge to the relief of the Army because I was a wreck with malaria by then. So, my mother took me to the civilian camp in Teheran and things started improving as there was a certain amount of medicine available there.

In Pahlavi, we could see beautiful villas, people beautifully dressed and going in the boats for rides. Some even threw us oranges and other fruits. The difference between us and them was so much that I remember telling myself, 'That is what paradise would be like'.

—Karol Huppert, 74, London

It was here in Pahlavi that many people came over to thank Mrs Zofia Morawska for her timely information to them about the transports leaving the USSR, recalled her daughter Barbara Morawska-Charuba of Canada.[53] Zofia had been in charge of a Polish orphanage near Bukhara. Once she was informed by the authorities to collect her daughter, Barbara, from the *kolhoz*, prior to moving the orphanage to Krasnovodsk; she informed several people about the impending move and probably the last chance to leave the USSR, walking miles on foot late in the night. General Anders visited Pahlavi on 28 August 1942 and remained for two days. On 29 August 1942, he attended a march past by 15,000 members of the fifth and sixth divisions. 'His presence had a most heartening effect on all the Poles in Pahlevi and the enthusiasm with which he was acclaimed bore witness to his inspiring leadership',[54] stated a British observer.

A second route of evacuation from Ashkabad (USSR) to Meshed and onwards to Tehran has been described by some former Polish refugees.[55] The orphanage was moving from Ashkabad to Meshed and several children were taken from their mothers or other guardians and evacuated with the orphanage. Stanislaus Harasymow of Perth says this arrangement released places for some adults to be evacuated out of the USSR.[56]

Królikowski maintained that the authorities in Tehran were not ready to receive such large number of refugees and had little conception of what a poor state they would be in on arrival. There were three major camps in Tehran, all extremely primitive, especially at the start, when epidemics of typhus and typhoid fever broke out once again. Accommodation was assigned as it could be found and ranged from an 'incomplete munitions factory' to 'veritable tent cities' scattered throughout Tehran. As a consequence, many people experienced both separation and reunion in Tehran. Janusz Dziurinski's (Connecticut, USA) parents met in Tehran after a long separation and could not even recognise each other for a long time. Janusz's older brother, Antoni, had died of typhus in the Guzar camp. Janusz was conceived in Tehran and was born in Karachi; his mother was moved out of Persia along with the other civilians, while his father was deployed with the Polish Army, only to meet again years later again.[57] Again in periods ranging from weeks to months, the people were moved to Ahvaz on the sea coast, in preparation for a transit whenever it fructified. 'At that time a visa to India was a visa to life', wrote Alicja Edwards.[58] According to official sources, there were about 18,000 Polish civilians in the former British East Africa.[59] Copies of her unused visas have been reproduced as Appendix 13.

People who stayed longer in Tehran found that, gradually, the relief effort was stepped up. 'Mattresses, lamps, and other essentials, as well as toys and candies for the children were brought in by Jews, Persians, British, and Americans' who were concerned about the plight of the Polish refugees.[60] Particular effort focused upon providing facilities for the growing numbers of orphans and children separated from one or both parents. Each of the three camps in Tehran had an orphanage, and many children resumed their schooling, initially squatting in the dust and using the ground as a writing tablet. When things became better organised, the trestle tables used at meal times were converted into school benches. But most people were beginning to be moved to Ahwaz on the seacoast to facilitate early transportation to the final destinations. Owing to availability of shipping lines to India, she became a natural choice as a transit or a permanent destination (see Appendix 12).

Transit Camp in Karachi

Owing to Britain's pressing need to move the first batch of 13,000 Polish civilians out of Persia to make room for the 26,000 expected from the USSR with the second group of Polish soldiers, a transit camp was established at Karachi Country Club. It was functional from 4 November 1942 to 2 October 1945.[61] The Polish civilians waited here from a few weeks to a few months awaiting transport to take them to the camps in British East Africa or Mexico. It is estimated that 20,000 of the 37,400 Polish civilians evacuated out of the USSR transited this camp in Karachi on their way to the permanent war-duration camps[62] during the entire period of its existence.

Transports out of Iran, to destinations as different as Mexico, India and the British colonies in East and South Africa began within weeks of the first Polish refugees' arrival there. The journeys by ship, all in convoy because of the treacherous wartime shipping conditions, proved to be memorable for many people, not only because of sea sickness but other factors. There are numerous recollections of the kindness shown by some sailors to children, especially to those who were fortunate enough to be aboard a Polish vessel. Most of the refugees passed through Karachi, although there were a few transports which went directly to Africa.

Kira Banasinska wrote in her autobiography,[63]

> Shiploads of deportees arrived every week. A transit camp with three thousand tents was built in Karachi. It was under command of the army, both British and American. Each new batch of refugees remained in the transit camp till they were shipped by sea to a number of other destinations.

Since the presence of Polish children in the USA would be embarrassing[64] to the much-needed Soviet Ally, President FD Roosevelt facilitated their settlement in Mexico, where their presence would attract less attention.[65] A pact between the Mexican government and General Sikorski, the Polish Premier, was brokered and it was agreed that 20,000 Poles were to be sent there from Persia. Out of the 1,586 people who finally reached the Santa Rosa camp, Mexico, most of who were children, reached there through India. The first transport to Mexico had children with parents and the second had only the orphanage in July and November 1943, respectively.

Some texts refer to Bombay too as transit points, but there is no record of a transit camp there. Captain AWT Webb mentions in his report dated 9 February 1943 that the GOI sanctioned the renting of a flat in Napean Sea Road, Bombay, as a reception centre for the Poles on a rental of ₹141 and 8 *annas* per month and a non-recurring expense of ₹1,008 and 8 *annas* for equipping the flat. He mentions, 'from time to time children have to be sent to Bombay enroute to sanatoria, for special reasons as fitting artificial limbs or visiting specialists, and enroute to join their parents who are going to Africa'.[66]

Subsequently, several other facilities were developed, which would be discussed in details in 'A Polish Village on an Indian Riverbank'. Several files available in the NAI, New Delhi, have lists of Polish refugees transiting Bombay. It has not yet been ascertained definitely whether they were the Polish Jewish refugees or those evacuated with Anders' Army and headed for different parts of the world under official schemes. One of the transports to Mexico caught the attention of the Government of New Zealand, who then offered to host Polish children in New Zealand. Seven hundred and thirty-six orphan children went from Istfahan and reached Wellington via Mumbai on 1 November 1944.[67]

The Country Club camp in Karachi had communal accommodation made of large tents and also communal facilities of kitchen and baths. A hospital and church soon became functional. Major Allan was the camp commander.

Indian Hospitality

In the course of 1942, the British government made exhaustive efforts to find countries which would accept the refugees. The USA and the Canadian governments were approached, as were several South American governments. All were either hostile to the idea or else hedged their offers with such conditions that they proved impracticable.[68] In June 1942, the British government came to an agreement with the East African governments on a policy of temporary settlement in the East African territories of Kenya, Uganda, Tanganyika (present day Tanzania) and Nyasaland, North and South Rhodesia and South Africa. The Nyasaland resettlement project never came to fruition.[69]

The Foreign Office then saw India as 'the most promising solution .... Either as a destination or a transit territory, or both.'[70] On 21 August 1942, AWG Randall of the Foreign Office wrote to WL Fraser, Treasury Office, about the decision of HMG. The 13,000 Polish civilians who had entered Persia from Russia without the consent of the British authorities were to be established in East Africa. Their places were to be taken by 26,000 Polish civilians arriving out of Russia with the full consent of the British authorities as a condition for securing 40,000 Polish soldiers.[71] The search for their permanent wartime home was also being pursued with the USA. 'The expenditure for the transport and maintenance of all these Polish civilians ha[d] been undertaken by the Polish government.'[72]

By this time, 1,000 children had been granted war-duration asylum in Nawanagar state at the Balachadi camp. Aware of the condition of the children, the rulers of Patiala and Nawanagar offered to accept a few thousand Polish children, on the political aspect of which the India Office were making the necessary enquiries, to which an objection of one kind or another could be expected.[73]

When Ambassador Rucinski was addressed on 17 August about the possibilities of Patiala and Nawanagar, he at once said that his government would wish to send to India more children from the Soviet Union and not those whose entry into Persia had been authorised.[74]

Seeking the views of the Treasury Department, Randall continued that the British authorities were now willing to tell the Poles that in view of all that the British were doing for their people outside, they, the British, could not help anymore with their people who remain behind.[75] There were also possibilities of American help since by now the Polish government was apparently relying almost entirely on the USA for supplies and money. General Sikorski had appealed to President FD Roosevelt to accept Polish children from the Soviet Union and the President was understood to have referred the question to the South African government, promising financial and material assistance of the American Red Cross.[76] The destination did not materialise and the Americans suggested South Persia as a domicile with a promise of American financial and material help, which did not suit the British for military reasons. Randall then felt clearly that while the British could count on the USA for sharing the financial burden, it was going to be British territory for hospitality.[77]

Accordingly, he wrote to the India Office, seeking to push for hospitality for the Poles amongst the larger Indian Princely States, like Hyderabad, Mysore, Baroda, etc.,[78] on the lines of the Nawanagar offer.

In a cipher telegram dated 25 November 1942, the Secretary of State for India wrote to the Viceroy of India,

> The War Cabinet for some time has been much exercised over the task of absorbing Polish refugees now in Persia. Inspite of a steady flow during recent months, there still remain some 25,000, mostly women and children, who, for military, political and economic reasons must be moved out as early as possible and certainly by the end of March. Arrangements had been made to absorb a large batch in Mexico and the balance in East Africa where room was to be made by the transfer of Italian prisoners to America, but this plan has failed from lack of shipping and military escorts. It is still hoped to transfer several thousand to America on vessels returning via Bombay or Karachi and also East Africa, which has already responded generously, but which will shortly reach saturation point. It will not however be possible to exhaust the number in this manner. I have accordingly been asked to appeal to you to take about 5,000, mostly women and children with some men above military age, till the end of the war. This number is over and above the quota of Polish children you have already agreed to take…. It has been suggested to me that some of the larger [Indian Princely] states such as Hyderabad and Mysore might agree to come to the rescue as Nawanagar and Patiala have done in the case of children, and if you do not find asylum anywhere in British India perhaps you might care to consider this course. The Russian reaction has surprised me, but I should think that it will still be possible to get the children out. Hence I doubt if it would be wise to assume that accommodation meant for children can now be turned over to the new influx now proposed. New sources would have to be tapped, and loathe as I am to add fresh burdens, I hope that you may find some corners for these unfortunates till the end of their exile.[79]

Accordingly an appeal was sent to several Indian rulers, including Baroda, Hyderabad, Patiala and Mysore amongst several others,[80] on 22 December 1942, both, inviting hospitality for the Poles[81] and seeking financial contribution and adoption of the five hundred Polish children already accepted and settled in Nawanagar (see Appendix 3).

A group of Maltese–Balkan refugees had been accommodated in India as also some Anglo-Burmese, when hostilities had spread to those regions. There was a camp for the Maltese–Balkans in Sewar, off Bharatpur, which was later moved to Coimbatore. The Anglo-Burmese were ostensibly accommodated in Nainital. A principal refugee officer—Captain AWT Webb—was already appointed to administer these people and their camps. The Poles were also made his charge once the British GOI accepted them.

The Political Department zeroed in on Kolhapur as a destination for the Poles, which while being a Princely State, was under complete British control, in contrast to the States suggested whose rulers were beginning to assert themselves and getting drawn into the Indian Nationalist movement. On 1 February 1943, Mr EW Parry, the Prime Minister of Kolhapur, informed the Kolhapur Residency about the Darbar's approval to grant a site for a camp for Polish women and children.[82] A large tract of land on the banks of the river Panchganga, formerly known as Gaikwad Park, near the village of Valivade, was made available for the Polish camp. M/s Hindustan Construction Company was granted the tender to construct the camp at Valivade for ₹30,85,000.[83] The Polish government-in-exile in London was to bear the entire financial responsibility for the camp, while the GOI was to act as their agents in the matter. The GOI assumed the charge of advancing all the money required for the camp and sent consolidated accounts to HMG to recover from the Polish credit.[84]

Once the British GOI accepted accommodating 5,000 Polish civilians in Valivade, Kolhapur, they were moved to a separate camp Malir, in Karachi. Malir was an American base and was lent for the purpose by the American forces. Those staying back in India were moved to the Malir camp and the rest had to carry on to British East Africa or Mexico. At Tehran, visas for both India and British East Africa were issued, as demonstrated by the unused visas of Alicja Edwards.

Banasinska wrote,

Before landing the refugees on board ships they had to be sorted out, those who were prepared to stay in India had to be separated and lodged at another transit camp—Malir—lent to us by the American Air Force. Those people remained there till a camp was built in Valivade, Kolhapur.[85]

There was also some kind of an option given to the deportees in Tehran. 'We chose India because it was the more exotic of the two', said Teresa Glazer of London.[86]

Some of the older girls were sent into the St Joseph's Convent, Karachi. Sister Margaret Hoogwerf of St Joseph's Convent, Bandra, recalled some of them in 2003. A few marriages between Polish girls and American soldiers were also solemnised at Karachi, according to her, but no records could be traced. There was a general difficulty in communicating owing to the language barrier. 'They were all extremely beautiful and talented, be it embroidery, singing or dancing', she recalled. She came across several

Polish refugee children again in Panchgani, when she was posted there in 1946. A rest home was established for the Polish children threatened with tuberculosis at Bel-Air Sanatorium at Panchgani. Some children also attended the Convent School there. The markings for Ootacamund and Nainital (see Map 6) are shown as places with suitable climate as destinations for Polish people in India, but they never worked out.

Map 6: Archival map of India showing Polish camps and other establishments, 1942

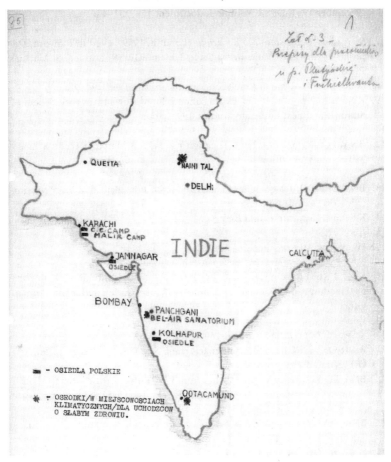

Source: Courtesy New Archives, Warsaw.
Note: This map is not to scale and does not represent authentic boundaries.

NOTES AND REFERENCES

1. Association of Poles in India, *A Short History of Poles in India 1942–48, In light of Reminiscences and Documents,* Polish (English translation underway).
2. Z Mendonca, interview to author, Pune, March 2002.
3. D Pniewska, interview to author, London, March 2004.
4. BNA, Document on Polish Soviet Relations (DPSR), Volume I (London, 1961), doc 132, 182.
5. 'Minute of the conversation held in the Kremlin between General Sikorski and M Stalin on the outstanding problems of Polish-Soviet relations', 3 December 1941, DPSR, Volume 1, document 159, 231–43.
6. Ibid.
7. W Anders, *Bez Ostatniego Rozdzialu* (London, 1959), cited in K Sword, *Deportation and Exile, Poles in the Soviet Union 1939–48* (London: St Martin's Press, 1994), 63.
8. W Anders, *An Army in Exile* (London: Macmillan, 1949), 94–95.
9. K Sword, *Deportation and Exile* (London: St. Martin's Press with School of Slavonic and East European Studies, 1994), 63.
10. Ibid., 65.
11. BNA, FO 371/31079 C2643, Telegram no. 3473; 8 March 1942, 30 Military Mission to War Office.
12. K Sword, *Deportation and Exile,* 65.
13. BNA, PREM 3, Telegram 3715, dated 19 March 1942, British Military Mission (Moscow) to War Office.
14. K Sword, *Deportation and Exile,* 66.
15. Ibid., 67.
16. W Anders, *An Army in Exile,* 98–102.
17. K Sword, *Deportation and Exile,* 67.
18. BNA, PREM 3, 354/1, this handwritten minute by Churchill was attached to telegram no. 407, dated 31 March 1942, Sir Reader Bullard to Foreign Office.
19. Ibid.
20. K Sword, *Deportation and Exile,* 68.
21. BL-I&OC, L/P&J/8/413, Cypher telegram No. 478, Kuibyshev to Foreign Office, dated 13 April 1942.
22. BNA, FO 371/32627 W 5163, Letter from WW Kulski, Cousellor at the Polish Embassy in London, to Sir A Cadogan, Permanent Under-Secretary of State at the Foreign Office, dated 31 March 1942.
23. BNA, FO 371/32627, W 5648. Sir A Clark Kerr (Kuibyshev) to Foreign Office. Telegram number 478 dated 12 April 1942.
24. K Sword, *Deportation and Exile,* 68.
25. BL-I&OC, L/P&J/8/413. Cypher telegram dated 13 April 1942, Sir A Clark Kerr to Foreign Office, 340 (possibly copy of communication mentioned in FN 25).
26. K Sword, *Deportation and Exile,* 71–72.

27. Ibid.
28. Ibid.
29. BNA, FO 371/42781, Ross Report on Polish Refugees April 1942–December 1943 (MERRA report), 11.
30. BL-I&OC, L/P&J/8/413, Cypher telegram No. 444 from Tehran to Foreign Office, dated 7 April 1942, Letter No. 346.
31. Ibid.
32. Ibid., Cypher Telegram No. 503, from Tehran to Foreign Office, dated 18 April 1942, Letter No. 337.
33. Ibid.
34. Ibid, Cypher Telegram No. 897, from Cairo to Foreign Office, dated 22 June 1942, Letter No. 319.
35. NAI, EA 276-X/42/Secret, 29.
36. Ibid., 30.
37. Ibid.
38. DPSR, Volume 1, document 219, dated 14 May 1942, 351–52.
39. DPSR, doc.233, 375.
40. Meaning 'civilian dependants', as interpreted by K Sword, *Deportation and Exile*, 78.
41. BNA, PREM3 354/7, Prime Minister's personal minute, dated 5 July 1942.
42. Ibid.
43. K Sword, *Deportation and Exile*, 79.
44. Ibid., 81 and 221.
45. BNA, WO 204/8711, *Evacuation of Polish Citizens from Krasnovodsk—A Report on the Refugee Camps*, 3.
46. Barbara Charuba, personal email to author. Barbara Charuba is the daughter of Barbara Morawska-Charuba and the granddaughter of Zofia Morawska.
47. M Jankowski, cited in R Umiastowsky, *Poland, Russia, Great Britain—A Study of Evidence* (London: Hollis & Carter, 1946), 107.
48. BNA, WO 204/8711, *Evacuation of Polish Citizens from Krasnovodsk—Report on the Refugee Camps*, 3.
49. BNA, FO 371/ 42781, W 8364, Ross Report on Polish Refugees April 1942–December 1943 (MERRA report), 7.
50. BNA, FO 371/34584 C 8076, Telegram No. 791, dated 13 July Tehran to Foreign Office.
51. L Krolikowski, *Stolen Childhood—A Saga of Polish War Children* (New York: Father Justin Rosary Hour, 1983), 72.
52. Ibid., 69.
53. B Charuba, *Memoirs of the Morawska Family*, email to author.
54. BNA, WO 204/8711.
55. S Harasymow, in email to author.
56. Ibid.
57. J Dziurinski, email to author.
58. AR Edwards, email to the author.

59. Fundacja Archiwum Fotograficzne, *Tulacze Dzieci—Exiled Children* (Warsaw: Fundacja Archiwum Fotograficzne, 1995), 128.
60. L Krolikowski, *Stolen Childhood*, 70.
61. KX Robbins, 'The Camp for Polish Refugee Children at Balachadi, Nawanagar (India)', *Journal of Indo-Judaic Studies* (Washington, July 2001), 99.
62. Jan Sielecki, email to author and video interview.
63. K Banasinska and G Verghese, *Autobiography of Kira Banasinska* (Mumbai: Kotak and Co., 1997), 98.
64. L Krolikowski, *Stolen Childhood*, 286.
65. Ibid.
66. NAI, 276(8)-X/42, 57.
67. BL-I&OC, L/P&J/ 8/414, 288 and Krolikowski, *Stolen Childhood*, 288.
68. K Sword, *Deportation and Exile*, 84.
69. MERRA Report, 8. Also cited in K Sword, *Deportation and Exile*, 221.
70. BL-I&OC, AWG Randall, Foreign Office, to JP Gibson, India Office, 20 August 1942 (POL 6251 1942) India Office letter file.
71. BNA, Ref. No. T 160/1204 8H177.
72. Ibid.
73. Ibid.
74. Ibid.
75. Ibid.
76. Ibid.
77. Ibid.
78. BL-I&OC, W 15133/5130/G, dated 17 November 1942, AWG Randall to Gibson.
79. BL-I&OC, L/P&J/110-N 19-1/412, Cipher telegram dated 25 November, the Secretary of State for India to Viceroy of India, 114.
80. NAI, EAD File No. 276-X/42/Secret, 51–54.
81. Extremely played down.
82. BL-I&OC, R2/952/76 C-70/43, Express Letter from PM Kolhapur to Decstates, Kolhapur Residency, 21.
83. Kolhapur Administration Report 1942–43, printed in 1944.
84. AAN, Amb RP-Londony no. 1812, Foreign Office to Polish Ambassador, dated 15 July 1942 and BL-I&OC, Letter no. POL 5646, GOI (Home) to Secretary of State (India), dated 6 August 1942, and POL 8924, Foreign Office to Polish Ambassador, dated 20 October 1942.
85. K Banasinska and G Verghese, *Autobiography of Kira Banasinska*, 98.
86. Glazer, interview to author, London, March 2004.

Franek in Valivade

❦

My first impressions of the Valivade camp were similar to Tadek's. In comparison with Balachadi, it was like a small town; a busy, noisy place with small shops and stalls, cafes and cinema. The nearest town was Kolhapur and you could get there by train in 20 minutes and the fare was only a few annas. There for one rupee you could rent a bicycle for 24 hours.

We were housed in the orphanage that occupied a complex of barracks in one section of the camp. Barracks were similar to the one in Balachadi, except a bit bigger. They had dirt floors, small stone wall about 3 feet above foundations and for walls bamboo mats all the way to the roof. No ceilings but better quality tiles on the roof that did not leak during monsoon. Before our arrival, the orphanage in Valivade had about 300 children, now with us there were over 700. Management was different. Only a few of our old guardians stayed with us. It did not take long to get accustomed to the new surrounding. Soon we made new friends and everything returned to normal.

Gimnazjum was also much bigger; it had 6 grades (4 of *gimnazjum* and 2 of *liceum*). Second grade had three concurrent classes. I was in the all boy class. As the curriculum was the same as in Balachadi, I did not find it difficult to readjust. The only thing I had to get used to was new teacher. They were better qualified for teaching *gimnazjum*, so the level of education rose.

Scouting was also at a higher level. There were many troops and what was more important, scout leaders were older boys. There were two young scoutmasters, B Pancewicz and Z Peszkovski, officers from the Polish Army; they revitalised the organization. I joined the Cub Masters Troop. There were about 30 of us, mainly girls, a very friendly bunch of people. We used to go on hikes and weekend bivouacs. I was helping Witek Olesiak to run one of the packs and we become good friends.

And what was going on with Wacek and Tadek that year? They were together in the school and had a lot of work and apparently not much free time. The school year for them lasted only six months. In June, both were promoted to the next grade. They went separately on a short vacation. In the meantime, the school changed location and now they were in Garelochhead near Perth. Tadek started thinking about finding place at some university, but for the moment his passion was theatre. At school theatre, he was the producer, director and also the lead actor.

In February, Tadek officially joined the Polish Army and now as a soldier (private) was on the army payroll which was much higher than that of a student. Wacek had the rank of Able Seaman (AB). Knowing my financial dilemma from time to time they would send me some money.

Some letters from Wacek and Tadek that kept me company.

Bridge of Allan
1-1-46

...a few words to describe how we live here, how we are managing and entertaining ourselves and as a last resource study when it's raining. Our new location is Bridge of Allan. We live in an old army camp in barracks made of corrugated metal sheets. It's very difficult to study here, some classes are held in the same barracks where we sleep, literally on beds. But the countryside is beautiful here and the town Sterling not too far. Tadek always drags me there to see some film, sometimes three times in a week. Once, after the film, when we had time waiting for the bus I took him to a pub for a beer. I couldn't persuade him to try it and eventually had to buy him lemonade.

Love—Wacek.

Bridge of Allan
24-2-46

...Recently I took Tadek for a visit to a Scottish family that I know. For the first time since prewar he was in a real home. No wonder he

was so thrilled. For a change next time I will take him for Easter to England to an English family. The added attraction: there are the two young girls. One of them I know well and I will try Tadek to get interested in the other one, or vice versa.

Not long ago I visited my old ship but I did not find too many old friends. I don't remember whether I told you that after the war, while still on the ship we made a few interesting trips. We went to Wilhelmshaven in Germany, city that surrounded to the Polish Panzer Division and to Oslo in Norway. I liked Norway very much.

—Wacek.

Garelochhead
8-8-46

Dear Niusiek.
The new school year already started. My vacations I spent in the south of England in Brighton. I enjoyed myself though we had only one week of good weather, the rest of the time it was raining and windy. The few sunny days I spent on the beach sunbathing and swimming. To tell the truth, during all my days in the navy I never swallowed so much sea water as now. I got beautiful tan and looked more like a native of Africa than Europe. English people could not believe that it was possible to get such a tan. In contrast they looked more like boiled lobsters.

Our school is now located in Garelochhead and it must be the proverbial 'end of the world'. There is nothing else around as but mountains and mountains. It's raining most of the time and sun comes out only for a few hours per week. Wherever you want to go is far, even to the post office you have to take bus.

My normal week looks like this. School lasts till dinner. After dinner I study or tinker with something. In the evening I rest or if there is some good film I will go there with Tadek. On weekends I might go with him to Perth to a friendly family where you can enjoy yourself as there are some pretty girls there and weather is generally better. I have one problem with Tadek as he is afraid of the opposite sex. He is so shy that once at a dance he nearly ran away when I wanted to introduce him to a girl.

—Wacek.

Bridge of Allan
19-4-46

…Two weeks ago I sent you L1. It was part of my first army pay. You know, since February I am in the army. No, I did not quit school I am still a student but now in a battle-dress and I get pay. Financially I am much better off than as a student in the navy school. Now our 'combine purse', Wacek's and mine is much heavier.

Recently during football match I had an accident. I pulled tandem in my right foot and now have my leg in a plaster. I could not go with Wacek to visit that English family. It was supposed to be my first real leave since I come to England.

In this letter I enclose L5 so you can buy yourself something more important than peanuts. Take this money without any scruples and spend it. If I would go with Wacek as originally planned, I would have spent it on trivia. For Wacek it's more difficult to save as he is smoking and that's very expensive in here.

—Tadzik.

Bridge of Allan
11-6-46

…I have written many poems but am aware that I was not borne to be a true and great poet. What I have written so far was just putting on paper what was in my mind and had to find an outlet in a visual form. I found that in writing poetry. Could I force myself to be a poet? Maybe after years of studying I could achieve some respected level. But would that be the real poetry, something that comes from your heart and mind. Writing poetry just for the sake of writing is not for me.

—Tadzik

Bridge of Allan
18-6-46

… for the school vacation that last a month I will not go anywhere special. I can get only two week leave from the army. I will use it to visit old friends in the navy school. Wacek wanted to take me to Brighton, but I did not fancy going to that 'port town'.

—Tadzik

Franek's Note: At the time Tadek did not know that Brighton was THE PLACE, famous seaside resort.)

Garelochhead
5-8-46

...On August 1 we started a new school year, for me probably the last one. After that I will try, at any price, to get to some university. You are doing fine by studying and not paying any attention to moving, or not moving to some other place.

Niusiek—if I could advise you it would be not to try to come to England. This island only looks appealing from a distance. I cannot see any future for you in here. If you want I could write you more regarding the situation that exists here.

—Tadzik

Garelochhead
15-9-46

...I was really surprised when you wrote to me about your eventual coming to England. I have no idea what you would be doing in here. Whatever it is don't expect that England would welcome you with open arms. I don't advise anybody to come here, especially to you being my brother. Both Wacek and I, though it would be our duty, we would not be able to guarantee you further education or any decent future.

On the other hand I have no idea what you would do in America. I hope that if you go there it would not be as a factory worker, the white slaves in place of Negroes, but that could happen. Whatever, I think in America you could get better a chance of decent living than in here.

—Tadek.

Year 1947

The way of life in the Valivade camp suited me. In the orphanage, we didn't feel closed in. Through scouting, I made some new friends.

Whenever I wanted, I could go visiting them or our guardians from Balachadi that now lived in the 'civilian' part of the camp.

At that time, I looked very much like Tadek, so some people thought that he has returned from England. I had to keep up the appearance as not to dishonor him or myself. Mrs Dobrostanska was preparing traditional Christmas play, and she engaged me to play one of the leading shepherds. Apparently, I performed very well.

My financial situation also improved. Now I was getting ₹3 per month pocket money. Beside, from time to time, Wacek and Tadek would send me something. In addition, I took a bookbinding course and after finishing it, I was doing some work for our local library. For every book done, I would get one and a half rupee and in a month I could bind four to five books. I was very frugal with my money and was never broke.

The new year 1947 I welcomed with scouts at a bivouac in Panhala, an old fortress of prince Shivajee of the Maratha nation.

In January 1947, Wacek received news about Uncle Jozek's arrest by the communist regime in Poland. He, with a group of other ex-officers, was accused of counterrevolutionary activities and spying for the Americans. He was sentenced to 15 years in prison, degraded to the rank of private and all the property was confiscated. During that political process, three death sentences were also carried out. Aunt Maria and her daughter Bozena, somehow managed to keep the flat, furniture and other things of value.

On the brighter side, Wacek made contact with mother's brother, Uncle Wacek, who survived the War and lived in Poznan.

Garelochhead,
7-1-47

...Niusiek, I am very glad that you are in Valivade. I remember that malaria left me when I got there. The same will happen to you. That's the first plus—your health. The second plus is that Valivade is much more opened to the world than Jamnagar was. It is bigger and has much bigger cross section of people, more organizations, there is the cinema, theatre, life is more vital etc, etc. There are shops and Kolhapur is nearby. We will try with Wacek to send you at least Pound 1 per month so you could go to cinema once a week, buy these peanut

briquettes covered in molasses (probably you know them by now, I loved them) or buy anything else. Well, I forgot about ice cream. You will have to make up for the 4 years of fasting in Balachadi. Well, have a good time.

As soon as I matriculate, I am going to join the Polish theatre that just come from Italy. I had a small test of my acting abilities and passed it. However, I will still try to get to the English theatre school. Don't tell that to anybody.

Describe to me in details your visit to Janiszawska (Marysia). You should visit her at least once, I am sure she would be very glad to see you. She is my dear friend.

Tadek

In April, the school year ended, and I was promoted to the 3rd grade. My last holidays in India started. At the time, the school year finished for Tadek and Wacek. Tadek matriculated, and Wacek was promoted to the *liceum*. Tadek wanted to get to a theatre school in London, but could not get scholarship. So he joined the Polish Army theatre and stayed there for a year. With that theatre, he toured Polish Army camps through England and Scotland. Right after matriculation, he had a chance to get scholarship for the Polish University in London to study Economics, but for the time being, did not apply. Theatre was his passion. The Polish proverbs says 'What must hung will not drawn'; in the end, in 1949, he went to the university to study economics. But for two years he was chasing his dreams. Tadek wrote:

Somewhere in England,
Spring '47

...After my matriculation everything went astray; I did not get scholarship to the Royal Academy of Dramatic Arts in London, so as a 'prodigal son' I had to go back to the Polish theatre.

Here in the 'beautiful Scotland' the atmosphere is very vague, meteorologically speaking, in the economy and politics. Meteorologically we had the most severe winter in the past 100 years and it still can't go back to the North Pole where it belongs. As a rule every day we have wind, rain, a little sunshine and from time to time hail and fog.

Wacek, towards the end of the year, was promoted to the last year of the *liceum*, and with his school, moved to the Bodney camp, near Thetford. He was hoping to matriculate in the first half of next year.

And now a few fragments from letters.

Garelochhead,
26-4-47

...For me one school year ended and a new one stared. Easter we spent together with Tadek in the camp, but soon after graduation he went to Perth to a Scottish family where he stayed till the end of April. I didn't feel like going there this time. Now I am in liceum and do nothing, I meant to say I do nothing but study. I selected the science curriculum and am very happy, as I don't have to take Latin any more and I always had trouble with that subject.

Probably I wrote to you that university is beyond my dreams. After matriculation I will look around. From the ship I have some experience with current and know how to operate the radar. Probably you heard about that marvelous invention of the XX century.

—Wacek

At the beginning of May, I went with a group of rover scouts on a two weeks bicycle trip pilgrimage to the tomb of St Francis Xavier in the Portuguese colony Goa in South India. There were 25 scouts and three adults, including the scoutmaster Peszkovski. Distance from Valivade to Goa was about 180 miles and most of it on dirt roads. On the return trip, we went by boat from Goa to a small port of Ratnagiri and then another 80 miles by road to the Valivade. That included one stage of 13 miles up the hill and none of us had a bicycle with gears.

A few days after returning from the trip, I went for three weeks' cub-scout camp as a councilor and then towards the end of the vacations, I went to the so-called 'rest camp' for those who had had responsibilities during the running of the summer camps. It lasted a week and was led by our scoutmaster Peszkovski. He knew a lot about star constellations and could talk about them at length. Once we had three alarms at night to observe changing pattern of stars, at midnight, 3 a.m. and then at dawn. That's what I call a 'rest camp', but we had fun.

I got the following letter from Wacek:

Garelochhead,
1-8-47

...Tadek is now in the theatre and was performing with success in London. Probably he wrote to you about this in details. Any day he is supposed to come to visit me.

I see that now you are quite a sportsman (your trip to Goa). I also have a bicycle and ride a lot, but in here there are mountains everywhere. Once I went with friends to the Loch Lomond. We did some 40 miles that day, it was nice but tiring.

Please write in details regarding your future plans. My advice to you is, if possible, go to America. Poland is out of the question and England as a last resort. There is no future here.

Now I have vacation, in fact I had as I just finished them. I went for a week to some friends in Perth. My day looked like this: I would get up around 10, have my breakfast, then sit in the garden talking to my hosts. After lunch I would go for a walk to town, park or for a hike to the nearby mountains. Then I would get back for supper around 6. In the evening I would go to a dance or cinema. I can't complain about monotony.

Regarding my future there is nothing new. British might close our school any moment. However, if miracles exist I might be able to get my matriculation beforehand. After that I will try to get to some university to study chemistry. If that won't work then I will get demobilized and look for work. If I won't find a good job then I will try and join the Merchant Marines. God willing, we will see each other here, in India, America or some other part of the world.

– Wacek

After such vacation, I felt a bit tired, but luckily the new school year started, so I could rest a little. Towards the end of 1946, the Polish Army from Italy and Middle East was shipped to England. Only families and dependant that had somebody in the army could join them. Soon after, school started the first transport, about 1000 people, went to England. As the first transport left for England, a noticeable emptiness could be observed in the camp. Classes were reorganised as some teachers also left; discipline in the camp started falling apart.

On 15 August 1947 India gained freedom from the British. There was jubilation everywhere. We too celebrated it in the camp since it was our day of Feast of Our Lady for the Miracle on the Vistula. We had the Indian scouts come over and exchanged gifts. Later, we heard of rioting in other parts of India and the formation of India and Pakistan—two countries out of one. There were all kinds of speculations about what the future would hold but none of that was my concern. I just wanted to be reunited with my brothers and whatever family there was left.

Soon the second transport to England was organised. I found myself on the list. We left Bombay on 9th November on board of a big troop's ship Empire Brent. There were about 1,000 of us. The voyage was very pleasant but uneventful and lasted about three weeks. We stopped in Aden and Suez and then without stopping all the way to England. We passed Gibraltar at night, and I did not see the famous Rock.

We docked in Liverpool at the end of November and were taken us to the army camp in Daglingworth near Gloucester. The start of my life in England was very miserable. It was cold, wet and foggy, and all I had for dress was my tropical clothing. I had just one sweater issued to me in India, which was seriously inadequate for the weather in England. The barracks in which we lived were 'the famous barrels of laughter', constructed from corrugated metal sheets with minimum insulation. There was one coal fired metal stove in the middle that was supposed to keep us warm. So we sat around it, rubbing our hands together. Luckily, after a week, we were issued, like other soldiers being demobilised, a suit, sweater, scarf, warm coat, pair of shoes and a hat.

In Poland, a 'barrel of laughter' was a tunnel constructed from sections of metal cylinders constructed at fairs. Each section of the tunnel would be rotating in different direction and at different speed. The idea was to walk through the tunnel without falling down.

A few days after our arrival at the camp, Peszkovski came and told us to write an application for admission to the Polish *gimnazjum*. He took them to London to the Polish Committee of Education where one of the directors was a friend of his, a scoutmaster.

After two weeks we were moved to another camp, West Chiltington, near Polborough in Surrey. From there I sent letters to Wacek and Tadek, telling them that I am in England. They were not expecting me. They had no idea whether they were supposed to be responsible for me, especially since they themselves were not quite sure about their own standing. The most important thing was that we were together again!!!

A Polish Village on an Indian Riverbank

☙❧

*K*olhapur in the Deccan peninsula was a part of the Bahmani kingdom, till it was wrested by Shivaji after killing Afzal Khan, one of the leading generals of Bijapur, on 10 November 1659. After the death of Shivaji in 1680, his son Sambhaji came to power. He was enticed and imprisoned by the Mughals in Delhi, as was his son, Shahu. After Aurangzeb's death, his son Azam released Shahu in 1708 with the expectation that his return to Maharashtra would cause a division amongst the Marathas, who were at that time united under the leadership of Tarabai, the widow of Rajaram, the second son of Shivaji. A war of succession ensued between Shahu and Tarabai, who was ruling on behalf of her young son Shivaji III. After Shahu was crowned in Satara in January 1708, Tarabai fell back upon Panhala fort, 20 kilometres from Kolhapur and made it the capital of the rival Maratha kingdom. Shivaji III died in 1712, and Tarabai was removed from the administration to be replaced by Rajas Bai, her co-wife and mother of Sambhaji II. Thus began the lineage of the Chhatrapatis of Kolhapur, but they no longer counted in the Maratha State, which was being ruled by the powerful Peshwas (prime ministers) by 1713. The Peshwas ruled from Poona and later formed the powerful Maratha confederacy which extended from Attock in the north to Goa in the south, Orissa in the east to Kutch in the west for a century thereafter, following the decline of the Mughals.

Several adoptions took place for the Kolhapur throne from time to time from amongst the Puar (Pawar) and the Bhosale lineages. Maharaj

Rajaram III of Kolhapur died in November 1940 and, as he had no son, the infant Pratapsingh of the Bhosale family was selected to succeed him. Pratapsingh was born on 22 November 1941 and was adopted with the customary ceremony on 18 November 1942. An official announcement of the minor ruler as the Maharajasahib of Kolhapur was made on the same day.[1] The senior Maharanisaheb was the Regent, with a Regency Council in place. Colonel Harvey, the Political Agent, was a very prominent and influential member of the Council. Mr Surve, the Dewan (Prime Minister) of the state had made way for Mr EW Parry. Kolhapur, on the banks of the river Panchganga, was a Princely State only in name. The British political agent and other officials of the Bombay Presidency had virtually complete control over the royal family and the state. All acts of the Durbar were a mere formality.

Valivade Camp, Kolhapur

The site of Valivade was unofficially selected by Captain AWT Webb, Principal Refugee Officer, GOI. Vide his report dated 11 February 1943, stated that Valivade had a good supply of water from the river Panchganga and was connected to Kolhapur city by way of a road and railway line. The site was cleared to be safe by an officer of the Malaria Institute provided a few simple precautions were taken. The contract for building the camp was given to M/s Hindustan Construction Company, Bombay.[2] They had to build:

> 140 family blocks, each to house 12 families
> 10 blocks, each containing 20 staff quarters
> 75 blocks of bathrooms, each containing 10 separate compartment with showers
> 70 blocks of latrines with 12 separate compartments, each block to serve 2 blocks of staff quarters
> 50 blocks of latrines with 5 separate compartments, each block to serve 2 blocks of staff quarters
> 6 officers' bungalows
> 1 storeroom
> 1 staff mess
> 10 school buildings

The specifications of the buildings were as under:

Foundations and Plinths:	Of local stone with brick corners in lime mortar
Floors:	Rammed murram except latrines, bathrooms and storerooms, where earth covered with bricks laid in lime mortar and rendered in 1 inch cement concrete 1–2–4.
Walls:	Rubble set in lime mortar up to 2 feet and thereafter uprights and crosspieces of bullies or thick bamboo covered with local bamboo trellis and matting, except in the case of officers' bungalows and storeroom, where the walls must be built in rubble set in lime mortar up to the roof.
Roof:	Bully trusses with rafters, covered with bamboo matting, bamboo trellis and local tiles.
Kitchen ranges:	These will only be required in the staff mess kitchen and should be of brick or local stone, constructed independently of bully uprights and plastered.
Finishing:	Inside whitewashed
Doors and Windows:	To be made of matting on bamboo frames except in the cases of officers' bungalows, storeroom and schools, where they should be made of country wood. Doors top one-third glazed, windows fully glazed.
General:	The bases of all uprights which are to be buried in the ground should be creosoted to the depth they are buried in the plinth.
Lighting:	By ordinary kerosene lamps.
Sanitation:	Dry-system Indian pattern with openings at the back of latrines for removal of pans by sweepers.

The Kolhapur state offered the Lal Risala Lines for conversion to hospital. The estimates provided by M/s Hindustan Construction

Company exclusive of water supply and furniture was ₹3,085,000. Madame Banasinska was advanced ₹300,000 for the purchase of clothing and equipment for 5,000 Polish women and children, on condition that all purchases were made through the supply department unless the relevant article could be purchased more cheaply through the open market. The total sum involved in furnishing these quarters was estimated at ₹3,300,000. Each family was provided a small kitchen and necessary cooking pots, crockery and cutlery and provision shops were to be opened in the camp. There were to be no servants, except sweepers, and the families had to do their own cooking and housework. A monthly maintenance allowance was given as per the following scale:

Adults, couple or single	₹45 each
Dependants up to 3, over 12 years old	₹40 each
Dependants over 3, over 12 years old	₹30 each
Children, up to 3, 6–11 years old	₹23 each
Children, over 3, 6–11 years old	₹20 each
Children under 6 years of age	₹20 each[3]

The Political Department strictly ensured that the PCG could not deal directly with any of the Princely States in spite of their dire need for hospitality which several Indian rulers were willing to extend. Their visits to states were also debarred except as personal guests of the ruler. The PCG was not allowed to visit Kolhapur where a camp for Polish people was set up at the cost of the Polish government in London. An unidentified entry of 10 January 1943 in an archival file states: 'The PM mentioned the Polish Consul General as coming here. We must draw his attention at once to the rules debarring States from corresponding direct(ly) with Foreign (sic) Countries or inviting foreign consuls to the State without the P.D's (Political Department) approval.'[4]

The rulers of the states, especially Kolhapur, were completely at the discretion of the Political Department of the GOI. While Kira Banasinska, the delegate of the Polish Ministry of Social Welfare, and wife of the PCG, hoped that the camp would be formally opened by the young Maharaja, the proposal was turned down firmly by the British GOI.[5] In an internal communication to the Crown Representative and the Principal Refugee Officer, the Resident of Kolhapur wrote,

It is unlikely that the Maharani Regent will be at Kolhapur in the beginning of January. I sincerely hope that she will not be there; and I would ask you in particular to ensure that no invitation to perform the opening ceremony (of the camp) is sent to her. Her Highness is at present at Bombay undergoing medical treatment. She is anxious to return to Kolhapur and would welcome any excuse to do so ... and that is why I ask you to take the greatest care to see that no invitation is sent to her.[6]

In the same letter, it was suggested that the opening of the camp be performed by Dr Khare, member of the Indians Overseas Department, and the distinguished visitor and the Prime Minister of Kolhapur district make a short speech on behalf of the Residency Council. Accordingly, Kira Banasinska informed Lieutenant Colonel CDN Edwards, the Resident of Kolhapur, about the proposed official opening of the Polish Evacuee Camp, Valivade, on 8 January 1944.[7] It is doubtful if the PCG attended the opening of the camp in his official capacity, since it is not mentioned anywhere in the said file. He may have been someone's personal guest at best or not been there at all.

The camp was divided into districts. Four districts were meant for families and the fifth district was designated as the orphanage. Initially, it was proposed that the orphanage at Istfahan would be moved there but soon that was rejected. Since no more children could be evacuated from the USSR, it came to house the orphan children from the later lot and the diminished Balachadi camp subsequently. Soon schools, kindergarten and chapel, in addition to the hospital, became functional. A shopping syndicate was set up and the contracts were given to the members of the prominent families of Kolhapur. Ghodke ran the fish and meat stall, Kittur bread and Mahagaonkar and Gaikwad stationery; Shivprasad Pardeshi a general grocery and Ingle kerosene and coal; Konde a cloth shop and Inamdar the watch shop. Pardeshi also ran the cinema hall later, which ran only one show daily from 6.00 p.m. to 9.00 p.m.[8]

Valivade camp was created by the GOI and was funded by the Legation of the Ministry of Labour and Social Services of the Polish government in London. The advance party of Poles arrived on 11 June 1943, from Malir, with Colonel Jageilliowicz as the camp commander. Their task was to create tolerable living conditions 'within this Indian wilderness'.[9] Mrs Button, an English lady, was the liaison officer.

Subsequently, the refugees began to arrive in batches. Mr Ramrao Ingle, now a retired lawyer of Kolhapur, recalls 'about 3-400 dishevelled people with grey faces and clothes hanging about their frames, carrying small bundles, disembarked from the train that brought them from Bombay. I was in the station trying to estimate what our average monthly sales of coal and kerosene would be and whether we would break even and make any profits', he explained.[10] Mr Rammaiah was the sanitary inspector and Mr Gune the resident engineer. Mr Shamrao Gaikwad was a clerk in the office of the Merchants' Syndicate.

Webb, however, notes in his reports that there were 'some murmurings' about the Poles not being accorded the same facilities as the other British evacuees in the Maltese camps and other camps for the Axis POWs in British India in places with salubrious weather all year round. He, however, brushes them aside with the trite remark that prices have gone up considerably since the setting up of the British evacuee camps at the beginning of the War.

The tone and tenor of the reports of the Principal Refugee Officer Captain AWT Webb are marked with an unwarranted hostility throughout and in the manner is more like dealing with an enemy than an ally. The British GOI insisted on retaining financial control over the camps, even though the expenses were being defrayed by the Polish government-in-exile in London. Webb's disapproval of Madame Banasinska's shopping list towards making the Polish refugee families comfortable is reflected in the following extract from his report dated 6 November 1943:

> From time to time there has been a certain amount of misunderstanding between the Polish Delegate and the Government of India as to the extent to which we can meet their wishes in the matter of expenditure on Polish refugees in this country without injury to the principles which the Government of India apply to their own employees and without placing an unnecessary strain on material resources. In the past delays and inconveniences have been occasioned to the Delegates by the examination of their proposals in the light of principles and rules which the Government of India would apply to similar proposals if made by one of their own officers. A reference was made to His Majesty's Government in the United Kingdom in the general matter of financial control, and the arrangement now accepted by both sides is that the Government of India will ordinarily concur in individual items of expenditure for which provision has been made in the budgets, unless they are of a nature which will seriously embarrass Government in one of their main lines of policy e.g. in regard to dearness allowance or anti-inflationary measures. As regards the proposal for expenditure which are not included in the budgets, the Government of India will in future offer their opinion on the merits of these proposals and will expect any objections of principle to be given serious consideration by the Polish Delegates. If however, after such consideration, the Delegates feel that the proposal should be pressed, Government will not, unless their objection raises issues of fundamental importance, insist on a reference from London. In such cases, however, it will be recorded that the expenditure is being incurred at the express request of the Delegates and after views of the Government of India have been communicated to them.[11]

The report continues and quotes Polish Delegate Victor Styburski's reply, where he points out that all the evacuees have lived through great hardships in the USSR and have greater average needs than the others, as their physical health as well as state of mind are far below normal and needs to be gradually built up to former standards.[12] This clearly indicates the resistance put up by the government towards extending succour to the refugees of the First Ally, who had suffered great hardships under another Ally.

Since the PCG could not have direct relations with any of the Princely States, who in turn were controlled by their respective political agents and residents of the British GOI, several offers of destination for Polish children remained unfructified. Noteworthy are the states of Baroda whose offer remained unutilised: Patiala, where the water supply for the proposed site was deemed inadequate, and Aundh. Maurice Frydman, a Lithuanian Jew, had come to India as an engineer with the Mysore state and was sucked into Indian philosophy and prevalent Gandhianism. Renamed Bharatanandji by Gandhi, he was at that time assisting the Pant Amatya of Aundh, Shriniwasrao II, in implementing the grassroot level democracy as suggested by Gandhi. The PCG approached Frydman through another Gandhian, Umadevi aka Wanda Dynowska, who had been active in the Theosophical Society of India for sometime, for Aundh as a destination for Polish evacuees,[13] but little happened as it probably did not meet the approval of the Resident or the GOI.

Over the next few years, Valivade grew into a remarkable community which is remembered fondly by those who lived there. Rows of indistinguishable barracks, made of metre-high stone walls topped by matting and tiled roofs, were transformed into picturesque homes surrounded by flower gardens, banana trees and ivy-covered walls which separated living quarters from the streets. Woven mats covered the earth floors and window curtains soon added both privacy and an individual touch to the anonymity of each family's allotted space. Most families prepared their own meals, in their kitchenettes, with the supplies they were able to purchase for themselves from the allowance they received. Some adults were able to supplement this income with paid employment around the settlement, either in administrative capacities as teachers, health workers or in one of the various workshops.

Antonina Harasymowa, mother of Stanislaus Harasymow of Perth, Australia, was the headmistress of one of the schools. Zofia Morawska, mother of Barabara Morawska-Charuba of Ottawa, Canada, was a teacher as was Janina Dobrostanska, mother of Tadeusz Dobrostanski of Melbourne, Australia. Janina came to Valivade after the closure of the camp in Balachadi. Janina Sulkowa's father was a clerk in the Legation Office while Janina was involved in bringing out 'The Little Red Elephant', a magazine for young people in the Valivade camp.[14] Francizska Kail, mother of Vanessa Kail of Melbourne, Australia, was also working in the Polish Legation Office.

The Legation Office continued to generate employment for the older residents of the camps. Several girls worked as typists or in other capacities in the legation office or as nurses in the Polish hospital, once that was established. Stefan Klosowski of Quebec, Canada, recalled that his older sister Stanislawa had left the camp at Balachadi and had been working in Bombay for some time when he was leaving for the UK in 1947.

Several older girls at the time trained as nurses at the Kolhapur hospital. Several members of Association of Poles in India (1942–48) (API), London, recalled a nasty incident of the prevailing apartheid in the country. The British matron of the hospital slapped the elderly Indian servant. The Poles were indignant and complained to the German Jewish doctor about the matron's behaviour. The doctor, however, pleaded his inability to intervene as he had been released from an internment camp to render medical services in the hospital and did not wish to disturb the applecart and be sent back to the internment camp.

The first annual report of the Valivade camp noted with satisfaction and pride that great progress had been made every month since June 1943. The indistinguishable rows of barracks metamorphosed into rows of homes with little gardens around them, in many cases the streets could be named according to the plant most abundant in that row, for example, silver aloe row or banana row. Other streets were named after the destination they led to, like Church Street, School Street, Co-op Street, etc.

The church, hospital, post office and fire brigade were the most important civic amenities, followed by 10 schools. There were three primary schools, three kindergartens, three secondary schools—a general education high school, a commercial high school, a school for instructors and a school for rural management as per the education system of pre-War Poland. In spite of insufficient school equipment and teaching aids, 1,028 children were being educated in the three primary schools. The availability of text books increased steadily till there was in an average one amongst four pupils.

The high school had 453 pupils of which 11 girls matriculated in the first year. They had an average of one book amongst 2–3 students. The commercial high school had 38 girl students and the school for rural management had 75 girl students. A three-hectare school farm was in place for the school for instructors of rural management.

There was a handicraft workshop, office of physical education, scout corps, office of cultural education, theatre and an orphanage. The co-operative and its numerous workshops were active in production. The administration was robust with a well-staffed administrative office.

The hospital had 200 beds with a chief medical officer, five doctors, one dentist, one hospital administrator, 16 nurses and 16 nursing assistants. In the first year, 2,045 patients were treated. There were 19 births and 15 deaths. A complete translation of the report was made by Mr Boguslaw Trella of Perth, Australia, in 2004.

Two more institutions need to be mentioned besides those mentioned above. The Merchants' Syndicate ensured that all goods used by Europeans were available, though at controlled rates. Some of the enterprising elderly men started stocking items for local consumption; best recalled is someone who started making sausages. Since beef and pork were and still are taboo in India, these men obtained special permission to source them from various sources for consumption of the people in the camp.

The post office was a busy place and Post Master Salokhe[15] is recalled, by the former residents, for his mastery over the difficult Polish names and knowing about status of their mail. Most former campers recall that he often held out hope of a 'letter soon' to a dejected person.

Letters in those periods often travelled to several destinations around the world before being delivered to the recipient finally, in a certain way marking the journey of the campers before finally arriving at Valivade destination. Some letters were from family members and friends left behind in the Soviet Union, trying to locate other members of the family or exchanging information about them. The information had to be couched in ways to be able to clear the strict war censorship. Often codenames were used. Other letters were sent to and received from Central Tracing Agency, IRC, seeking information about fathers, husbands, brothers and, possibly, also sons caught behind enemy lines and held captive. The Agency also helped to trace other separated family members. After the battle of Monte Cassino and the Uprising in Warsaw, there was much bad news from the agencies involved and the number of widows and orphans increased substantially. At other times, letters came from complete strangers giving information about a close family member, unable to establish contact, as in the following letter (Photograph 14 (a & b)).

Interaction with the Locals

Though all the Polish refugees were mentally tuned to the developments in the War and the events taking place in their home country, and trying to locate their scattered families, they interacted with the locals as best as they could after overcoming the language barrier. Most Indians who interacted with the Poles in Valivade too remember them fondly. Shamrao Gaikwad, the clerk in the Merchants' Syndicate, soon learnt Polish and became virtually indispensable. Other Indians in regular touch with the Polish people too started picking up the language. 'Initially we used to communicate using sign language, and there were many a laughs', recalled Mr Ramrao Ingle.[16] 'But soon we began to understand the language and they some English. They even helped us to overcome our initial hesitation to speak and even corrected our usage and pronunciation,' reminisced Gaikwad.[17]

Initially, interaction between the Polish campers and the local Indians was restricted. Firstly, there was a language barrier. Most campers spoke only Polish and only some Indians spoke English. Besides, the British administrators did not favour interaction, even when both sides attempted to overcome the language barrier. The children, however, were the first to overcome this 'minor hurdle'. Stanislaus Harasymow recalls that it was the swear words first. In one of his articles, he mentions provoking the local boys with the choicest Marathi abuses and they retaliated with 'White monkeys' in perfect Polish.[18]

According to both Ingle and Gaikwad, the Polish families, mainly women and children, treated the Indians with respect and did not hesitate to interact with them socially. They invited the Indians to their homes, parties, celebrations and other social occasions throughout the year. They also accepted invitations to Indian homes, outings and other get-togethers. 'They often carried little gifts of their embroidery or items only available in the camps, while visiting us', recalled Mrs Nirmala Nesrikar,[19] holding up an embroidered cushion cover, whose families had business and social relations with the campers. Colonel Vijay Gaikwad, who was an 8-year-old boy then, recalled[20] the Polish visitors at his home bringing in gifts of sweets, sugar, butter, cheese and other such items which were no longer available in the Indian market owing to wartime rationing.

'The Polish people treated us as equals, unlike the British, who looked down on us regardless of our social standing,' maintains Ramrao Ingle.[21]

'Through them we got a chance to see the European way of life quite closely', says Shamrao Gaikwad.[22]

Several members of the API 1942–48 said,

> It was a 'home away from home', a sunny, peaceful refuge after the harrowing depravations of years spent in forced exile in the U.S.S.R. Of course, there was no running water or electricity, no glass windows or solid doors and only a charcoal stove for cooking. But the mat doors could be closed and even locked with a padlock, giving us the much longed for privacy and semblance of normal life after years and years of communal living. What a joy it was to tend the narrow slips of gardens along the cool verandahs, to grow one's own banana, papaya or canna trees.[23]

The Polish boy scouts and girl guides participated in the march past to commemorate the coronation of the new king of Kolhapur. The infant Pratapsingh Bhosale had been ailing for some time and later died.

Advanced Schooling

The facilities at the camp became better functional over the years and all the important tenets of pre-War Polish society not only became functional, but also more and more efficient—church, schools and scouting. The schools got Polish and other books from the Legation in Tehran. Teachers and older students made copies of them. No one had a complete set of books and sharing a copy by a group of five or six pupils was the rule.[24] Several books used were developed on Indian themes by Madame Wanda Dynowska, aka Umadevi, who was highly respected in Polish society. See the book on Indian Geography in Polish developed for use in the Polish camp in Photograph 15.

Several older children were sent to Catholic institutions for higher education, to avail facilities not available in the camp. Initially, in 1944, 6 boys attended St Mary's High School; 7 girls St Joseph's High School, Karachi; 11 girls St Joseph's High School, Panchgani and 24 children St Joseph's High School, Saugor. In 1946, 9 girls attended JJ School of Art, Bombay; 8 girls went to YWCA Commercial School; 11 boys attended St Mary's European Boy's High School, Bombay; 1 went to St Xavier's College, 2 girls attended Cathedral Girls High School, 57 children went to St Joseph's Convent School, Panchgani, of which five were day-scholars; 13 boys attended St Peter's Boy's High School.[25] No list for 1945 was located.

Possibly the children stayed a two-year term till they either completed schooling or left to join the forces or their families. At the end of schooling, most boys joined the Polish Forces deployed in various parts of the world. In 1944, 40 boys from both the Kolhapur and Balachadi camps were granted visas to travel to the UK for training in the Polish Marine services.[26] They included the six boys who had attended St Mary's High School, Bombay, besides some from St Mary's High School, Mt Abu, one of whom, Henryk Baczyk from Perth Australia, older brother of Alina Baczyk Haus, referred to earlier, confirmed the above.[27] The girls usually went in for nurse training or learnt typing and joined some work in some administrative capacity in the Polish Consulate in Bombay or in the camp office in Kolhapur.

The atmosphere in the Valivade camp was that of a Polish village and the school curriculum also was completely Polish. Those who had the exposure of English schools while in India reflected back that it had a great positive impact in their lives. 'The only English that I learnt was in India sixty years ago', recalled Wieslaw Stypula in Warsaw.[28] 'The knowledge of English that I had gained in India gave me an edge over the other Poles in securing admission to a professional college when we reached England in 1947', said Jan Siedlecki, a retired architect in Kent, UK.[29] His name appears in the list of boys attending St Mary's School, Bombay, in 1946.[30] Two Indian teachers were also appointed at the Valivade camp to teach English to the inmates, one of who was Ms Manorama Gaikwad.[31]

Life in the Camp

Victor Styburski, the Delegate of the Polish Ministry of Social Welfare, noted that while Valivade was complete in itself as a Polish village, the biggest challenge was channelising the energy of the teenage group. Several scouting and other trips were arranged for the children to nearby and distant locales, besides a slew of sporting, cultural and religious activities.

Since, the overall financial control of the camp rested with the British GOI, acting as agents of the Polish government in London, they insisted on some cut-backs on the allowances being paid to the families, especially those whose menfolk were in active service.

While several types of activities filled the days, the male family members were sorely missed. Most former campers recall that women and girls greatly outnumbered men. Only men over age for military service or disabled were the ones in the camp. The number of grown-up boys was also very small as they all left regularly to join the Polish forces in various theatres of war regularly. Most families comprised merely of mothers with children or children in the orphanage. But, there were a few aunts with nieces and nephews and yet fewer grandparents with grandchildren. Since growing boys needed role models, the gap was filled in by the scoutmasters—Lieutenant Pancewicz and Lieutenant Peszkovski. Discipline was strictly maintained, to the extent that licences were issued to ride a bicycle in the camp to ensure the safety of the pedestrians.[32]

The organised market inside the camp and a makeshift one outside thrived as both the Poles and the Indians got to know each other better. Flowers, fruits and vegetables, fabric and dairy products saw brisk trade. Enterprising inhabitants started procuring or making items of Polish consumption, and they also entered the trade zone.

The cuisine at the camp was essentially Polish and several Indians recall being invited and initiated to it. Shamrao Gaikwad and Ramrao Ingle recall being invited to parties and picnics and 'getting to see the European way of life' closely.[33] As mentioned earlier, there were very few Polish men and older boys in the camps. Thus, interaction with Indian men grew as the language barrier was overcome.

Facilities in Mumbai

After the Polish Consulate at 30, Napean Sea Road, another office for the Polish Red Cross and delegates of the Ministry of Social Welfare became functional at 15, Napean Sea Road. A nearby flat was also hired to act as a transit camp for the children travelling to and from the rest home in Panchgani, needing specialised medical attention or coming in or proceeding to the UK.

Subsequently, the need for a Polish hospital became pressing as the Polish patients could not communicate with the staff in other hospitals generating an air of discontent. On 1 June 1944, a 35-bedded Polish Red Cross Hospital was opened in Bombay. No details about the ownership holding of the building is known, but repairs and installation of equipment cost amounted to ₹56,000 of which ₹36,000 was received from the USA and the rest was collected in Mumbai.[34] The Tatas donated ₹2,500 towards this hospital.[35]

Eighteen doctors, amongst whom were Dr Moos, Dr RN Cooper, Major Puller and Major Waters gave their services voluntarily. Several nurses, both trained and probationers, and ten other staff from the Polish camps were appointed. The hospital received a large consignment of medicines and X-ray equipment from the USA. Dr Bazergan, an Iranian who had married a Polish girl in Persia, was the resident doctor. This fulfilled a longstanding need of the Polish population then in India. The Army released an ambulance and a lorry for the hospital.

Panchgani

The Bel-Air sanatorium under the Tuberculosis Association of India had accepted several children threatened by tuberculosis from Bandra and Balachadi camps in 1942. As more and more Polish people came into India, several people had to be accommodated there. A house was rented to accommodate all the people needing to be there. Several children were accommodated in the St Joseph's and St Peter's Convent schools. Later, a rest home was created there and staffed from the two camps—Balachadi and Valivade. Polish Minister of Social Welfare, Mr Jan Stancyk, also visited Panchgani during his visit in 1943. Thus, Panchgani became an important place for the Polish refugees in India. Panchgani was also the holiday location of the staff at Valivade, being a salubrious location not too far from Kolhapur. Stanislaus Harasymow recalled spending a few weeks holidays there with his cousin and mother, the former being the principal of one of the schools.[36] It was also the holiday destination for the rare soldier who got leave and came to meet his family living in Valivade. K Keczynski was in charge of the Panchgani centre.

Some Polish residents even attended a few prayer meetings held by Mahatma Gandhi at Panchgani and recall being couriers for communication between Wanda Dynovska and Mahatma Gandhi.[37] Janina Mineyko recalls being censured by the camp officials at the behest of the British[38] authorities. Some members of API have autographed photographs of Mahatma Gandhi from the period. The meetings left some deep and indelible impression on the people who met the Mahatma. Even Lieutenant Peszkovski recalls meeting Mahatma Gandhi four times, thanks to Wanda Dynowska's proximity to him. The Mahatma was acutely aware of the Polish situation and had made some accurate predictions.[39]

Change of Guard

Minister Jan Stanczyk returned to London less than satisfied with the arrangements the PCG Eugene Banasinski and his wife Kira, as delegate of the Polish Ministry of Social Welfare and the Polish Red Cross, had organised for the children in India in 1943. Balachadi, as a destination for the children, was condemned. The Chela camp, ready and waiting, had to be dismissed. The Balachadi camp was to be closed down and merged with the Valivade camp. Dr Banasinski was posted in London in 1944. He handed over the charge of the Consulate to Consul Litewski and Kira handed over the affairs of the Polish Red Cross to Mr Golawski. They left India in October 1944 to sail to the UK. Map 6 in 'The Transit Camps and War-duration Domicile' indicates the preferred destinations for Polish evacuees as Nainital and Ootacamund, which did not materialise with the British authorities. Delegate Victor Styburski was posted in Dakar even before Banasinski was posted in London. Delegate Darlewski replaced him.

By this time, serious differences were cropping up between the British GOI and the Delegate of the Polish Ministry of Social Welfare. The British GOI felt that the camp staff was being paid too much as salary. This in turn was even communicated to HMG, London, who in turn, took it up with the Polish government. Delegate Darlewski sought some clarifications on the expenses being incurred in the camps, which gave Webb the much needed impetus to clamp down on salaries of camp staff in 1944.[40] In 1944, Dr L Grosfeld, the Polish Minister of Finance, was censured by WL Fraser of HMG for high expenses incurred on the salary and the administration of Polish staff.[41] HMG in London sought the view of the GOI about handing over the charge of these people to the UNRRA.[42] It can be surmised that the gold reserves smuggled out by the Polish government and deposited with HMG was running out.

As the War drew to a close, the USSR's claim to a large section of eastern Poland, usually referred to as the Kresy region, was upheld at the Tehran and Yalta conferences. The new communist government in Poland did not protest and was happy to receive some territory on the west, at the cost of Germany. Most Poles in India had no homes left to go back to, as they mostly hailed from the Kresy region. They were not at all keen to return to either the USSR or Poland, fearing prosecution for having left with Anders' Army. Overnight General Ander, the hero, became a persona non-grata like the member of the former Polish government-in-exile, Dr Eugene Banasinska and Kira. They feared persecution in communist Poland.

In December 1944, Britain shifted recognition from the Polish government-in-exile in London to the new communist government in Lublin, led by Wanda Wasilieska, after some kind of elections had been held there. The new government was supported by the USSR. Soon the Warsaw Uprising broke out and it lasted till August 1945. The Provisional Government of National Unity set up in Warsaw with Soviet support did not want to accept financial responsibilities for its citizens abroad.[43] Britain then handed over the charge of this huge group of Poles all over the British dominions—unwilling to return to their countries—to the UNRRA from August 1946. The financial responsibility of these people then rested with the ITC of the UNRRA till they were handed over to International Refugee Organisation (IRO) formed for the purpose in July 1947.[44]

A slew of austerity measures followed in the camps, to the delight of the British GOI who had all along felt that the Polish government was being overtly generous in terms of allowances, salaries and the number of people employed in the camps. Uncertainty about the future hung heavy in the camps. Political changes began to sweep India. In 1946, the UNRRA limited its liability for all refugees in India, including the Maltese–Balkan and Anglo-Burmese people to £1,700,000 per annum, exclusive of the repatriation costs and advised all refugees to be repatriated. The India Office accordingly informed the Principal Refugee Officer in India to limit costs to £5 per capita per month.[45]

The GOI stated in the Agenda of Polish Forces Official Committee meeting of 13 December 1946 that the Poles were accepted by the GOI at the pressing request of HMG who had been financially responsible for their maintenance. In all, 5,080 Poles were sent to India, of which 2,075 were women, 2,000 children and 420 men. Out of that, 3,610 were relatives of members of the Polish Second Corps. The GOI wanted them moved to either intermediate camps outside India or to the UK with the dependants of the Polish Second Corps.[46]

The Secretary of State for Colonies, Government of Palestine, stated in a confidential report in January 1947 that there were three categories of Polish refugees:

1. Those who had opted or were likely to opt for repatriation to Poland.
2. Dependants of members of the Polish Second Corps.
3. People who neither came under classification/category (1) nor under classification/category (2) and should be regarded as a part of the world problem of displaced persons or refugees, and therefore, handed over to the IRO.[47]

A representative of the new government visited the camps of India, urging the people to return to Poland. There was a great ferment in the camps. Adults and children alike were doggedly resistant about returning to Poland under the communist rule. All residents had had a first-hand experience of a communist government in the USSR and loathed it severely. One teenaged boy ostensibly threatened to jump out of the ship if he was forcibly taken back to Poland, recalling his mother dying of starvation in the streets of Russia.[48] Another boy wanted to know why his father would send a typewritten letter to a stranger and not a handwritten one to him if he wished to be reunited with his son, when shown a letter ostensibly from his father wanting his son's return to Poland.[49]

Visits and Tours in India—The Scouts' Visit to Goa

The Polish people who came to India were poor refugees living off meagre doles supplemented by some income from employment generated by their government, vehemently opposed by the administrating British GOI. Travel was a luxury and had to be carefully weighed against a number of other pressing requirements—food and clothes for the immediate and extended family—besides saving for repatriation day. Sending parcels with items of food, clothes and money to family members in the USSR and Poland was a common and regular feature; hence, travel was not a priority activity. In those days, Europeans were not expected to travel in third-class railway compartments which had the lowest fares. They were the sole prerogative of Indians. So, travel needed to be very carefully planned in an unknown country after considering all aspects.

However, treks and scouting camps at Panhala and Rukadi were carried out often. Stanislaus Harasymow recalled the folklore that they heard about Shivaji's guerrilla tactics and heroic deeds against the imperial Mughal army, which greatly inspired and motivated them.[50] He even recalled the boys trying out some daredevil acts of swinging by banyan ropes and walking on the fort ramparts.

Only two major outings for the children took place—a bicycling trip to Goa for the Boy Scouts organised by Lt Z Peszkovski and a trip of South India for older Polish girls by Madame Wanda Dynowska aka Umadevi.

Franek Herzog, Weislaw Stypula and Zbignew Bartosz of Warsaw, Poland, recalled a bicycling trip to Goa organised by Lieutenant Peszkovski.[51] The objective of the trip was to visit the cemetery of St Francis Xavier in Goa, the patron saint of India. The group consisted of 23 senior scout boys, on hired bicycles and three adults—Lieutenant Z Peszkovski, Scoutmaster Reverend Jankowski and Salesian Brother Orysiuk. Lieutenant Peszkovski carried all the tents and other camping requirements in a van that he drove himself. See Photograph 16.

Umadevi and the Trip to South India

Wanda Dynowska, a philosopher, had come to India in 1930, before the outbreak of the Second World War, as did Maurice Frydman. They were both associated with the Theosophical Society of India and translated many Indian books, poems, songs and legends to Polish, after learning Sanskrit. Wanda Dynowska was greatly influenced by Mahatma Gandhi, and she spent considerable time in Wardha Ashram, where the Mahatma rechristened her Umadevi.

After the War broke out, she offered her services to the Polish Consulate in Bombay, being fluent in English. She took charge of publication and publicity. She made many trips around India giving lectures about Poland, her people, conditions and its complex political position at the time, and was an advisor to the PCG in India, Dr E Banasinski. She used to bring out the Polish newspaper *Polacy w Indach* (Poles in India), till it was closed down in 1947. She was instrumental in setting up the 'Bibloteka Polso-Indyjaska' (Indo-Polish Library) in Bombay. She wrote one of the books on Indian geography used by Polish children during their stay in the Valivade camp.

Umadevi was not involved in the administration of the Valivade camp, but was a regular visitor and often held prayer sessions. In 1946, she took a group of girls on a trip to South India to the Theosophical Society headquarters in Adyar, Madras, and the Arunachalam Hills Ashram of Ramanna Maharishi, besides the numerous temples of South India. It was a month-long tour and has been described in details by some participants.[52] Twenty-five people including Dynowska, Z Wilczynska, a teacher, three boys and 20 senior Girl Guides embarked on a 3,000 kilometres trip on 7 October 1946. They started with ₹100 per person and had to raise the remaining money through guest performances. This trip has been erroneously referred to by some scholars as a means of earning livelihood.[53] The objective of the trip was to see India and spread awareness about Poland through their cultural activities.

They were in Bangalore from 8 to 11 October 1946 and had an invitation to perform by the mayor. Dynowska was using this opportunity to explain to the Indian people why the Poles were not returning to Poland, though the War was over. The group reached Tirunmalai at the ashram of Ramanna Maharishi on 11 October and were there till 14 October. The chanting of the mantras during the evening *aarti* was a unique experience for many. Some considered it as an ancient link with their Aryan forefathers, but Ramanna Maharishi's philosophy was thought too heavy for the young Polish teenagers. The performance in Tiruvanmalai brought in the necessary funds to continue their journey. From 15 to 21 October, the group was in Madras where they stayed in a film studio. It was here that they were joined by Sitaram Puranik, whose article on the problem of the Poles later appeared in the *Mahratta*.[54] It was here that the two pictures (Photographs 17 and 18) were taken.

The visit to Adyar at the Theosophical Society left them wishing that there were no wars, partitions, occupations, NKVD, Curzon Line, atom bombs and similar calamities.[55] From there they went to Madurai, Tenkasi, Kottayam, Trivandrum, Nagercoil and Cape Comorin, where they met members of the American Salvation Army. The return route was Mysore and Bangalore where they stopped to see the Vrindavan Gardens, the Wodeyar Palace and Seringapatam.

Though limited in their scope due to several constraints, these trips left a great impact on those who participated. While it created homesickness in some, others felt enriched by the contact with so many religions and philosophies. Several people have returned to explore other parts of India as adults after attaining financial security. Jan Siedlecki, President of the API 1942–48, London, felt that the Polish evacuees had not benefited fully from the stay in India to familiarise themselves with this country.

Closure of Valivade and Dispersal

There was great uncertainty about the future amongst the residents of
the camp after the War ended and Poland was firmly in the camp of the
USSR. It was strengthened by the fact that most people hailing from
the Kresy—or eastern borderlands—region of pre-War Poland had no
homes left to go back to as the region had been ceded to Ukraine and
other countries. They had all come out of the USSR along with General
Anders' troops who had been decried at the end of the War by the new
communist government in Warsaw, which had won international recognition, much to the dismay of all the Poles outside of Poland.

In his report of 1 November 1944, Captain Webb writes, 'The Poles
are convinced that there is a plan afoot to transfer them to the clutches
of either the Russian (Soviet) or Lublin Governments.'[56] The special representative of UNRRA, Mr Durrant's visit to the Polish camps caused
great angst in the camps and 'nearly resulted in a riot'.[57] On 17 March
1945, he was 'urged to leave camp in his own interest'.[58] The Poles in the
Indian camps who had communication from their friends, relations and
acquaintances in the camps in East Africa, had been were advised against
Durrant and 'recommended strong personal action, should he turn up
in Kolhapur'.[59]

Thereafter, Poles who tried to seek employment outside the camps,
in 1945, in a bid to settle down in India permanently or raise capital for
a subsequent passage to some other western country, were firmly discouraged. A new Polish commandant of the camp was appointed, but
stripped off his power to grant permission to leave the camp vide a letter
addressed to the PCG from the Principal Refugee Officer.[60] Permission
to leave the camp then had to be taken from the Liaison Officer, who in
turn, could grant it for medical or educational reasons only. The tone of
this letter is rather hostile and quite unlike one that would usually be to
the Consulate of an allied country. The British GOI strongly enforced
the condition that these refugees had been accepted in India for wartime
duration and had to live in camps. Webb mentions that local authorities
on 'several occasions had complained that European refugees are taking
the bread from Indian's mouths and it is no part of government policy to
encourage Europeans either to compete against Indians for employment
or to settle here permanently.'[61]

There were several marriages around this time—27 to British partners
and 41 to Polish partners.[62] The Poles were the sailors of *M.S. Batory*

and only one of the grooms was a disabled older boy who was not in the Army. There were approximately six marriages with Indian men and one with a Chinese man. The Valivade camp was then made an 'out of bounds area' for army, navy and air-force personnel.

Barbara Krawiec married Dr Sunil Shinde and Danuta married Salim Mujawar, who had the transport contract for the merchants of Valivade. Shamrao Gaikwad was engaged to Roma (see Photograph 19). The British GOI then keenly considered putting the town out of bounds to all inmates of the camp. Several marriages also took place in Bombay. Wanda Kashikar nee Nowicka recalled that when she got married to Vasant Kashikar, Colonel Harvey, Resident of Kolhapur, not only threatened them both with dire consequences but also ensured that Vasant became and remained jobless for two years till Vasant's family came to their rescue.[63]

In 1946, M Buraczkiewicz, the representative of the Warsaw government, wrote in a report to the Cairo Mission,

> Pandit Nehru told me, that a deputation from the Camp visited him asking for permission to stay in Kolhapur. He told them that they could stay for the time being, but they should not regard India as a place of permanent settlement, as the war ended two years ago and it was time to return home, or settle wherever they would be welcome—India had enough of its own population.[64]

M Buraczkiewicz has been described by Fr Pluta as a communist, who was booed by the residents of the camps.[65] With Mahatma Gandhi's known sympathy towards the Poles and even the generosity towards the average British people, the statement attributed to Pandit Nehru is rather unlikely or out of context. Even the Kolhapur Durbar postponed the closure of the Valivade camp till June 1948, when approached by the GOI on behalf of the Poles in July 1947.[66] Hence, the Buraczkiewicz report seems rather dubious. It may have been made either to suit the new Polish government or the British administrators of India or both. Besides, in 1946, the former to India, Dr E Banasinski and his wife Kira, returned to Mumbai after spending two years in London trying to find a suitable job after losing their diplomatic job with the derecognition of the Polish government-in-exile in London.[67] Wanda Dynowska's visits to the camp were also frowned upon by the British administrators. In his report dated 31 August 1946, Webb writes,

> Some [Poles] it is rumoured, are turning an ear to the hazy blandishments of a certain crack-brained Pole of feminine gender, who has

turned theosophist, apes Indian mode of dress, and would have as many Poles as possible remain in India 'to help in India's fight for freedom'. By this, presumably, she means remain behind and fight the British![68]

After the charge of these Polish people was handed over to the UNRRA, the expenses in the camp were to remain within the budgeted amount of £5 per month. In a communication discussing the finances of the camp, Webb stated categorically that the Indian people had contributed to the tune of ₹0.6 million towards the upkeep of the Poles in India, hosting them through the years which saw the famine of Bengal.[69] A host of austerity measures followed, primarily the closing down of the Balachadi and Panchgani camps and concentrating all the Poles to Kolhapur. All children studying in the various colleges, technical schools and convents were recalled. The complete Polish staff was asked to render their services merely in exchange of board, lodging and double pocket money. The notices of retrenchment of the Indian staff and the new arrangement for the Polish staff in the Polish camps were issued on 1 November 1946.[70]

All these measures were adopted to coerce the Polish population in India to return to Poland. Those who felt less fearful of the new regime opted to return to Poland, but they were a minority, including the parents of Zofia Mendonca. They had located their eldest daughter Filomena in Poland through the Red Cross. By this time, several Polish families were being returned to Poland from the Soviet labour camps. Several children from Balachadi camp, like Roman Gutowski, Wieslaw Stypula and Zbigniew Bartosz, and virtually all members of the present API, Warsaw, located their families in Poland and were repatriated.

Since the Polish troops had battled alongside the British in the Allied cause, the British government was obliged to take charge of all the Poles doggedly declining to go back to Poland due to the political reasons. The British government created the Polish Resettlement Corps from the de-mobilised Polish troops. The families of these soldiers could join them in the UK. Once again there was a great scramble amongst the people in Valivade to locate members of family willing to sponsor them to the UK. The British government imposed more and more stringent parameters about the dependants of Polish troops to be accepted into the UK.

The second round of admission into the UK was for the dependants of Polish soldiers killed in action in allied campaigns, where several families from Valivade qualified. The date for India's independence was drawing close and the British administration wanted to reduce their charge in India, especially after the Naval Ratings Mutiny of 1946, and was pressing the Poles hard. Umadevi's visits to the camp and discussion about the Indian

Nationalist Movement against occupiers were viewed very unkindly by the British officials, and this is reported by Webb. Several Poles had started identifying with the Indian freedom struggle against occupiers, which made the British administration even more nervous. Members of the API 1942–48 recalled several instances of apartheid and the Poles' complete identification with the Indians, which made the British administrators more and more nervous about the Polish presence in India. They were afraid that the Poles may join the Indians in their struggle against the British or may be motivated to do something that might be terribly embarrassing for the British worldwide. It must be recalled here that these Poles had had firsthand experience of the conditions in the USSR, who had been a tacit ally of Nazi Germany in 1939 at the beginning of the War and finished on the winning side with the Allies in 1945 at the end of the War, changing course midway and gaining tremendously from the Lend-Lease Agreement.

According to international law, all orphans are the charge of the country to which they belong, hence the children in the orphanages of Balachadi and Valivade were to be repatriated to Poland. There was great resistance about repatriation to Poland amongst the children. While those over 16 years (legal age for adulthood at the time) 'refused to consider repatriation, guardians were appointed with the consent of Polish Consul General in India just before closing down of the consulate, for those under sixteen years of age.'[71] A legal adoption of the orphaned children was worked out in the courts of Nawanagar, between Fr Francisek Pluta, Jam Saheb Digvijaysinghji and Lieutenant Colonel Geoffrey Clark to facilitate the transfer of these children. The children were moved out of the court's jurisdiction with permission, first to Kolhapur and later overseas. The Legislative Department, GOI, 'considered this transaction valid in law'.[72] At that time, it was a move to direct some children to Australia. It is not clear whether the move to Australia materialised or not.

Fr Pluta arranged for 81 children from the orphanages to be sponsored by two American missionary organisations. Fifty girls were sponsored by the Bernadine Sisters of Pennsylvania, amongst them Alina Baczyk Haus and 31 boys by Orchard Lake Seminary, Michigan. As mentioned in the chapter 'Franek and Tadek in Balachadi' and even previously, the adoption facilitated the transfer of 81 children to the USA.

HMG had no objections to such moves and RN Gilchrist of HMG informed Rhea Radin of the UNRRA accordingly. The GOI acted as agents of HMG and raised no objections to this scheme.[73] The UNRRA then demanded to know the legal standing of such an arrangement. Selene Gifford, Director, Displaced Persons Division, UNRRA, and Rhea Radin,

Chief, Repatriation and Care Division, UNRRA, were informed, 'the position of the children under present guardianship (was) absolutely safe
and easy to defend'.[74] The formal documents of the case were 'water-tight
from a legal point of view', according to Webb.[75] Ms Burakiewicz showed
the telegram from Polish Legation, Cairo, asking them to try and stop
their departure, but the children had already left Valivade camp en route
for the USA. Fr Pluta was later declared an 'international kidnapper' by
the new Polish government. He rushed back to the USA once he learnt of
his status at Cairo,[76] and remained there till the end of his life.

Ostensibly Ms Burakiewicz approached Pandit Jawaharlal Nehru to
let the Poles without any families left elsewhere in the world remain in
India, which he declined.[77] The Commonwealth countries of Australia
and Canada were approached to absorb this large body of Polish
deportees, now termed as 'Displaced Persons' (DPs). While both these
countries sought various kinds of details to process the request, the
camp at Valivade had become uneconomical for the UNRRA to support
individually as more and more people were being encouraged to return to
Poland. Amongst those who were determined not to, many were leaving
for the UK qualifying under the categories being accepted there.

Table 4: Total number of Poles in India

Date	Strength in Balachadi Camp	Strength in Valivade Camp	Total Number of Poles in India
13 September 1943	588	2,534	
1 November 1944	459	3,621	
16 June 1945	327	3,914	
31 August 1946	–	–	4,600

Source: Captain AWT Webb's reports, BNA, FO 371.51153, report dated 31
August 1946.

While it was 'the ardent desire of the G.O.I. to be relieved of all European refugees by the end of 1946'[78] only half-a-dozen Poles had agreed to
return to Poland. Two hundred and fifty families had applied for permission to settle in Canada in January 1946. In August 1946, Webb reports
that 400 Polish orphan children had a possibility of being accepted into
Australia. Of the remaining 4,600 Poles in Valivade, 2,750 could claim to
be dependants of the members of Polish Second Corps, 100 dependants
of other members of Polish forces who served under British command,

170 willing to return to Poland and about 680 falling into the general pool of DPs.

The approximate leave-taking figures from Valivade are: 83 dead, 500 to Poland, 3,500 to the UK, 100 to Australia, 150 to the USA and the rest without relatives or in special situations to the camps in Africa and Lebanon, from where they were accepted eventually into the UK or other Commonwealth countries of Australia and Canada[79] as DP.

The Union Jack was lowered in India on 15 August 1947. The day was celebrated with great élan at the Polish camp at Valivade. It coincided with the Polish Feast of Our Lady and the Miracle on the Vistula, where the Poles had defeated the mighty Bolsheviks in 1921.

The assassination of Mahatma Gandhi on 30 January 1948 sent shockwaves throughout the world, including the Polish camp in Valivade. A man of peace had been shot dead by a Hindu fanatic. The last ship to leave India was in March 1948. The last people to leave the camp were the families in special circumstances, definitely unwilling to return to Poland, not qualifying as 'orphan children' and sponsored by the missionary organisations of the USA and no relative to sponsor them to the UK. Among them was Tadeusz Dobrostanski with his mother Janina and older brother Jerzy and Stanislaus Harasymow, also with his mother Antonina and a cousin.

This last group of Poles were present during the funeral of Gandhi held all over the country. The scouts from the camp formed a special contingent when the ashes were received for immersion in the river Panchganga. Stanislaw Harasymow wrote,

> News of the assassination of India's spiritual and political Leader shocked the nation. His policy of passive resistance, together with his political strength and determination, brought forward the liberation of India from British rule. We learned of Gandhi's death around 6.00 p.m. on the 30th of January 1948. In accordance with Hindu custom, his body was cremated on a funeral pyre and his ashes placed in several urns to be distributed all over India and emptied into rivers, as a symbol of his boundless devotion to his nation's cause. He always believed in humanity as a brotherhood of nations, and he proved this with his life.
>
> Mahatma Gandhi's ashes were brought to Kolhapur by train. At the station, a funeral procession was assembled ready to accompany the urn on its way to the Panchganga river. A spot in front of the station was reserved for the Polish scouts. We got there long before the arrival of the ashes. We stood in rows together with lots of Indian students and other chosen guests. A huge crowd waited alongside the route of the funeral procession. The prevailing feeling was that of deep mourning.

At last the ashes arrived and we all moved forward. There were government, civil and religious dignitaries, army and police units in colourful uniforms, as well as parading elephants. We joined the solemn march and soon found ourselves surrounded by the huge crowd of mourners, all moving towards the river. On one of the wider streets, which sloped gently down, we could cast our eyes over the sea of human heads and appreciate the immensity of the crowd. The funeral cortege finally stopped, the crowd thickened and stood in silence. We were too far away to hear the speeches or to witness the scattering of Gandhi's ashes into the Panchganga River. But I will never forget the countless number of people who, by their presence, paid their last respects to the great Man of our times.[80]

The last few months in Valivade have been described by Leszek Trzaska, a resident of Krakow in Poland, as:

A feeling of sadness came upon Valivade. The inevitable closing down of the Camp was drawing nearer. A few transports had already left our settlement. We had been so happy here. More and more vacant rooms and window openings looked with envy upon the inhabited quarters, knowing they too will soon join them. It was the end of 1947 and beginning of 1948. Education was still proceeding, based on a shortened school year. Life was slowly becoming melancholy and the remaining residents were feeling lost. We had to decide what to do next? For those who had their close relatives in England, it was an obvious choice to join them there. Only they were eligible to settle in Great Britain. And so it happened without any problems or hesitation. This was the only way to take for them, with no alternatives. But the remaining majority of the people had to battle it out in their consciences, where to go?

There were three alternatives. The first alternative was the Polish refugee camps in Africa, with an uncertain future, because the war had ended three years previously. The second possibility was the American Occupation Zone in Germany, with promised immigration later on to the U.S.A. Again, there was an uncertain future as to work prospects, securing living quarters, getting qualifications, carrying on with studies, wages etc. The families consisted usually of mothers and children, because the fathers had died in Russia or were killed during the war. And the third choice was to return to Poland, but to what? The whole of our possessions had perished with the 'selling off' of the eastern part of Poland to Stalin. In my case, the Germans occupied our home and there was nothing there to come back to. On top of that, those who were contemplating repatriation were regarded by some in Valivade as traitors, because it meant abandoning the Polish Government in Exile in London and accepting the Communist Government set up by the U.S.S.R in Poland. Our mothers (sisters) and 5 children ranging in age from 8–14 were puzzled as to what to do? My uncle in Poland came to a decision. He resolved categorically that his brother's children would not wander all over the world with an uncertain future. Return to Poland and the family will support you. Live here with me, we were told. Even then it wasn't an easy decision to take. Seven persons to squeeze into someone's home! My uncle's family had also lost all their possessions. Before the war, he was a high ranking staff officer in the Military Head Office in Warsaw. During the hostilities he was interned in a prisoner of war camp. His wife returned from Lvov to our native Krakow, where she felt more secure among the family members. Similarly, her siblings left Lvov behind and their big house and large shop. And so, after five peaceful, happy and adventurous years, we left our Camp in February 1948, together with a large group of Poles from Valivade via Poona to Bombay. We boarded a troopship General M.B. Steward and were on our way. Among us there were three groups of passengers. One, and the most numerous, was to disembark on the African continent. The other significant group was on its way to the American Occupation Zone in Germany, with the promise of later immigration to the U.S.A. The smallest group was returning to Poland. After a couple of weeks we reached Mombasa and received certificates for crossing the Equator. This is where we farewelled the group from Valivade and welcomed new Polish passengers on their way to their Homeland.'[81]

Tadeusz Dobrostanski, who with his family was in this last group of Poles to leave Valivade, describes that after disembarkation in Mombasa, the Poles were sent by train to Kampala, and further, driven by trucks to the Polish settlement of Koja, in the jungle on the banks of Lake Victoria. The accommodation was straw-roofed clay huts[82] and primitive. At one point of time, the young people demanded to be sent back to Valivade, where they had enjoyed better standards of living, but were told that Valivade had been closed forever.[83] In 1949, they were accepted into Australia and arrived in Freemantle aboard *U.S.A.T. General Langfitt* on 14 February 1950, ending a decade of peregrinations around the world, starting a new life from the very beginning. A similar experience awaited those who reached Canada. Several others reached Canada from the UK and the USA from occupied Germany. Testimony of this is detailed in 'Voices form the Past'.

The Valivade camp was used to accommodate the Sindhi refugees ousted from Pakistan following the partition of the Indian sub-continent and the ensuing riots. It was renamed 'Gandhinagar' and stands to this day, retaining its original use of being a shelter for displaced people!!

Most barracks in the new Gandhinagar have been concretised. The roads are no longer green and tree lined, but is a huge urban slum.

The Valivade camp has been mentioned as a high-standard camp by all residents in later years and has been particularly mentioned in a commemorative book on the subject in Poland.[84] All surviving residents across the world recall it as a sunny peaceful place, where they spent the best years of their life, which prompted them to form associations, have regular biennial reunions, issue commemorative bulletins, revisit India and put a memorial plaque in the town centre after the dismantling of the communist government in Poland and the USSR. The revisits are dealt with in detail in 'Looking Back'.

NOTES AND REFERENCES

1. Kolhapur Administration Report, 1942–43, printed in 1944.
2. NAI, 276 (8)-X/42, Captain AWT Webb, Principal Refugee Officer, GOI, Report dated 11 February 1943.
3. Ibid.
4. BL-I&OC, R2/952/76 C-70/43, Notes.
5. K Banasinska and G Verghese, *Autobiography of Kira Banasinska* (Mumbai: Kotak & Co., 1997), 98.
6. BL-I&OC, R2/952/76 C-70/43, Resident of Kolhapur to Sir Kenneth Fitze and Captain AWT Webb, Document No. C 2508/43-D, dated 29 November 1943.
7. Ibid., 46.
8. R Ingle, interview to author, Kolhapur, September 2003.
9. PIGSM, *Polak w Indiach*, No. 18–19, 15 September–1 October, 1944.
10. R Ingle, interview to author.
11. BNA, FO.371/42882/PRO, Webb's Report.
12. NAI, 276(8)-X/42, 90.
13. PIGSM, Banasinski Collection.
14. *A Holocaust and a Gulag—Letters of Chris and Janina Sulkova*. Available at http://info-poland.buffalo.edu/web/history/WWII/gehenna/link.shtml
15. Possibly Salunkhe.
16. R Ingle, interview to author.
17. S Gaikwad, interview to author, Kolhapur, October 2002.
18. Association of Poles in India 1942–48, *A Short History of Poles in India 1942–48, In Light of Reminiscences and Documents*, Polish (English translation underway) (London, n.d.). Hereafter API Book.
19. N Nesrikar, interview to author, Kolhapur, October 2002.
20. Colonel Vijay Gaikwad, interview to author, Kolhapur, October 2002.
21. R Ingle, interview to author.
22. Ibid.

23. Special Supplement to API Book bulletin number 16.
24. S Harasymow, email to author.
25. BL-I&OC, L/AG/40/1/169(PRC/A-25).
26. NAI, 218(72)-G/44, 1–4.
27. H Baczyk, email to author.
28. In email correspondence to author.
29. J Siedlecki, videotaped interview, London, March 2004.
30. BL-I&OC, L/AG/40/1/169 (PRC/A-25).
31. API Book.
32. S Harasymow, email to scholar and API Book.
33. R Ingle, interview to author and Gaikwad, interview to author.
34. K Banasinska and G Verghese, *Autobiography of Kira Banasinska*, 119.
35. TCA, DTT Collection, Minutes of 74th meeting, 11 July 1944.
36. S Harasymow, email to author.
37. Memories of Rena Jagiellowicz-Kuszel, 'Valivade Me Jawan', commemorative volume in Polish, translation courtesy Barbara Charuba, Canada.
38. API Book.
39. Z Peszkovski, cited in API Book, 456.
40. BNA, FO.371/42882, Captain AWT Webb's Report of 1 November 1944.
41. BL-I&OC, L/P&J/8/413, p 123, WL Fraser to L Grosfeld.
42. BNA, FO.371/42882, Captain AWT Webb's Report of 1 November 1944.
43. BL-I&OC, L/AG/40/1/131 (RRO A-5), HH Eggers to AWT Webb.
44. Ibid.
45. BL-I&OC, L/P&J/8/415, 582.
46. Ibid., 559.
47. Ibid., 522.
48. SS Puranik, 'Why the Poles Do Not Want to Leave India,' *The Maratha*, 10 January 1949.
49. Ibid.
50. S Harasymow, email to author.
51. F Herzog, excerpted diary, email to author.
52. API Book.
53. K Tokarski, *Wanda Dynowska—Umadevi: A Biographical Essay* (Fullerton, 1994).
54. Puranik, 'Why the Poles Do Not Want to Leave India'.
55. Konrad cited in API Book, 472.
56. BNA, FO 371.51153, Captain AWT Webb's Report.
57. Ibid.
58. BL-I&OC, L/P&J/8/415, 125–131.
59. Ibid., 139, A.W.T. Webb to JH Thomson, Residency Office, Kolhapur.
60. BL-I&OC, L/AG/40/1/169/PRC/A-25, Captain AWT Webb to PCG, dated 16 May 1945.
61. Captain AWT Webb's report dated 16 June 1945, FO 371.51153, PRO, London.

62. Michal Golawski, *Polak w Indiach* (Poles in India), No. 8 (66) April 1946 (translated by Stanislaus Harasymow) (Bombay: Polish Red Cross).
63. Wanda Kashikar, personal interview to author, Kolhapur, 2003.
64. AAN, 417, Report of M Buraczkiewicz.
65. F Pluta, *Reunion speech of July 18, 1989*, transcript courtesy of Franek Herzog.
66. BL-I&OC, L/P&J/8/415, Telegram GOI to Secretary of State India, dated 17 July 1947.
67. K Banasinska and G Verghese, *Autobiography of Kira Banasinska*, 123.
68. BNA, FO 371.51153, Captain Webb's Report of 31 August 1946.
69. PIGSM, C811c, Memorandum to Webb's Report.
70. BL-I&OC, L/P&J/8/414/Coll 110 N3, GOI Commonwealth Relations Department to Secretary of State, India.
71. BL-I&OC, L/P&J/8/415, p- 341, Telegram dated 2 July 1947, GOI to Secretary of State, India.
72. Ibid.
73. Ibid., telegram dated 10 January 1947, Captain AWT Webb to L Findlay, UNRRA, 410.
74. Ibid., telegram dated 30 January 1947, CRD to Secretary of State, India, 491.
75. BL-I&OC, Letter no. POL 8103, Webb quoted in Eggers to Gilchrist, 23 May 1947.
76. F Pluta, Reunion speech of July 18, 1989.
77. AAN, 417, Report of M Buraczkiewicz.
78. Ibid.
79. Cass Glodek in Kresy Siberia discussion site, 12 August 2003.
80. Harasymow, API Book, 461.
81. L Trzaska, personal correspondence to author.
82. Testimony of Tadeusz Dobrostanski.
83. T Dobrostanski, email to author.
84. Fundacja Archiwum Fotograficzne, *Exiled Children (Tulacze Dzieci)* (Warsaw: Fundacja Archiwum Fotograficzne, 1995), 317.

Reminiscences and Reflections

CRROO

Franek's Epilogue

⋆⋇⋆

Once in England a new chapter in my life started. The care free kind of life came to an abrupt end. Till now somebody else had been looking after me—in Poland, it was my family; even in Russia, I could rely on Mother and my older brothers; in India, it was the orphanage, its staff and the patronage of Maharaja Jam Saheb. Now that had come to an end. I had to start looking after myself and start thinking seriously about the future. In life, a lot depends on fate and luck, but sometimes you have to guide and nudge it a bit to reach your goal. Also one must not rule out God's hand and guidance.

In 1948, over 200,000 Poles found themselves in England. That number included all the Polish Army that was under the British Command, that is, the Second Polish Corps from Italy, the Panzer Division of General S Maczek, the Parachute Brigade of General S Sosabowski, the Air Force and the Navy. In addition to them, were the soldiers of the Uderground Army held in the German POW camps. Then the women, children and dependants from the Middle East, India, Africa and other parts of the world came to join their husbands, brothers or relatives who had been in the Polish Army.

Only a small percentage of people returned to Poland. At that time, the only places for emigration were Argentina, Australia and Canada. For emigration to the US, Displaced Persons (DP) were on the priority list rather than the Polish comrades-in arm and the Polish ex-servicemen. The British government formed the Polish Resettlement Corps (PKPR). That allowed the Polish servicemen to stay, if they wished so, on the military payroll for two years to learn some new trade and adapt themselves to civilian life in England. They also established the Polish Education Committee that was operating four Polish high schools and the Polish University College (PUC) in London. The Committee was also granting scholarships. Thanks to those, my brother Tadek graduated from the PUC, and I had a grant for a part of my college education.

Without proper knowledge of the English language, finding a good job was difficult. At the same time, about two million or more British ex-soldiers were also looking for jobs. So the Labor Exchange was directing Poles to mines, farming, fishing and building or the lowest paid jobs in factories and in London, to Lyons tea-shops. You could find ex-officers and other highly educated people as dishwashers or sweepers in factories. For my brothers and me, returning to Poland was not an option as we did not have anything or anybody to return to.

The borders of Poland were redrawn again at the end of World War II, ceding the eastern region to the Soviet Union and some regions from Germany appended on the western side. These decisions (and the overall silence shrouding the matter) caused some strange experiences in our life. In later years, when asked about the place of birth, it was entered in our documents as Belarus for my wife and Lithuania for my brothers. But they were never Belarusian or Lithenians—they were born in cities which were in Poland at the time they were born.

In UK, I knew that first of all I had to finish high school. I managed to get to one that was run in a military fashion in an ex-army camp. In three years, I finished it and with a high school diploma in my hand and a few pounds sterling in my pocket, I was ready to conquer the world. I went to London to be closer to my brothers and for a year worked as an unskilled labourer in a factory. But that's not what I wanted to do for the rest of my life. I enrolled in a college, got scholarship for two years and then with many more years of evening studies, I eventually graduated with a degree in Electrical Engineering. That has been my profession for the rest of my working days. I continued devoting lot of time to scouting activities and that became my life's passion.

While in England, I met a wonderful Polish girl, Kama Mikucka, and after a few years of courting, she became my wife. Three years ago, we celebrated our golden wedding anniversary. We have one daughter Ivona and three grandchildren. In 1968, we immigrated to the US, and now it is our permanent home, but Poland, which I visit frequently, is and always will be my fatherland. And India? It is my second homeland. It was the place where I had been a child again, after Poland, though in a slightly different way.

In my diary, I use the term Siberia liberally. Geographically speaking, Siberia is the northern third of Asia stretching from the Urals in the west to the Pacific Ocean, from the Kazakh steppes in the south to the Arctic Ocean. But to the Polish people, Siberia means all the areas of the Russian Empire where Polish people were forcibly deported and sent to *gulag*s and prisons. It could be Kazakhstan, Kamchatka, Altaj near Mongolian border or the forest areas in the Archangelsk region, Tundras of northern Siberia or coal mines in the Ural Mountains.

Now, as I ponder over the events of my life, I can better understand the events of the past and see that many things did not happen automatically and my life would have been quite different but for them. The following are just a few of them.

Somehow Mother's cousin Marian Strumillo knew our whereabouts in Russia; so when he came to Kuibyshev with the Polish Embassy, he contacted us immediately and even sent some monetary help. Soon after Wacek notified him of Mother's death, we received a telegram from him advising us to go to Aktiubinsk as soon as possible. A friend of his from the Polish Embassy would be going to Tashkent and would have railway tickets for us. In Tashkent, a Polish orphanage was being assembled which would be evacuated to India.

Sometimes I wonder what would have happened to me if Uncle Strumillo would not have helped. Wacek would have joined the Polish Army while Tadek and I would have remained in that collective farm. Probably I would have been sent to some Russian orphanage. At that time I was still only ten. How would I have grown up and matured? Would the grain of attachment to religion, Poland and its heritage planted in me have sprouted or rotted in that 'inhumane land'?

How did it then happen, that we went to India and were saved? All because someone in India was sympathetic to Poland. As it happened, after the First World War, the future maharaja of Nawanagar as a youngster was visiting his uncle who had an estate in

Switzerland next to the estate of the great Polish pianist and patriot, Jan Paderewski. A friendly relationship was established between the two families. When Jam Saheb, remembering his friendship with Paderewski, learned that there was an idea of bringing Polish orphans from Russia to India, he persuaded other maharajas to declare that they would pay to a central fund a sum of money to support 5, 10, 20, 30 or more children till the end of the War.

Over the number of years the API 1942–48 has been organizing reunions. Not counting the transit camps near Karachi, there were two permanent camps for Polish refugees in India. There was the big camp with over 5,000 inhabitants in Valivade near Kolhapur, mainly for families and much smaller in Balachadi with 600, mainly orphans. There is a marked difference between the Valivade people and the Balachadi people. Though I am not a self appointed voice or representative of the Balachadi group but I am sure the majority of the people from Balachadi would agree with my comments and observations.

At our reunions, which are very friendly, it seems some sort of antagonism exists between the two groups. The group from Valivade is a bunch of good friends, whereas we from Balachadi feel more like a family. Valivade was built and maintained with funds provided by the Polish government in England. Balachadi was built on hospitable Indian soil and maintained by the generosity of people of India. We therefore feel closer to India and to its people.

In 1990, we erected memorial plaque on the grounds of Sainik School in Balachadi. The plaque, in bronze, weighing more than 800 pounds, reads 'In homage to the land of Jamnagar which in difficult years of Second World War gave shelter and hospitality to a thousand of homeless Polish children. Hail to the Far Land, Friendly Land, Human Land, Good Land.' We named one of the more prestigious high schools in Warsaw after Maharaja Jam Saheb, in memory of the camp in Balachadi. After all, Maharaja had told us to call him 'Bapu'—father in Hindustani. He was father to us not only in the name, but many of us were adopted by him to give us a chance to stay in the free world. For that we will be always be grateful and never forget him.

In later years, it was always a pleasure to meet and talk to Fr F Pluta, scoutmaster (by then a priest) Z Peszkovski and our beloved Ms J Ptakowa who really organised scouting in Balachadi. In the

USA, I could talk to them as an adult and get a different overview of the days of Balachadi.

But some larger issues remain unresolved. In April 1943, the Germans discovered in Katyn, near Smolensk in Russia, mass graves of Polish officers from Kozielsk POW camp who were executed by the Russians. One of the bodies identified was that of my Father's brother, Captain Stefan Herzog. We were sure that the same thing must have happened to our Father. But where?

Today, after Russia admitted to the crime, we know what happened to them and where. Practically, all the POWs from Starobielsk camp were murdered in Charkov by the NKWD and buried in the woods in the nearby village of Piatichatka; those from Kozielsk in Katyn near Smolensk and from Ostaszcov in Miednoje, near Twer. Many more educated Poles, not just military officers, were executed in various Russian prisons; altogether about 22,000 people. The whole hideous crime is generally referred to as the Katyn Massacre.

It was always my earnest desire to visit my parents' gravesites. In 1990, Gorbachev and then, Yeltsin in 1995, admitted that the Russian NKVD was responsible for Katyn. In 2000, Reverend Peszkovski, who had missed being executed in Katyn by a whisker, commemorated the cemetery in Katyn. Same year, after more excavations and exhumations, the Polish Military Cemetery was established near Charkov in the Piatichatka woods. I visited the place where my Father's unidentified body lay buried in one of the mass graves. [See Photograph 20.] The questions regarding the whole Katyn episode became persistent in my mind.

In 1990, after the Russian admission of responsibility for Katyn, I wrote to President George Bush asking him 'please, look at the facts again and then in the name of US Government apologise to the Polish People and families of the victims for sheltering the criminals for fifty years'. It took 18 months and an intervention of my senator to get a reply from the state department which said 'US Government never accepted the Soviet Government's claim that they were not responsible for the massacre'.

At the Nuremberg Trials, Germany was never officially blamed for the murder. Who but the Soviets could then have executed 15,000 POW officers?

In his last postcard from the Starobielsk camp, Father told us that they were being transferred and not to worry if we didn't hear

from him for some time. Since then, we did not receive any correspondence from Father. History of that postcard written on 6 April
1940 always puzzled me. There were two reasons for that:

1. The return address on the postcard was crossed out, but not
   Voroshilovski Rejon (Region). Charkov is located in that region. The person who crossed out the return address must have
   known where they were taking prisoners. He also added that
   note in Russian 'left Starobielsk'. On the backside of the card, he
   also added similar note in Polish.

   Since details of Katyn had never become public, my Father
   had been lost to that unknown event. It had always puzzled me.
   More recently I read the book Katyn—Genocide of Polish Officers by Natalia Lebiedova. Ostensibly, while researching the subject of Nuremberg Trials, she stumbled for the first time upon
   Katyn. In 1998, she started gathering materials from the Russian
   archives regarding the Massacre, and the findings are published
   in the above mentioned book. There I found some explanation
   to the mystery of that last postcard from Father. Here are some
   excerpts from her book.

In the process of closing the three POW camps numerous NKWD
personal from districts of Smolensk (for Kozielsk), Charkov (for
Starobielsk) and Kaliningrad (for Ostaszkow) as well as execution
squads and transportation units were involved. All these people for the
past 50 years kept silent. No one dared to reveal this hideous crime.

   Danil L Czecholski, a Pole born in 1904, member of the Communist Party since 1926, was employed in the Starobielsk camp as a
translator. He was not afraid of the consequences and dared to break
party discipline. In a roundabout way, he tried to notify some families
that prisoners were moved from the camp. On June 10, Suprunienko
(Chief of the NKWD Dept. for POWs) notified commandant of the
Starobielsk camp that the local Post Office stopped 20 postcards sent
from the camp in June. All outgoing correspondence was closed
from March 16 1940. Camp official conducted investigation and it
was revealed that it was Czecholski who had mailed a number of
postcards written by the officers in April. Since there were no prisoners left in the camp after mid May, when asked, how the correspondence found its way to the post offices (not necessarily Starobielsk)
with crossed out senders address, Czecholski answered: 'I did this to
pacify families and to stop any intervention by the families.' Under
directives from Moscow on July 23, Czecholski was dismissed from

his services in Starobielsk. What happened to him thereafter is not known, and we can only speculate. [1]

Documents in the archives indicate that some of the correspondence reached addressees, as in the case of my Father's postcard.

2. And now the second question to which so far I have no documented answer. The postcard was mailed to our address in Lubaczow, but it never arrived there. There is no Lubaczow postmark on the last postcard, as on all the other postcards; yet, somewhere, somebody new exactly to where we will be deported. That person crossed out our Lubaczow address and readdressed it to Lugawoje in Kazakhstan. It could not have been somebody in Lubaczow, as we had not had time to contact anybody back home, nor did we have any family there. This indicates that deportations were not done in a haphazard way but were done with precision and were planed to the last detail.

Lebiedova's book suggests that based on the outgoing correspondence and interrogations of the prisoners, the NKVD prepared list of the officers' families to be deported on 13 April. Maybe in the camp they also had list of destination of individual families. Maybe Czacholski had an access to such a list and redirected cards to the new address. Unfortunately, from the postmark, it is impossible to read at what day the postcard was sent and from what post office. The postcard arrived in Alga on 26 June 1940, and we received it soon afterward.

After the 2000 trip to the Polish Military Cemetery in Charkow to pray at my Father's symbolic grave, I also wanted to visit my mother's grave in Kazakhstan. But that wish has remained unfulfilled to date due to visa restrictions. In 2009, a friend went to Kazakhstan and visited Lugawoje village and sent me a few photographs, including some from the devastated cemetery, with broken crosses and sunken graves. In one of them, my mother lies buried.

Since joining the organisation Zwiazek Harcerstwa Polskiego (Polish Scouting Organization) in Balachadi, I am still an active member, and scouting has been my life's passion. Through the years, I held various posts from patrol leader to the top executive position. Our scout law says, 'A scout considers everybody to be his neighbour and regards another scout as his brother.' I call it the 'Scout mafia'. A few days after I came to England, Scoutmaster Peszkovski came to our camp and said, 'There is Polish high school in England

and a friend of mine, also a scoutmaster is responsible for placing students in that school. Write applications and I will take it to him.' I was accepted without any delay. When I arrived in the US in 1968, the first Polish people I met were scouts. Through the scouting connections, I visited Lithuania and Latvia. The Polish scoutmaster from Lvov in Ukraine drove me in his car all the way to Charkow. Naturally I reciprocated.

My wife laughs and says, 'Franek, you have three families: your own, Balachadi and scouts.'

Over the years, I have met a few people from the past that I mentioned in my diary. They were always very moving experiences and bring tears to my eyes.

In England in the office where I worked, there was another Pole, Jan Zielinski. One day he approached me and asked whether my Father was a Lieutenant Colonel in the Polish Army and was taken a prisoner by the Russians. When I replied in the affirmative, he told me that as a young boy he used to carry bread and cigarettes and passed them to the prisoners held temporarily in Tarnopol. Our Father had asked him to send a note to us in Lubaczow about his whereabouts. He told me that he had sent two postcards, but by then we were living at a different address and had never received them.

I also had a few occasions to meet with soldiers and officers from Father's battalion. They always spoke very highly of him.

During the War, afraid of antagonizing Russia, the British and the American press would not print articles about the massacre of Polish officers by Russia in Katyn or the mass deportation of the Polish people to Siberia. Even after the War, the subject remained a taboo in the 'free' western democracies.

That situation today is not much better even today. History of the Second World War is rarely thought in its entirety at any level. The consideration might be that if the subject is left out, in time it might be forgotten that Great Britain and America betrayed their staunchest ally—Poland. In later years, I have often been asked by my British and American friends and neighbours, why did Russia deport a million and a half Polish people to Siberia? The answer is very simple. If you remove from the society all the intelligentsia, military leaders, clergy and all the people with some standing in a community, then all that is left are masses who can be easily controlled and manipulated.

There are some writers, however few and far between, who probe into the truth about that dark and camouflaged period of the Second World War in Poland: British historian Norman Davies, author of several monumental books on Polish history and especially Warsaw Uprising in 1944; publicist L Rees, with his book Behind Closed Doors and American reporters Lynn Olsen and Stanley Cloude with their book Question of Honor. Therefore, this work by Anuradha, an Indian, means a lot to those of us who got a second lease of life because of an Indian initiative.

Over the years, I have observed that almost everybody knows about the Holocaust and the six million Jews killed by the Germans, but hardly is it ever mentioned anywhere that three million Poles were also killed outright or died in the German and the Russian prisons and concentration camps or as a result of being deported to harsh regions of the USSR.

After the War, the Great Powers compensated the Jewish people, though at the expense of the Palestinian people, with the Jewish state of Israel. Over the years, Israel accepted from Germany, the UK and the USA millions of dollars in aid, but there has not been anything similar in Poland for the Polish people. Though there can be no compensation adequate for the death of my parents for me, at least an acknowledgement of the history would make me feel a little better. The silence surrounding the subject is as if nothing happened at all, and we all travelled through Kazakhstan, Persia and India and reached the UK in November 1947 with nothing besides the single set of summer clothes on our back, on a personal adventure trip, losing our parents, property and comfortable lives by our own volition and choice. It is almost suggestive that we chose to be displaced persons after the War and were not really so and were thus treated with disdain in both the UK and the USA.

During my days as a stateless person in the UK, I would often think about my citizenship options. I had three: Polish, because I was born in Poland; Russian, because it was forced on me and million others when Russia occupied eastern Poland in 1939 and Indian, as an adopted son of Jam Saheb! I acquired British citizenship in 1961 and American in 1973. But in my heart I am and will always be a Pole, because I cannot be anything else.

Usually it is written that the crimes of the Second World War were committed by the Nazis or the communists. These crimes were committed by the Germans and Russians in the name of ideology and because they had power and the system allowed them to do so. While the crimes committed by the Nazis were penalised by the Great Powers, those committed by the Bolsheviks of the USSR have not even been acknowledged even to date, neither by democratic Russia nor by the UK and the USA, the champions of democracy and freedom. I wonder why the losses of the Polish people under the Soviet Bolsheviks are not comparable to the losses of the Polish Jewish people under the Nazis. Was it because Poland was no longer important for the Great Power countries?

In 2010, there was some hope of Russia accepting full responsibility for the Katyn Forest Massacre. A commemorative event to be attended by the Polish and Russian presidents was planned for 10 April 2010 to mark the 70th anniversary of Katyn. As the sole registered direct heir of one of those killed there, I was invited to go as well. [2] Then I thought that I would rather visit Katyn Military Cemetery at some later date when there are no crowds and pray in silence at my Uncle's symbolic grave, same as I did in Charkov. The plane carrying the Polish president, the crème of the country's decision-makers from all departments of the government and business and family members of those killed in Katyn, 96 people in all, crashed at Smolensk, killing all aboard. Katyn has once again claimed the blood of the best in Poland. Now there will be two memorials. Reports of Russian solidarity have swamped the television channels. Reportedly, Andrej Wajda's 2008 Oscar nominated film 'Katyn' has been shown on Russian television channels. But will Russia take full responsibility for Katyn and the deportations? I wonder, especially whether it will happen within the lifetime of even the youngest of us, affected by the events.

There is a Chinese curse, 'Hope you will live in interesting times.' I do not wish anybody to have an interesting life as mine, especially as a young boy.

NOTES AND REFERENCES

1. Natalia Lebiedova, *Katyn—Genocide of Polish Officers* (Warsaw: Dom Wydawniczy Bellona, 1998).
2. At the time of Franek writing this epilogue, in early 2010, this incident of the plane crash had just happened. He was an invitee to the event and was supposed to have been on the ill-fated flight. Providentially, he had dropped out almost at the last minute.

Looking Back

꧁꧂

hough Franek Herzog has never returned to India since 1948, several of his compatriots from Balachadi have. In April 1989, during a visit of the President of Poland to India, Weislaw Stypula, Stefan Bukowski, their children and a few other Balachadi children from Warsaw returned to install a commemorative plaque at the venue of their former camp (see Photographs 21 and 22). By that time, it was a Sainik School, run in the same military style as the camp had been. Only now, it was a fully boys' school.

The cemeteries at Jamnagar and Kolhapur were also refurbished. The complete project was undertaken by the Poles themselves. The Polish Consul at Bombay was present at both the occasions, signifying the political acceptance of this part of Polish history.

Kira Banasinska, wife of the first PCG to India in 1942, who had spearheaded the mission to get the children to India, was a very special invitee to the occasion. She was 88 years old by then and had been a naturalised citizen of India since 1964. She wrote in her autobiography:

Recently some of my past caught up with me. The children who had lived in our refugee camps, now grown men and women, periodically hold small reunions in various parts of the world, where they have settled. After the war ended and the children departed, the Balachadi camp was not used for any other purpose. Gradually a school came up at the old campsite. In April 1989, when the President of Poland visited India, I was invited to Jamnagar for a function to mark the presentation of a memorial plaque brought from Poland to commemorate the refugee camp there. In Jamnagar the memorial plaque was fixed at the entrance of the new school at a ceremonial function in the presence of a great gathering, which included important dignitaries. At Kolhapur instead of plaque, memorial marble carving were fixed at the graves in the cemetery.

Though there are no visible signs remaining in Balachadi to indicate the site of the camp. Yet the memory of the Polish children who had lived there is still alive in the hearts of the local people. I was present at the function for the installation of the plaque at the school in Jamnagar and I saw an old man pushing his way through the crowds towards one of the Polish visitors who had lived as a child at Balachadi. The two men looked at each other for a while and then embraced each other affectionately. I was told that the old man had been one of the servants at the camp and he looked after the children. The memory of those days even after almost fifty years was still alive in their hearts. It was a touching sight to see the joy of recognition on their faces.

.... The President of Poland told me great changes were likely to be there in Poland after the elections, later that year.[1]

The democratic government of Poland in an acknowledgement of her contribution towards preserving Polish national life, honoured Kira with the Polonia Restituta, Poland's highest civilian award in 1990. Kira was 90 years old by then and had chosen to return and live in India since 1948 with her husband Dr Euginisusz Banasinski. She wrote in her autobiography:

I really do not know how it all happened, but the Embassy came to know about my wartime work and in August 1990, when Poland emerged from behind the Iron Curtain, the Polish Ambassador came to Hyderabad to give me the 'Polonia Restituta' in recognition of the work that I had done for the refugees. It came as a surprise and I was deeply moved to find that after so many years the Polish Government had chosen to recognize my work.[2]

She is probably the only person to have been recognised for her wartime work by the democratic Polish government during her lifetime. The autobiography was commissioned after this at the behest of JRD Tata. She died in 2002 and rests besides her husband in Mahalaxmi cemetery, Bombay.

In 1997, one of the new premier private schools in Warsaw was named after Jam Saheb Digvijaysinghji. 'The pupils of this school will be the custodians of this valuable piece of our common history for generation,' insisted Dr Maria K Byrski, the first Ambassador of sovereign Poland to sovereign India and the Dean, Department of Indology, University of Warsaw.[3] The school already has two campuses and is one of the elite schools of Warsaw, teaching English and foreign languages, which is still a rarity in Poland.

The former Balachadi boys patronise the school and take great pride in its achievements. They invite guests from India and bring school groups to India on a fairly regular basis.

It would be an honour if my daughter, Marysia, is accepted in the Maharaja Jam Saheb School. I would work very hard to help her to qualify. It would be very nice if she goes there and can learn about the history of her grandfather and family.

—Evelyna Gutowski, daughter of Roman Gutowski, Warsaw

In 1994, a group of members of API, London, visited India and Kolhapur in particular. The idea of a monument to commemorate the stay of Poles in India came up during a civic reception, which was hastily grabbed by all present. Colonel Vijay Gaikwad and Vasant Kashikar became actively involved in the project from the Indian side in Kolhapur. Mahavir Garden in Kolhapur city was chosen as the venue for better visibility.

The project was funded from contributions from the members of API spread across the UK, the USA, Canada and Australia. Jan Siedlecki, a former resident of Valivade, an architect by profession and the vice president API, London, designed the monument. It was a column based on the columns from the Mahalaxmi Temple, Kolhapur, but also embodying Christian and Polish elements, with inscription in three languages—Polish, English and Marathi.

The monument was unveiled on 3 February 1998, jointly by Chhatrapati Shahu, Maharaj of Kolhapur, and Polish Consul Ireneusz Makles. Polish charge d'affaires, Dr Krzysztof Debnicki, was present on the occasion. Kira Banasinska, though invited, did not attend this function due to health reasons arising out of old age. A large number of former residents of Valivade travelled to India in a large group for the occasion. This was the second revisit. Most travelled around India as tourists after this function, 'seeing the beautiful country that had been missed earlier'.[4]

Danuta Pniewska reminisces:[5]

It was a long overdue need in us. We were poor refugees then, with little money. Firstly, there was little money to spare for travel, besides we needed a multitude of permissions from the British authorities to be able to. In those days white people had to travel First Class or Second Class. They were not allowed to travel Third Class with ordinary Indians, which obviously cost more and we could not afford it. We have all had jobs now for many years and have retired from active work and it is now possible to travel in India freely without restriction, so we had to make the most of this visit.

When news of the Gujarat earthquake of 26 January 2002 spread, the decision to help with money and resources went around like lightening amongst the former children from Balachadi. An undefined sum of money was raised and sent, which was later untraceable.[6] Subsequently, the Government of Poland decided to sponsor a drinking-water project for Jamnagar. The foundation stone for the 'Samarpan Elevated Drinking Water Storage Reservoir' was laid on 19 August 2001, and it was completed and opened on 10 May 2002.

In April 2003, Franek's friend Stefan Klosowski made the pilgrimage to Balachadi to pay his respects to Jam Saheb and the land that gave him a lease of life. Stefan had just retired from an active career as an aeronautical engineer at Canada.

Franek and Stefan met later that year and relived many memories with Stefan.

On 11 January 2003, a granite plaque was installed at the St Andrews Bobola Church, London, to mark the deliverance of the Poles from Siberia to India, which gave them a lease of life.
The translated text reads:

To the Mother of God
  With thanks for
Our escape from Soviet enslavement
And safe haven in the land of India
—Association of Poles in India, 1943–48

There is now an ongoing discussion about creating a memorial monument for Catherine Clarke, the liaison officer at Balachadi. The matter is still at a nascent stage and is nowhere near fruition at the time of writing this thesis.

Reunions

The Polish people from all over the world had to start from the very beginning all over again. They struggled to make a living, being stripped off their lands, assets, family members, citizenship and often even dignity at the altar of world politics. The 'displaced' Poles formed clubs to be able to socialise amongst themselves without being sneered at, regardless of the jobs they were doing, to keep the home fires burning. At the Polish Hearth Club in Kensington, London, and other such clubs, the men used to address each other with their full wartime rank and decorations, as a measure of recuperating their self-worth.

It is probably in these clubs that the origin of the API 1942–48 can be traced. All those who survived Siberia called themselves the *Sybiryakis*, and those who cherished the dignified existence in India, in spite of the other losses, called themselves the *Indacys*.

In communist Poland, cut off from virtually the rest of the world, the *Indacys* from Balachadi and Valivade banded together. In the late 1970s, a 'Jamnagar Club' was legally set up by Wieslaw Stypula, which functioned under the umbrella of 'Indo-Polish Friendship Society'.[7]

Once these clubs and societies were set up, they started meeting more regularly. The Jamnagar Club started holding its reunions every two years with regularity, a fact confirmed by Indian diplomats posted to Warsaw at different times. With the dismantling of the communist structure in Poland and other democratic rights restored, including contact with foreign nationals, the Jamnagar Club became the Warsaw chapter of the API 1942–48. Since then, the participation at these reunions is fervent (see Photograph 23—members of the API with HE Mr Anil Wadhwa and Reverend Z Peszkovski at Katowicz, Poland in 2004).

In the Western World

While no details are available about the date of the first reunion, the second meeting of the API 1943–48 resulted in the production of the commemorative album *Youth in Valivade* in 1973. The album is a compilation of old pictures, memories and snippets of information from the years spent in India and the activities carried out then.

Subsequently, a biannual bulletin of the API 1942–48 began to be brought out. It is published in Polish from the UK and is privately circulated amongst the members. It usually carries information about any links with India, including visits, activities of the API, reunions, etc., besides translations of documents by members and memories. Though members from Australia contribute articles and subscribe to the API bulletin from London, they also bring out an annual magazine of their own around Christmas every year.

The fact that the practices are continuing 60 years since the Poles' departure from India, in spite of declining number of survivors, reflects the strength of their bonds and the love for the time spent in India. More recently, membership to the API has been opened to the children of survivors. It was during such reunions that the idea of revisiting India, the land of their childhood, came up.

The Third Revisit

The third revisit of the members of the API took place in February 2005, after more than a year of planning. Roman Gutowski, the former Balachadi child, was accompanied by his wife, daughter and son-in-law in a group dominated by former Valivade campers. While no new monument was installed anywhere, it was full of nostalgia and warmth in the two days spent in Kolhapur on 8 and 9 February 2005. Amongst the 24 member group, 11 were true 'Indians' (former campers), five were second generation 'Indians' (either parent was an 'Indian') and the rest were spouses.

The visit was a melee of receptions organised by the local people of Kolhapur and the places the visitors wanted to revisit—Valivade Station where they first disembarked; Valivade camp, Panhala, where they went for scouting and the Panchganga riverside, the venue of childhood pranks. There were also wreath-laying functions at the cemetery, monument and St Xavier's School.

Polish Consul at Bombay, Mr Marek Moroni, attended all the functions on 8 February, starting with a wreath laying at the cemetery, the monument and at St Xavier's school, civic reception in Town Hall and at Mahavir Garden and the private dinner hosted by Colonel Gaikwad. This visit was duly recorded in the local press. On 9 February 2005, the visitors were invited to tea at the palace by Chhatrapati Shahu Maharaj, as had been done on the occasion of their earlier visit.

The warmth and fervour showed by the Indians was heartening. The Poles were well received not only by the who's who of the city but also common people.

Former vegetable vendors, milkmen and ice-cream vendors turned up at one or either public function. Teresa Bereznicka, a second generation 'Indian', met the ice-cream vendor Solanke at one of the public functions, where he came calling out 'Aniela! Aniela' and recited the names of all the children of the family. It turned out to be Teresa's aunt, mother and uncle. Similarly, Roman Gutowski met the milkman who used to supply milk at the orphanage. 'He used to let us drink extra milk every other day by rotation', said an emotional Gutowski. Sonawane, a vegetable vendor, turned up with a boyhood picture with Polish customers. 'They always put a few extra coins in my pocket after their purchase', he said looking to find familiar faces amongst the visitors. Hubert Bock, one of the spouses, was impressed by the invitation from Shahu Maharaj. He said, 'I have never been entertained by a Maharaja and cannot imagine once poor refugees in the State being received as guests of honour by a person of such stature several years later, in the West.'[8]

A fortnight later, the visitors were hosted to a reception in New Delhi by His Excellency the Ambassador of Poland to India, in spite of most of them being citizens of other countries.

While leaving from Delhi, Roman Gutowski commented,

> We could not go to Balachadi since it was not on the itinerary. That is the most important place in India for me. We are so few of us from Balachadi that our voice does not count in the large group of those from Valivade. Balachadi was an experience for us that even those from Valivade, who have very similar experiences like us, cannot understand. We were only children without families there and were children the only time other than when we were with our families in Poland.

NOTES AND REFERENCES

1. K Banasinska and G Verghese, *Autobiography of Kira Banasinska* (Mumbai: Kotak & Co., 1997), 137–38.
2. Ibid., 138.
3. MK Byrski, interview to author, Warsaw, March 2004.
4. J Siedlecki, interview to author, London, 2004.
5. D Pniewska, interview to author, London, May 2005.
6. S Klosowski, interview to author, Balachadi, 2002.
7. A Neizgoda, '1000 children of the Maharaja', *Polityka* (2001), dated 2 June. English translation of article by Jan Siedlecki.
8. H Bock, videotaped interview to author, Kolhapur, 9 February 2005.

Voices from the Past

CRXO

hile the diary of Franek Herzog accompanies us throughout the narrative, the testimonies of some others have been
included in this chapter to present a range of experiences
that engulfed the children of Balachadi as they left India. Their perspec-
tives and reminiscences 60 years later have been presented here to give a
sense of the dispersion that followed the event presented in this work. All
these people have remained in the country they had reached after leaving
India.

There are children of Balachadi who live in Canada, Argentina and
South Africa, having reached there from the UK, besides those in the
countries mentioned above. There were several others who generously
shared their memories in interviews that could not be published here
due to various constraints but whose contribution is just as important
and significant.

Hershad Kumariji, Daughter of Jam Saheb Digvijaysinghji

Jam Saheb's eldest daughter, Hershad Kumariji (see Photographs 24 and
25) was interviewed in June 2004. She was about six years old at the time
and had been a part of the entourage that had received the Polish children
at Jamnagar. These interviews were carried out in New Delhi between June
2003 and June 2004.

I am Hershad Kumari, the late Jam Saheb's eldest daughter. I was six years old and present when the Polish children came to Nawanagar. They were a bunch of miserable looking, sad lot, slightly afraid of what was there, not knowing what awaited them. We, that is, my brother, about four years old then, and I, were there with my governess AnnieBa, Colonel Geoffrey Clarke, my father's liaison officer and Cathy, his wife when they arrived. I don't know how much my brother remembers about that day, but the most I remember is them scrambling out of their train looking totally terrified coming into this land where everything was so different. Soon they were quite happy as they received the warmth, and knowing those days and the traditions, they would have been given something to nibble at. So, that must have cheered them up a bit because they really looked underfed when they came. They were very emaciated. We were told that they had been cared for for some weeks now, and I wondered how they had been before that, for they were such a sad and miserable-looking bunch.

My memories are childhood memories, of children who looked miserable and were very different from us, who seemed terrified of everything around them. Then we saw them come out of it and become happy children. We thought of them as one more lot of the extended family that was there. We used to go and play with them and see them on their festivals. They used to celebrate all the festivals. They had a Polish school in that place. They were and became literate by the time they left, even the little ones. The youngest, I think, when this lot came, must have been two or three years old or less. There were a couple of kids that were being carried, not walking yet.

We received them, saw them go off to Balachadi, which had been quickly built temporary huts at that time. Most of it was still unfinished. We just saw them as a batch and wondered who they were why they were there till we started going to the camps and meeting with them, and till they started learning some [English] language and had some people to translate to gradually understand what they had undergone.

The next time we saw them, they were all in their uniforms, all wearing the same clothes, running around, hustling and bustling. Their routine had been worked out. They had a bunch of very sincere and loving adults who had come with them. I remember a lady called Yasha or was she Sasha. My brother and I used to go there with our governesses, at first a little taken aback. Gradually, we learnt to communicate in a childish fashion—different languages—but we communicated and learnt that they had suffered, they didn't have parents, some knew that they had lost them, including that they had been killed. These are all vague childhood memories.

On Visiting the Camp

In summer, we stayed a stone's throw away from them, at our seaside summer resort. We used to go sometimes in March to be there till the rains came. So, during those months, we saw them all the time, because there was just a little bit of a beach between them and us. We were on a little island which had been joined by a little roadway and they were on the mainland on the other side of the beach. So, we saw them at the beach, in the camp, they'd come over to our place. I think they came only once in my memory, but we went there all the time—when we went for our rides or walks. When we were not in the summer camp, when we were back in Jamnagar, we used to go there for special occasions—Sunday when something was happening, we'd go across and see them. So, we never got to know them intimately because there was the language barrier. It was more child language and body language that we got by with. We saw them more frequently than we saw other children of other schools. This was just like any other group. We didn't think of them as foreigners for more than a few days. We thought of them as one lot of unhappy Jamnagaris who needed looking after. They used to come for my father's birthday. They came for my brother's birthday and they came for what used to be the National Day of Nawanagar—Tilak Day.

On the Nawanagar Offer

I can't tell you with certainty, but what we were told was that my father used to know some of the Polish people, especially one their most famous pianists, when my father and uncles used to spend time at Ranji's chateau in Switzerland as a boy. During the lunch breaks of one of the IWC meetings in London, he heard the details about the circumstances of the Polish children—that they had nowhere to go, no country was willing to receive them, etc., and offered to take on their responsibility. It apparently upset the British government because they were not quite in tune with this offer. So, he said that he was not asking them but inviting them to Nawanagar as his guests. Finally, after a lot of correspondence, etc., which I learnt later from Colonel Clarke that it was finally said, 'you can receive them and we cannot agree about them being looked after by the State'. He said, 'they will be my personal guests'. They were actually paid for from his allowance or whatever it was called in those days but not from the State Treasury. They were totally maintained by my father.

I know that the camp was built against everybody's wishes. Even the State Treasury had objections. But that camp was built, I don't recall ever hearing of any money collected anywhere coming there.

On Feasibility of Maintaining a Child on ₹40 Per Month

In those days, ₹40 per month wouldn't have fed a child. By that time grain and things had gone so much up in price that our domestics, etc., were all bemoaning the price of *bajra* (the staple food of our side), terribly upset as that which had been 6 *anna*s a *maund* had become 14 *anna*s a *maund* (a *maund* is about 40 kg and an *anna* was four paisa or a sixteenth of a rupee before it converted to the metric system). They lamented, 'how are we going to make both ends meet?' And [the Polish children] would have used wheat for their camp which would be more expensive compared to *bajra*. Veggies were not expensive. In my estimate, per day, a child's food would have cost ₹3 with milk and all. They used to be given milk and sugar was rationed towards the end of the War. Those facts I can't tell for sure as they would not have interested a child of six. I just remember the bemoaning of all the servants about *bajra* becoming 14 *anna*s a *maund*.

On Jam Saheb Donating Money to the Camp Directly

That sounds very plausible because if he was putting up the camp, then why would he go through all this rigmarole of some [system] that was obviously not disbursing enough. In those days, even ₹50 wouldn't have fed them for a month. However, I do remember some sports equipment being bought—football, volleyball, etc. They had learnt some Indian games as well—kho kho and hockey. The sticks were a problem as one couldn't get junior-size hockey sticks—it was wartime and there were no stocks coming in and we [Indians] were not manufacturing them at that time.

So, all the sports equipment was bought by my father because I remember we children looking at all this sports equipment that was going somewhere. That was when we realized that no one else could have sports equipment. I was six and my brother was still very young. The only thing that my brother had was a small cricket bat that he hit tennis balls with. So, we suddenly realized that this has come to make some games possible. So, after that, we started indenting to our father what we wanted depending on the games we wanted to play. That's how we got a mini ping-pong table. Then we were told to play badminton, then we got little hockey sticks which our uncle, Himmatsinghji brought for us. But a lot of equipment had come for the Polish children.

On the Use of Royal Buildings for the Polish Camp

They began their school in one of my uncle's premises that was next to the camp. He had a sort of a summer palace which was a pool with some rooms around it. It had a little courtyard and some outhouses. The school began there and towards the end they had a school building inside the camp itself. To begin with, they were at Himmatkaka's, what he used to call, his farmhouse.

When we were not there, they had free use of the tennis and squash courts. When we were staying there in the summer, they were limited to some timing that suited the family. When we used to go there for the summers, the whole administration used to move there, so everything used to move there. We were a sporting lot, so they must have worked out some fixed timing.

On Visiting Jamnagar

I think they came for my brother's birthday which was at the Pratap Vilas Palace. There were children's parties in the grounds. I think they also came for my father's birthday, but perhaps not to the palace. There used to be celebrations in line with the Sports Day in March each year—10 days of sports to mark Raja-Rani's birthdays. There used to be parades and celebrations. I think the Polish kids took part in the parades. They came and celebrated that day at the Sports Grounds.

On Christmas Celebrations

My most vivid memories are of the St Niklaus Day and seeing them all dressed up. They had put as many as they could in their Polish costumes, and dances. Three camels came in bearing the incense and things for the celebrations, as they visualized it from the Bible. There was no Father Christmas, but St Niklaus, followed after Jesus Christ, was born.

There was a nativity scene and the camels decorated the way they were visualized, from Middle Asian kings coming to see baby Jesus Christ—all bedecked in orange and green—all kinds of things that they visualized; half was the local tradition and the extra touches they wanted given. That image is still with me—the Polish children coming up on the slat, up the incline. That day we got the dolls. The next festival we got the dresses—both my brother and I. I don't know what my brother has done with his, but I still have mine. Once we had a meal with them without any festivities. My brother didn't eat anything, but I ate happily.

On Warm Memories of Balachadi

Yes, they are bound to. If they had the sort of rough time that they had before, then they are bound to. Here at least they were at peace, no doubt. They had a very good medical system in Jamnagar and a diminished, but a very good one, in the camp itself. There was everything possible in Jamnagar itself. In Rajkot maybe X-rays and things as that was where the British seat was. Rajkot was the centre of the AGG—assistant governor general for Kathiawar. I believe they have named a street after my father. [It is a school in fact.].

The last time they were there, they said that they would like to do something to express their gratitude. The present Jam Saheb (my brother) told them about the water shortage in the area and they contributed a water-storage tank in an area that did not have a direct water supply. So, now a whole section of Jamnagar enjoys the water that comes through their taps.

On the Chela Camp

There was a lack of proper homework or research. It was meant for the RAF. They wanted to build an airstrip, so this area, Chela, was identified as there were no farmlands that had to be moved away to proceed. But, there was something wrong with the soil. When the first rains came, it all sank. So, when the plan for the airstrip was cancelled, they might have thought that this would make a good camp for the children. But the first monsoons came and the buildings also started sinking. So, nobody did ever stay there.

On Colonel Clarke's Position towards the Camp

Besides the fact that it was costing my Father's private accounts, he was very keen on seeing to their welfare. He was very proud about having so many children. Geoffrey and Cathy were there practically every day because she used to look after the health side of it till they were completely organized. Geoffrey and Bapu used to go there very often. In fact, Geoffrey used to go there even when Bapu was not there.

On the Poles as Citizens of Nawanagar

Yes, Bapu had made them all—children and adults alike—citizens of Nawanagar. He used to tell us that they are Jamnagaris just as you or the others. That way he had adopted the whole jing-bang lot.

Alina Baczyk Haus

Alina Baczyk Haus (see Photographs 26 and 27) was amongst the orphaned children who reached Balachadi. She was one of the 50 girls adopted by the Bernadine Sisters of Pennsylvania, USA. She has lived and raised a family in Pennsylvania ever since after. This interview was carried out over extensive emails after Alina had put up her story 'Alina's Odyssey' on the Internet for a while in 2003–04.

I was born in Wolkowysk, Bialystok, Poland. It is now in Belarus; the eastern part of the country has changed hands many, many times. My parents were Antoni and Albertyna Baczyk. I was a sickly child; they said, I had a 'nervous heart'. We now know it was a congenital heart defect, a bicuspid aortic valve.

My very early childhood was uneventful until 1939 when the attack on Poland by Hitler and then Stalin happened. Since Bialystok was in the eastern part of Poland, in 1940, we were occupied by the USSR. As my father was a city official (Henryk and I think he was the Police Chief of Wolkowysk), he was considered a political enemy by the Soviet government and was arrested. Later, my mother, brother and myself were deported to Siberia, where mother, and later my brother, were used as forced labour. This was the second time for my mother, as she had also been deported during the First World War.

We were moved to wherever there was work to be done. The Russian people tried to help us whenever possible, but they risked being deported to Siberia if they were found out. I received about two years of intermittent Soviet schooling since I was often sick. My brother also tells me that I almost died from dysentery. Food was always scarce; I can remember having to eat soup made of grass fed to the dromedaries.

We were able to make our way south to seek refuge with relatives who lived there. I think it was at Samarkand, where one of mother's brothers who had been taken prisoner in the First World War had married a local girl and settled there. He had prospered and was by then an official of some kind. He helped us, but when it was discovered by the communist party that he had a German as well as Polish background, he was deported to Siberia. We never saw him again. I have recently come to know that he was finally released and allowed to return to Samarkand. Mother's family name was 'Resh' and although my mother was born in Poland, some of her older siblings apparently were born in Germany! [Poland had emerged from territories held under Germany, Austria and parts of Tsarist Russia at the end of the First World War.]

Henryk tells me that a Polish army was formed in the USSR to help fight the Germans. Several thousand former prisoners of war and deportees from the Soviet Union became the Polish Second Corps. We were in the first wave of evacuation and got separated in the USSR. Mother went to Palestine with the Polish Army and we children went to India as orphans.

Henryk relates that the Prime Minister of Poland in exile in London, Ignacy Paderewski, the famous pianist and composer, was a personal friend of the Maharaja of Nawanagar, and after the Russians were attacked by the Germans, the Maharaja offered a part of his estate to establish a camp for Polish children in 1942. Somehow transportation was found and we were sent with a convoy across the mountains of Persia (now Iran) and Afghanistan to India and reached the camp for Polish children at Jamnagar.

I spent the years 1942–47 in India, as one of about 500 Polish orphans that escaped from Siberia. Because the Maharaja was personally acquainted with the Polish Prime Minister and musician, Ignacy Paderewski, he allowed a camp to be built on his land for the Polish orphans. I was 10 years old when we arrived in Bombay. We stayed there for some months until the camp was ready to house all the children and the adults who took care of us. The camp was in Balachadi, off Jamnagar.

Having to live in an orphanage did not afford me a chance to see India as a tourist would. We simply attended school from 7 a.m. each morning until 1 p.m. After that, we had to stay indoors and actually were made to lie down because of being the hottest part of the day. In those days, air-conditioning was unheard of! After 3 p.m., we usually went swimming in the ocean, which was very enjoyable. Occasionally, the Maharajas would invite children to visit the palace and a few of us were selected to go. The flowers and greenery at and surrounding his estate were beautiful.

The part I enjoyed the most was camping as a Girl Scout, the beauty of the country, the climate and the moonlit nights. Being

young and romantic, as most girls that age are, I used to write poetry by the light of the moon. Another thing that stands out in
my memory is the electrical storms we sometime experienced. It
seemed the whole sky was lit up. The monsoon season was another
thing, with the scorpions crawling under our feet afterwards. One
of the few things that took some getting used to was that the cows
were allowed to roam the streets; also the poor and homeless beggars. I must say that every country has its share of the poor and
homeless, so India isn't alone in that respect.

After the War was over and the Indian people started demanding their independence, the people in charge of us started looking
to place us into different parts of the world. I left India in 1947 for
the United States. I loved living in India and have most pleasant
memories of my time there. My memories of the camp in India
are pleasant.

In 1944, Henryk finally got a letter from our mother, who had
located us with the help of the International Red Cross. My mother
had managed to get out of the USSR after joining the Polish Army
and was then in Palestine. However, we were unable to join her
there. By 1946, arrangements were made to send us to other countries. Henryk was to join the Polish Navy after a training in the UK.
[His name appears in a list of boys scheduled to go to the Polish
Maritime Training Academy in the UK.] I was accepted amongst a
group of 50 girls by the Bernadine Sisters at Mt Alveria Convent,
Reading, Pennsylvania.

Life in the USA

I landed at San Francisco on 27 February 1947. We travelled by
rail to Villa Maria in Stamford, Connecticut, for a rush course in
English. After learning enough to get by, we came to Reading in
August of 1947 and were enrolled in the orphanage and parochial
high school there. All classes were in English (there were no English
as a second language courses then) but I did fine in school. The big
shock, however, was when we were told that the Mother Superior
expected us all to become nuns! My faith in God was strong, but I
had no desire to live the life of a nun.

Intervention, Divine or otherwise, was on the way. There was an infirmary at the convent for nuns who were ill with tuberculosis. However, they were allowed to walk the grounds and mingle with others. We were taken on a trip to give a Polish play at various catholic parishes throughout America in order to raise money to defray the cost of bringing us here. The schedule was too much for me and I became very ill, and finally, was diagnosed with pneumonia. We returned to Mt Alvernia and I was admitted to the Infirmary. In my weakened condition, I contracted tuberculosis from the sick nuns and was finally sent to the Berks Count (Pennsylvania) Tuberculosis Sanatorium for treatment. I was terribly lonely there but I did make some friends, among them a student nurse, Joan, who also had TB and was in the bed next to mine. Among her visitors were an aunt and her husband who were usually driven there by her stepson, Frank Haus.

Frank and I were married on 26 October 1952. In 1954, our first son, Jere Robert was born at the Ephrata Community Hospital, and in September of the same year, we purchased our first home. On Friday, 16 November 1956, in a group of 25 excited people, I became a citizen of the greatest nation in the world, the United States of America. In 1957, our second son Mark Anthony was born. Time went by, and Frank continued to advance in his chosen profession. Things generally were good, naturally with a few bumps along the way. After a little over 12 years, wonder of wonders, I was pregnant again! We thought it would be a girl this time. In February of 1970, our third son, Christopher Franklin arrived before the remodelling work in the house was quite finished. Having a new baby again made us young.

Reunion

Henryk joined the Polish Maritime services from India. By the time he finished training, the War was over. So he stayed in the UK doing some jobs. When immigration for Australia was allowed, he moved there and lived in Melbourne till he died recently. In Australia, he has formally changed his name to Henry Bonshek.

In 1972, we were able to fly to England and travel to Huddersfield in Yorkshire. After 32 years, I saw my mother again. I met my stepfather Stefan (also a Baczyk) and half-sister Kazia and her husband Stanislaw (Stash) Brzezinski for the first time. It sounded a bit odd that my mother married two men with the same last name! What a grand time at the reunion! The week went by so fast it seemed like a dream.

It hardly seems possible that by Thanksgiving of 2009 it will be 31 years that we have lived here! The boys are all married and on their own. Our oldest son lives in North Carolina, the second one lives in Alabama and the youngest lives all the way 1.8 miles from us! And now we have a big bonus. They have a son, Spencer Christopher, and a daughter, Danielle Marie. Finally, to have both a grandson and granddaughter is like icing on the cake.

Marian Raba

Marian Raba (see Photographs 28 and 29) stayed on in the UK after reaching there, as described by Franek, helped along by the scouting fraternity. He lived in Leicester and was very ill at the time of the interview in 2005. The interview was carried out against medical advice. He died soon after.

My name is Marian Bronislaw Raba. I was born on 13th of April 1936 in Lvov, which was a Polish city at that time. My father was from a noble family of Poland and was a member of the House of Lords. My family of my mother, two sisters and two brothers besides myself were deported to Russia, where I lost my mother and younger brother. My father, who was in the Polish Army, had left during the mobilization. We never really knew his whereabouts since then. So after our mother's death, we became orphans. I reached India from Kazakhstan, Uzbekistan and Persia, with the Polish Army via Meshed, Persia, through Afghanistan to Balachadi, Gujarat, in India. It was an orphanage in Balachadi, where there were 600 or so Polish orphan boys and girls. We were looked after by a Polish priest called Father Franciszek Pluta. The immediate lady who looked after me was Pani Dobrostanska [mother of Tadeusz Dobrostanski]. At Balachadi my brother Henry was with me. We had two sisters, but they were in the Polish Army in Palestine.

Our campus was situated on hill which overlooked the sea. The school was situated in one of the Maharaja's palaces or hunting lodge. There was also a lake nearby which used to get filled with ducks and once a year there was shooting of the ducks there. There was a school and a hospital there. The hospital was one of the barracks and the hunting lodge was converted into school. From Jamnagar, there were outings to Maharaja's palaces. Once or twice we visited. I was lucky enough to participate in the jubilee celebrations of his rule, with another Polish girl, Bozena. Once we had an opportunity to visit the British fleet. They sent lorries, who took us onto the boats. There for the first time in my life, I saw a film. They were all Micky Mouse and Walt Disney's film. I was just amazed. I thought it was something out of this world. Every Christmas, we used to put up a show, the Christmas nativity show which was more enjoyed by the Maharaja and his entourage than us, because we knew it by heart.

We were taught or at least I was taught, as one of the youngest boys, by two Catholic Brothers, Brother Oskar and Brother Eustachy. They were very severe and if we didn't learn our English words, we were punished. We were lucky enough to be allowed to go to the sea once in a while.

We seldom kept with the main group and roamed the place freely. Often we escaped and went to the palace. I think, it was built on a rock on the sea and it was a picture of luxury to us after living in the mud houses and camps, in Kazakhstan. It had a golf course. The grass was cut everyday and it shimmered like glass. There we also saw for the first time, two elephants with their *mahouts*, sitting over them. Being boys, we escaped from the camp and would come back with these discoveries. We often got a good beating for escaping, but that didn't help. We continued, because we wanted to know what lay beyond the farthest hill.

While in Balachadi, I caught malaria. I didn't know what it was when I started shivering. I thought that the Devil had possessed me. I was hiding in the room. The other boys found me, took me to hospital. Thanks to fatherly care of the wonderful doctor, Dr Ashani, who was helped by Dr Joshi, after two or three days, the temperature dropped. Later, we were given another Polish doctor from the Polish Army whose name I cannot recall. And my stay in Balachadi, Jamnagar, was the best part of my life. We had plenty to do. There was schooling every day, exercises, scouting and cultural activities.

I was accepted as a scout on 11th November 1944. I was very proud when for the occasion of our swearing in, the scoutmaster Zladyslaw Peszkovski flew in from Middle East. His scouting name was Rhys Zuch, which means 'wild cat'. After that, I felt I was grown up because I had the scout cross on my shirt and lapels to show.

Balachadi is the happiest period of my life when we mixed with the local children and learnt to speak a few dirty words in Gujarati. The joy didn't last very long. After three and half years, we were told that we will be moved to another camp, so everybody was very sad and in tears because we got to know local people. They were all simple people from the village like *dobi*, the laundryman and he had two white oxen on the cart with which again, he used to come to collect the wash. He would load them and smack them, they went to the village to his wife, where she unloaded them, loaded them back again and smack the oxen's bottom and they would come back. Sometimes, we used to jump on and have a free ride from the camp to the village Balachadi. We also had this *chaukidar*, with his big waxed moustaches and tight trousers. He held us down as a policeman while we were smacked. No grudges against him. Then there was a mendicant I had never forgotten. He had red hair and a red beard. I thought that he was thousand years old because he never moved. And people who helped in the kitchen—our cook was from Goa.

Maharaja Jam Saheb came on special occasions for which we used to be collected in the square with the Polish flag on it. That was our central point and meeting with the guests. Once the Pope came. [It was the Bishop of Poona]. Otherwise, every morning, we did a bit of gymnastics at the square, after which we have to have a shower and reassemble for prayers after breakfast. The Polish flag was raised up on a pole in the morning. And the same thing was repeated during the evening prayers when the Polish flag was lowered and tied for the night, after which we went to the barracks for sleep.

Now, we were taught to address all elderly men and women as Mr and Mrs respectively, and when we applied that to the Indian people, they were surprised that white people addressing them respectfully in those occupied days of India, especially when the English were kicking them around.

We used to go to Balachadi often, and there were many peacocks in the lodge. In fact, they used to chase us. We collected their feathers and used them in our Polish Cracovian costumes. Once one of the boys desecrated the temple, and the whole village was very upset. We were all smacked. I stole the food in the temple a few times though. Boys are boys and always hungry. We used to have bread for breakfast and yellow rice with meat and spices for lunch [biryani]. The Goan cooks made it in a very special way, and we could never find it again in England. In the evening, it was tea and fruits, mostly bananas. I never looked at bananas again after reaching England. Every day they told us that millions of people starve in India and in my young mind I wondered how, with the abundance of fruits around—sugarcane, bananas, coconuts and dates—all that could be had by merely reaching out.

Yes, looking back now, the food was mean, but after Russia, it was heaven. I don't know whether we have bigger stomachs or bigger mouths that we need to fill, but Indians also eat that much and work in the fields all day.

Just after we reached, we were told not to associate with the villagers. But what is the first thing that you do at that age—rebel. Children don't discriminate between black, brown or pink. So, there we were playing with the village words. We learnt some swear words in Gujrati from the local boys; they teased us with '*Lolo*, cut, cut', implying circumcised. I remember, a knife is *chakoo*, isn't it? And a pigeon *kabootar*, *sosa* is rabbit, *kutra*, a dog. It was very easy for us to pick it. I could even write my name in Hindi, but I don't think I will be able to do that now. The numbers are *ek, do, teen, char, panch, chha, saat, aath, nao, das.*

We all sang the Nawanagar anthem once when the Maharaja was visiting, and he seemed quite pleased. Now he was a large man and it was difficult to find a comfortable enough chair for him till [ND] Marshall got a large enough cane chair for him from Jamnagar.

Since the Indians told us not to kill any animals, we had them for pets in the camp—a little roedeer, Basia; she was found as a baby and the cooks fed her milk with the children's bottle. She used to follow us everywhere like a dog. We also had a bulldog who had to be shot; a shaggy dog, Abu; a mongoose who used to have these long duels with the cobras around and a stork [flamingo] from the lake. The stork had a broken wing and the other storks nearly killed him. We rescued him and got him to our hospital where Dr Ashani put a piece of wood under his wing and bandaged it. It took one season to recover. In the second season, he flew away. Maharaja presented us with a pair of speckled birds on his return from perhaps States. We almost had a small zoo in the camp with so many animals including a few ducks. In fact, Basia muzzled Maharaja during one of his visits to the camp. He was so affectionate. He would call us all to sit around him. Of course, [ND] Marshall was always there to tell us what not to do include touch him. But he was very affectionate. He accepted whatever we children did. Balachadi was the happiest time of my childhood. I don't remember my father, and my mother's face is hazy now since I was only four years old when we were taken to Russia. My father had been taken first by the Russians to Kolyma. Later, we came to know that he had joined Berling's Army and had marched to Berlin. My mother, of course, had been with me in Russia till she died. So, the memories of early childhood in Poland are very few, and all the other happy ones are from Balachadi. Jam Saheb was a father figure to all of us. He was the Maharaja and everybody respected him, but I respected him like a father.

During one of the visits, there was Polish music. Maharaja enjoyed it and he was clapping very enthusiastically. You know how solemn they are, majestic. Suddenly he became one of us. He was just normal. He was human being. We didn't have to bow in front of him. There was always this twinkle in his eyes and a big smile when he was around. He'd pat here, pat down there for us kids. We needed that. You know we were orphans. He was a big man, but we were not afraid of him. I'm sure, if he'd put his arms out, I would run in and hug him, but the Polish priest—no. But seeing him and being told that he was king, but finding all this humanity in him was very warm.

His children, two of them, used to come with medicines and things, especially at Christmas time for the nativity play.

After all our journeys through Uzbekistan, Tashkent, Ashkabad, Meshed and Afghanistan to India, we felt like lepers or beggars, very degraded. I did not like the pity that we got from the English, 'Oh! Poor boy' and all that. I threw away the chocolate that I was given, even though I was hungry. But we accepted the presents from Maharaja Jam Saheb, because we knew they were from the heart. I don't know how we knew it, but we did.

Yes, then when we were leaving, then too Maharaja came. We all got a little basket of food each, half a duck, I suppose the ones that were shot in the lake. And then we all said goodbye amidst a lot of crying. The only thing that struck in my mind he said that if ever we were in trouble we have to turn to him and he will give us a hope and look after us. So he was like a father to us. Many times in life I have wanted to go back to India.

After this farewell, I think we spent two or three days in the train to reach Kolhapur. Many times in life I have wanted to go back to India. Valivade, in Kolhapur, was a big Polish camp with about 5,000 people. Our orphanage was also within the camp site. There were schools—primary, secondary and special schools. There were lot of girls there, and they had High School, Commercial School and Sewing School for the girls and a Gardening School, with their own gardens. We used to pinch the papaya, tomatoes, cucumbers that they grew there. Papaya and mangoes were my favourite fruits. It was quite an easy and interesting time … was never as good as Balachadi in Jamnagar. In Balachadi we were only 600 and in Valivade, there were 5,000 people.

From Valivade, in March 1948, I reached UK as my sister's dependant. She was a nurse in the military at Cairo. We were quarantined off Southampton. The neon sign said *Osram* which is a swear word in Polish. It did give us a strange feeling about whether we were being welcomed at all in UK. It was still winter and we had no warm clothes. It was especially hard after the warm climate of India.

It was my dream to go back to India, just to lead the simple life of the village—eat simple chapatti and *bhaji*, onion *bhaji* or meat *bhaji*. But for the paperwork needed to travel, I would love to simply go and live the simple village life. Just keep the mosquitoes out. How can we ever repay the kindness that we had received from the simple Indian village people as children. We learnt so much from them.

Several times I have eaten at their houses, when I was late in returning to the camp after wandering around near the sea and bushes. I knew I wouldn't get food in the camp and would have to sleep on a hungry stomach. I had had enough of hunger in Russia. So I would go into one of the houses and say 'Mama, *chapatti*'. And the woman would put a little mat for me to sit and give a few chapatti with some *bhaji* or the hot pickle on a metal plate with some water, *paani*. I have probably done that three or four times in my three years in Balachadi. I wouldn't have heart to take something from them now, they had so little. But the happiest memories of my childhood are those from India, Balachadi. It was absolutely different from Russia. It was human response to us. Because before you were a number, as a slave labour. Nobody cared about you. If you were in a ditch, they would kick you in and leave you there. In India, it was kindness, from everybody. In India, it was, if you are hungry, you are fed, if you are thirsty, you get water, if you are sick, you get treated. So much like the Poles where it is 'guest at home is God at home', which is once someone comes through your door should be treated like God.

And all that time there was a war going on in Europe. We didn't know much because we were kids then. They didn't tell us much to keep us from being upset. They just said, your father, your brother, your mother, they are fighting for your country. The news coming in through the radio was in English, so those who knew English knew. The teachers wouldn't tell us very much because we were very young then.

But my heart is there in India. That smell, the air, you know when you approach the village, whether it was the smoke, I don't know. That smell is still there, you can smell something in the air. I can't explain that. But there is a special comradeship that all of us from Balachadi share—helping each other out during times of need. We were a few hundred in Balachadi and three fourths went from here to Canada and USA and other places, so we are maybe a hundred or less from Balachadi in England now. But it is a special bond.

Ok I'm soft, but when we all meet in London and remember Balachadi, everybody goes yes, yes. My best friend in London is from Valivade. He is jealous when we talk about Maharaja in Jamnagar. He says, 'Even I was in India why didn't I have all these?' Well I say, don't you see, this warmth, you come from Russia and its mud house. People dropping dead here and there. Suddenly this human being, the king, smiles at you, pats you, takes your hand. For us, it was like nearest thing to our Polish Pope [Pope John Paul II] whom the young people loved so much.

On Reuniting with His Father in 1961

My father had been transported to Kolyma in the northeast part of Russia, where he was made to work in the gold mines. He left the place to join the Polish Army being formed down in south, in Uzbekistan, Kazakhstan. By the time he travelled south, he was too late; no more Poles were being allowed to leave Russia. So he joined the Berling's Army [which was formed after the Anders' Army left USSR]. He went to battle with them to the western front in Germany and won Berlin. He was decorated with the highest medals then. But it is interesting the way I found him.

During my first holiday after getting my first job, I went to Poland as I had always promised myself. I went to the Church of the Our Black Lady to thank her for keeping me alive. Then I went to the main Red Cross Office in Poland, left my address saying that I was looking for my father, or any surviving family. Poland was under communist rule then, so the secret police caught up with me and questioned me for three days about what I was doing in Poland and why I had come back after leaving.

Some weeks later my friend went to Poland to attend the funeral of her mother. When she came back she said, 'When you went to Poland, you had wished that someone from your family who survived might still be living in Poland. Well, there is one such person—your father'. I went into a complete state of shock. After twenty years? She said a doctor in her late mother's village had told her that a Colonel Bronislaw Raba was looking for his children Henry, Marian, Ireana, Helena and Piotr. Well, it matched all our names, though Piotr had died in Russia. So I sent a reply paid telegram to that doctor, 'Dear doctor, you told Mrs. X. that my father Mr B Raba was alive. I want his address, full name and my address is....' Three days later, a telegram arrived with the name of my father and his address. So I sent another telegram to that address. In those days, there was danger that it might land in the hands of imposters who might want a passage to England; so it read, 'Mr Raba, You claim to be my father. I want documentary proof for that'. Several days later I got a letter, 'Dear son, I was glad to hear from you but I was so sad that my son is asking me a proof that I am his father'. The letter had many parts cut out by the censors. The same day there was a letter from the Polish Red Cross that said, 'Dear Raba, you were enquiring about your father. Your father is alive'. The censors had got the communication, checked with the local authorities whether he was really there, and so, there were two letters the same day; one from my father and the other from the Polish Red Cross.

Then after some days, my father gets a letter from the British Embassy saying that your son is looking for you. If you come to the Embassy, you will get a visa straight away. In the meanwhile, I had two visitors from the Foreign Office, black suits and bowler hats, the perfect English gentlemen, asking me when I was expecting him. They gave some details which would hasten the issuance of his visa, but the same question again. Then it occurred to me that he had no money to travel. Nor did we, in those days but all of us chipped in and sent him a train ticket, through an agent in Poland.

The communists issued a passport to my father quite quickly. He went to the British Embassy with somebody who spoke English because he was fluent in Russian, bit of French, bit of German which saved his life, but not a word of English. So he went there and 'Congratulations!' The visa was issued straight away. I couldn't remember his face as I didn't have a photograph, but I knew it was him when I saw him come off train. There were a few Eastern Europeans, fully dressed but shrunken cheeks. I just pushed the guards and ran in and fell into his arms. I had just moved to London and had lived alone, with little money. This was in the newspapers and everybody came to know and helped with all that we needed for a large family gathering. My sisters came from America and my brother from Scotland. The neighbours were very kind helping with crockery and cutlery and mattresses. It was around Christmas and was the best that we ever had.

He was a highly decorated soldier and was even awarded the *Polonia Restituta* [Poland's highest civilian award].

Reverend Zadyslaw Peszkovski

Reverend Z Peszkovski (see Photographs 30 and 31) was the sole surviving adult from the period and events described in this work. He was a young officer in the Polish Army, a prisoner of Kozielsk who narrowly missed being executed at Katyn and reached India as a scoutmaster. Roman Gutowski persuaded Reverend Z Peszkovski to see me for a short while in spite of his failing health. The 20 minutes allotted for the interview stretched to 90 minutes. This interview was carried out at Warsaw in May 2004.

If it were possible for me to say that the culture of one country influenced me better than Poland, Palestine and Jerusalem, it would be India.

I am a survivor of the concentration camp called Kozielsk, where I was one amongst 1,500 Polish officers, most of who were killed in Katyn in 1940. I saw the state of affairs when Germans and Russians were allies and was later asked to be in the Polish Army in Russia to fight the Germans after the special agreement between the Polish government-in-exile and the Russians came into effect. It is a long story, but for the first time in the history of Russia, at that time Poles were allowed to leave Russia and go to Iran, Iraq and Palestine on a special mission, to maintain the safety of places like Kirkuk and Mosul. We were sent as occupying force to protect Persia. The Poles and others were also there to protect the lives of the Iraqi people. It was a difficult situation for the Allies because the Germans were just across the border of Turkey.

In May 1942, I was sent to India for three weeks to help with the setting up of the camps. I was asked to organise the Polish youths there for War. At that time General Andrew was talking to Churchill and telling him that we would be better off stationed in Palestine and that it would be impossible for us to return to Poland in case we went into Russian controlled areas once again. It would be impossible for us to survive if we were located in areas controlled by them.

They needed me to help with structuring the Polish youth in India. Thereafter, I was in India for four years. The Balachadi children were the closest to my heart, because they were all orphans with little or no living family. I was assured to see that they were in good hands because there was a priest and a very good staff of people working within the camps. I was sure that everything was under control in the best possible way, under the conditions, especially with Maharaja Jam Saheb taking a lot of interest in their welfare.

He was a quite person. His father was close to Ignacy Padrewski. He was friends with some of the Poles who were outside of Poland and Padrewski was a pianist at that time. Because of this friendship with the Polish people he had met in Switzerland and at other such instances, his attitude towards the Polish people was very good. He influenced the people around him too and everybody had kind feelings about the Balachadi children. He made very good gestures to tell us that he understood the situation of Poland fully at that time. He and Gandhi understood our occupation under the Germans and the Bolsheviks was the worst possible thing. It was heartening that in spite of their own situation, they were doing something for others. That was the beginning of a relationship.

My interaction with Maharaja was very pleasant. He wanted to see me and find out some secrets that I had, especially about the Russians and the concentration camps. He asked many questions about how I survived and what was Katyn. It is the place where 4,200 [Polish] officers from the Kozielsk camp were killed in Stalin's way. They called it special action. By some kind of law, it was not necessary to have any normal procedure for sentence of death but only an order. To say 'Kill them' was enough.

It is so unbelievable as it was the worst thing that could happen in the world. This place is testimony that it is possible to kill people without even trying to show why or for what reason. This was one of Stalin's new style of killing people—called Katyn. It is the name of the place where they were killed and we didn't know whether there was only one Katyn or more [such summary executions]. Altogether about 15,000 people were killed and being a survivor of that horror, everybody was asking me for as many details. It was the worst possible thing, but since I was a Polish officer, they believed whatever I was telling them, however terrible.

Maharaja was personally in the camp on several occasions to check on the condition of the war-ravaged children. The children had had terrible experiences in Russia and were without any families in Balachadi. But with all the care and the best possible arrangements, it was a little paradise to be free and be in hands of Poles only. The feeling was that the brown people were good. There were children as young as two years old who were outside of Poland, without parents, without family, in a different country, a different way of life, different kind of religion for the next four years. But yet, Balachadi for them it was a wonderful experience. I know that the time they have spent in Jamnagar is very close to their hearts. It's an important part of their life, where they felt safe and in good hands, not only Polish but also friends. In my opinion and experience, 'Jamnagar' is the name of something very good.

So, once the children had a safe place, with good people around, I tried to teach them how to live together as boy scouts and they were so happy that someone from outside, a real veteran, is coming and teaching them scouting.

I was in Kolhapur during that period of four years. Besides official work, I used to spend my annual one month's vacation to travel. I had the opportunity to meet Gandhi several times through the auspices of two Polish people who were very close to him—Maurice Frydman and Wanda Dynowska. Both loved India immensely and had Indian names given by Gandhi and were his close associates [Bharatanandji and Umadevi, respectively].

Maurice Frydman had stayed back in India to study the Indian philosophy and way of life. We met several times in Kolhapur and Bombay and had the most interesting and enriching discussions with him, learning the way of non-violence from Mahatma and I, having been in Poland till the very last minute, defending the country in a battle against two armies. Wanda Dynowska was also there. In fact, Frydman took me to the ashram of Maharishi Ramanna and the experience has remained with me always.

I remember that during my meeting with Gandhi, he said, 'I'm always thinking of your nation and your people. It's a problem of blood. They are always trying to kill you, to destroy you. It is difficult for me to be connected with problems where there is blood (shed).' I said, 'When we are dealing with Russians or Germans, their attitudes are very different. "Ahimsa" is beautiful and if we have a special attitude or way of life, we can follow it but at the same time we know that they are murderers or killers.' He was sceptical about the safety of the 16 representatives of the Polish underground movement who had been invited by Russian for talks.

Later they were arrested. Gandhi had foretold both me and some of his close friends that those people would not be safe but would be killed instead.' And soon he was proved right.

Poles have experienced both the worst kinds of murderers—the Nazi Germans and the Russian Bolsheviks. It is best not to call them people—they are animals, murderers. There were two fearsome words of that time—'Auschwitz', by the Germans who created the Holocaust for the Polish people and 'Katyn', the place where you can kill people without any explanations. And both these events are connected with Poland. If my nation survives today, it is because of Providence or Holy Intervention. Under these circumstances, it was a very unusual and special situation for the Poles in India. We were completely in the hands of the British, who had helped us to find a safe place for our people. But there was no doubt with the Poles in Kolhapur and Jamnagar that they were waiting to return to Poland.

Now this day, 15 August, is the Polish Feast of Our Lady or the Miracle on the Vistula. So, when we were having that feast in our camp in Kolhapur on 15 August 1947, the English woman in charge of our camp, Mrs Button, and other Britishers were very intrigued and nervous asking repeatedly, why we were so happy. For us Poles it was a very special day because on 15 August 1920, Poland had managed to stop the advance of the Bolsheviks into Europe after a bloody battle on the banks of the River Vistula. It was one of the important days in Polish history. The Bolsheviks had wanted to conquer the whole world and revolutionalise it. For that they had to cross over Poland. For nearly 150 years after the partitions of Poland, we were free and we were going to fight to retain our freedom. A country that had become free in just 1918 from three countries—Austria, Germany and Russia—went to war in 1920 to preserve its freedom. The day 15 August 1920 when the Bolsheviks were stopped from any further advance into Poland and Europe, is known as the Miracle on the Vistula. It is celebrated in a very special way.

So, on the same day, so many years later, another country, India, becomes free. The joy we felt was indescribable. We had special meetings, special parade, and I gave many gifts to the [Indian] Boy Scouts to express our joy about independence of India. I feel such joy to have been a part of those celebrations. In fact, later there were problems. The people in charge of us from the British side were so angry about why we were celebrating. But from our side it was just joy, joy and joy that we were a witness to a very special day to India on a day special to us too. I remember how happy we were. For us it was the miracle on the Vistula, once again, one of the greatest events that shaped destiny. India in the hands of the British was one of its most important colonies.

In India, the Poles were under the protection of the British. Our Army, with the British Army, was fighting against the Germans and was in the closest possible relationship. Our position was that while we were happy that India was free, but we were always a charge of the British Army. So, it was not difficult for us to accept the changed situation. For victory against Hitler, this friendship and cooperation was very important but apart from that, we were very happy that we were witnessing the moment when India became a free country. I remember with fondness the farewell parade for the British Army in Bombay at the time of our leaving.

It was a dilemma for the Poles because they knew that Poland was lost. They loved the country and probably still had some parents or families in Poland, but how to return to the country which was in the hands of communists and become slaves like the others before them. The Polish communists were doing exactly what the Bolsheviks wanted them to do. So, to return to Poland was walking into an uncertain future about how one would be accepted. At that time, if anybody had been out of USSR, even for a few hours, it was as if you were in some way 'contaminated' by the west and, therefore, become too dangerous for the Bolsheviks or the communists.

It was a dilemma for so many people. As a matter of fact, the Polish government sent special people to Polish camps like Jamnagar and Valivade to demand their return to Poland. The same happened in New Zealand and other places too, wherever there were Polish camps. People had to make choices between returning to Poland or staying in the west. For many people, it was dangerous enough that they were outside of Poland, and they faced the likelihood of being sent [again] to Siberia or some such place.

While everybody wanted to return to Poland badly, the Bolsheviks were such, that they were doing everything possible to remain in the free world. They were looking for a place outside of Poland to live till Poland became free of the Bolsheviks.

On Asking Gandhi for Residency in India

They were facing many problems connected with the freedom movement in India. There were so many changes vital for India at that time and the numerous problems connected with them. It was very difficult to talk to anybody and ask Gandhi or others, because they were preoccupied with their own problems.

We must also remember our dilemma. We were going to ask India for something, when we had always been the charge of the British. How could we negotiate with India when we were British responsibility? I know there was some kind of promise that they would be good to the Poles. It was a very delicate problem and for us at that time and it was enough that the Indians were free and also sympathetic to our problem.

On Gandhi's Assassination

For us Poles, the end of his life in this way, especially when he was killed by his own people, signalled that we are a mankind in a situation that whenever there is a beginning of a new way of life, there must be so many martyrs, just as it is necessary to work, pray and think together. Such a pure, great person, one of the greatest of his time, it was necessary for him to give his blood. So, whenever anybody tries to be different, they have to be martyrs. The most beautiful person who has given answers for many things in today's world had become a martyr.

Personally, exactly a year before he was killed, I was talking and praying with him at the same place. That's something I'll remember all my life.

The problem of the Poles outside Poland was a headache for everybody, including Maharaja Jam Saheb, the Polish government in Poland, the Polish government outside Poland and the group of people trying to do something to help the people. All were looking for a good solution. If the people went back to Poland, they might be persecuted in some way. If they were to remain outside, who was going to help them and in what way? So there was seesawing all the time. It was one of the worst times in the history of mankind. Poles outside of Poland were a big headache for the Polish government, USSR, the British and Americans.

The Poles all over the world had been under the umbrella of the Polish government. The Polish Army in Italy had been sterling in the allied forces. Many good people wanted to help. But you cannot raise Polish children, longing for parents in Poland to be raised in a foreign culture. Law is law and is often against human beings.

Life after Leaving India

As a Polish officer, I returned to England during the demobilization. After four years in England, I went to study in Oxford where I studied Psychology and Philosophy. I had some very good experiences in the time I spent in Oxford. Most people were grappling to understand the meaning of life. There I was better off having had the experience of India.

I realized that I could not return to Poland as my country had become a slave to the worst thing of mankind—the Bolsheviks. She was no longer the country I knew. I decided to go to Rome and then to the USA—Orchard Lake Seminary—to prepare young people to become priests. About 40 boys from Valivade had also gone there. The idea was to send them to good schools. Some offers came from convents. In India, I was a Polish officer when I interacted with the camp priests, but later, I too became one.

I returned to Poland permanently in 1996. My mother used to be here, so I used to visit her earlier. Now my most important role is taking care of the Katyn forest matter and the persecution of Poles. Now I am working towards documenting the experiences of Poles under the USSR. A third of the Poles were killed in the USSR. There is no family in Poland who has not lost someone in the USSR and no family who has not had a victim to the Germans. Two words will remain through history—'Auschwitz' and 'Katyn'.

Auschwitz is not only for the Jews, though it has become synonymous with the Holocaust. It was for the Poles at large. One day the Germans decided to go only for the Jews as they had differentiated people and the Holocaust has become a special chapter.

In a special conference of the NKVD and Gestapo held and on the orders of Stalin and Hitler, where after in six weeks they prepared the list of people they wanted. Sixty years later it is a good idea to know that Hitler and Stalin decided to remove Poland from the map of Europe and kill all the people—the ovens of Auschwitz, work in *Gulags* and shot in Katyn where they killed so many of my friends. We need to know whether there were other Katyns. This country was not to exist as per the plans of Hitler and Stalin.

Tadeusz Dobrostanski

Tadeusz Dobrostanski (see Photographs 32 and 33) was born on 17 March 1933 to Jozek Dobrostanski, editor-in-chief of *Kurier Baltyki*, a daily newspaper in Gydnia, and Janina Dobrostanska, a theatre actress, in the Polish city of Bydgoszcz. The family, along with Tadeusz's older brother Jerzy Dobrostanski, lived in Gydnia on the Baltic sea port till the Second World War broke out.

Dobrostanski is one of the surviving Polish children who reached Balachadi, India, in 1942. Later, he reached Australia with his mother and older brother categorised as a DP at the end of the War and the ensuing policies. Through the timbre of Tadeusz's voice, one can gauge the courage displayed by scores of Polish women, like his mother who chose to brave the unknown vagaries at the far end of the earth rather than go back to communist Poland with nothing but only their conviction and belief in their own selves.

Dobrostanski has been living in Melbourne, Australia, since 1950, with his wife and grown-up daughters and two grandchildren. The story of his peregrinations is narrated here in his own words.

Three days before the War started, my father was called to arms as a lieutenant in the Polish Army; so, my mother, 36, brother Jerzy, 10, and myself, 6, travelled to L'wow in south-eastern Poland to escape the Nazi invasion. On 17 September 1939, Soviets entered Poland in accordance with the secret Ribbentrop-Molotov Pact. Poland was divided by the two occupants at the Bug river line (later known as the Curzon Line). A Soviet administration was installed. Father survived the War and rejoined the family in occupied L'wow. He worked as a waiter in a restaurant organised by a group of lawyers, journalists and actors. Mother worked in the kitchen as a cook.

About 26 June 1940, at one o'clock at night, the NKVD arrested my father with the guarantee that he was wanted for interrogation only and would soon return home. We did not see him till two years later. A few days later, the NKVD arrested my mother, brother and myself. We were taken to the railway station and forced into cattle carriages together with hundreds of other unfortunate Polish people.

After a two-week journey, we reached somewhere north of Svierdlosk [now Ecaterinberg] and disembarked in the provincial town Novaja Ljalja. We journeyed further by horse-driven cart to a small settlement called Ust Lobva Posiolek. Ust Lobva was designated 'Spec' or Special, intended as a penal settlement for [undesirable] Russian, Ukrainian and other citizens of the Soviet Union, in the eyes of the communist party. The deportees were taken to log cabins where they were to share half a house with another family. Mother was issued with an axe and a saw and was assigned to a woodchopper's brigade. We, the children were enrolled at the local school, where we were subjected to communist doctrines and strange ideologies. In my estimation, besides us, there were about 25 other Polish families in Ust Lobva.

With the approach of the severe Siberian winter our family suffered, not only the cold, but also hunger, since food was rationed and available only to working people. My mother and we two boys had to share one ration of basic staple. From the letters she received from our family in Lvov, we got information about father and later established some direct but limited correspondence with him. From that, we learned that father had been deported to Rybinsk, near Vologda (north of Moscow).

In 1941, in accordance with an agreement between Stalin, the Soviet premier and General Wladyslaw Sikorski, the Polish Prime Minister in exile, hundreds of thousands of deportees were issued with the so called 'Amnesty', which included a travel document and a personal ID. We had been set free and allowed to travel within the Soviet Union. During the same time, the Polish Army, under the command of General Wladyslaw Anders was being organised in Tatiszczevo, Buzuluk Tockoje and other places. Thousands of able-bodied Polish men and youth journeyed south to join army units. With them, thousands of woman and children travelled south to Uzbekistan with the hope of escaping from the Soviet Union.

At this time, father joined the 5th Infantry Division in Tatiszczevo and organised a divisional newspaper 'W marszu' (Marching On). Mother, Jerzy and I travelled south to Samarkand with the hope of reuniting with father. The train was overflowing with Polish deportees and half way to Samarkand, it was redirected by the Soviet authorities to Bukhara with the intention of using cheap labour for the cotton fields. We escaped from a guarded train in Samarkand

and shared a life with the gypsies on the side streets of the city. With the approach of winter, we moved to an Uzbek village on the outskirts of Samarkand. We shared a pigsty with a few other Polish people and often visited the Polish Legation for help and information. The Polish Legations in the Soviet Union were organised by the Polish government-in-exile in London to help deportees and to distribute scarce food, medication and clothing. Medicines were being delivered by the Polish and Indian Red Cross from India in the city where we hoped to get information about father.

In January 1942, at the Polish Legation, mother was finally reunited with father and he at once organised proper accommodation for us all. As an Allied officer, he was entitled to secure such accommodation. He was also issued with a special pass that allowed him to shop for food at 'Voyentorg', the special food stores for army officers only. It must be understood that in those days, it was extremely difficult to obtain any food at all in the shops, and what little food was available, was at black-market prices. Mother, Jerzy and I contracted typhoid fever and were confined to bed. Father requested an extension of his army leave and nursed the sick family as best as he could. The family survived the sickness and in mid-February, 1942, father returned to his unit in Tatiszczevo. Soon after his return to the Army, we were transported by the Polish army to Ashkabad, in Turkmenistan. Here, mother was informed that her 43-year-old husband had died of typhoid fever on 6 March 1942. He was buried at the Polish Army cemetery in Tatiszczevo.

In 1942, we were evacuated from Ashkabad across the border to Meshed in Persia [present Iran]. After some rest there, we were transported with about 200 Polish children, mostly orphans, by lorries, along the Afghanistan borders to Zahidan in the south and onwards to Quetta [formerly India, at present Pakistan], where we again rested for few weeks. Our destination was a newly built children's camp in Balachadi, near the city of Jamnagar.

My older brother Jerzy had been included in the first transport of Polish children to India. I was too sick to travel by truck at that time. Three months later, mother and I were transported by the Polish Army transport unit to India. We crossed the border of the Soviet Union and Persia and were taken along with others to the orphanage in Meshed where we rested for some time and were nursed by the Red Cross and British authorities.

The whole group continued their journey to India by trucks driven by Persian drivers. The next stop was in Quetta, where we were looked after by British authorities and allowed further time to rest and recover. The children were hosted by British families residing in Quetta and were often invited to their homes for picnics. When we were sufficiently recovered, our journey progressed by train to Jamnagar, on the Kathiavar peninsula, where we reached our destination at the Polish children's camp, Balachadi.

The Balachadi camp was built and placed at the disposal of the Polish people by His Highness Jam Sahib, the Maharaja of Nawanagar state. He was a man of culture, a proven friend and protector of Polish orphans. He often visited the camp, donating money. Mother and I were finally reunited with Jerzy. She soon took over the responsibilities for the kindergarten and cultural matters in the camp. For one of the events she got someone to teach the Polish children to sing the anthem of Nawanagar, which greatly pleased the Maharaja when the children sang it during his next visit to the camp. In all there were about 400–450 children in the Balachadi camp, from 3 to 15 years of age. Most of them were orphans, often brothers and sisters; some had their fathers in the Polish Army in the Middle East.

The camp at Balachadi provided the safe refuge for all the sick and war-torn children. The Polish government in London in co-operation with the Indian government, was responsible for the financial matters. However, the prime benefactor was Maharaja Jam Saheb of Nawanagar state. Thanks to his kindness and generosity the occupants of the Polish children's camp in Balachadi were offered a safe refuge. The Maharaja was a frequent visitor in the Balachadi camp and often the children were invited to his palace in Jamnagar or his summer retreat in Balachadi. According to the records, there were four transports of children to Balachadi.

I do remember playing with Maharaja's son and a little girl at the summer residence in Balachadi, but I do not remember their names. Both were younger than me. I was 11 years old then. I would be glad if they remember me.

In Balachadi, besides studying in the school and playing pranks with the other boys, I joined clubs and my leader was Franek Herzog. Later in Valivade, I belonged to scouts.

The camp commander at Balachadi was Father Pluta, a man of high integrity, high morality and honesty. Though he was a strict disciplinarian, at no time were there any suggestions of inappropriate moral behaviour or excessive physical abuse. He demonstrated a great respect for Maharaja Jam Saheb and his family remembering the kindness and care that Maharaja offered to the orphaned Polish children. Mrs Ptakowa was a young widow. She lost her husband and an infant son in the Soviet Union. She was in charge of the Scouts. Dr Konarski was a doctor of medicine. He travelled with us from Ashkabad to Quetta. He saved my life in Samarkand when I was dying of red typhus. He was a very kind and caring doctor, devoted to his profession, saving many hundreds of young lives in the Soviet Union. He did not live with us in Balachadi. Hanka Ordonowna was a well-known singer before the War. She was very attractive but of poor health. She devoted her life to the Polish orphaned children, standing in for their lost mothers. I remember having met her in Ashkabad, when she was there with her husband, Count Michal Tyszkiewicz, who was a Polish diplomat. She died in Lebanon and is buried at Warsaw's Powazki cemetery in the Avenue of Honor. Mr Henryk Hadala was an official, possibly a representative of the Polish Legation in Samarkand. I remember him from Valivade, not Balachadi.

Some other people from that period are Mr Banasinski, the Polish Consul, stationed in Bombay. He was married to Kira. She was a Polish Red Cross representative in Bombay. I only meet them when they were visiting the Balachadi camp.

After two years at Balachadi, we were transferred to another Polish settlement, Valivade near the city of Kolhapur. This settlement was much larger than Balachadi—about 3,500–4,000 people, mainly women and children. Mother was given the important post of director of the Cultural and Educational Department. The children attended at first, primary and later, secondary school. The education system followed Polish school programmes, guided by the ministry of education in London, but was under British general supervision. By the end of the War, it became obvious that post-War Poland was to be placed in the Soviet zone of influence. All the people in Valivade were faced with the serious decision of whether to return to a communist Poland and face a possible second deportation to the Soviet Union or to stay in India and face an unknown future.

There was also Umadevi (Wanda Dynowska), a frequent visitor in Valivade. She was very involved in introducing Polish girls to Indian history and [cultural] traditions. She was a close friend of Mahatma Gandhi and she has contributed significantly to the Indo-Polish friendship. I do not recall Mahatma visiting either Balachadi or Valivade, however, he spent some time with Polish people in Panchgani.

I obtained many documents and photographs of the period from my mother. All the photographs in Quetta, Balachadi, Valivade and elsewhere were taken by some lucky fellow with a camera, for instance, in Quetta by a professional Indian photographer called Mulik [of Malik and Co., Quetta].

About 1947, the Warsaw government issued an ultimatum to Polish people abroad to either return to the Polish People's Republic or their Polish citizenship would be revoked, hence, the people in Valivade were proclaimed stateless and became DPs, to be taken care of by the UNRRA. The authorities, not certain what to do with the DPs, finally decided to send them to the Polish settlements in British East Africa, in Uganda.

In 1947, India was granted independence. In 1948, we were transported to Uganda, after which the Valivade settlement was liquidated. The only Polish people that stayed in India after 1948 were some girls who had married Indian men and a few businessmen that were operating factories or companies in India [Mr Gabriel of Gabriel Shock Absorbers among them].

Some people were reunited with their husbands, who had been demobilised in England; a minority decided to return to communist Poland for family reasons. By then the British government had revoked the legitimacy of the Polish government in London and recognised the new Polish communist government that was a puppet of the Soviet Union. The custody of people in Valivade was taken over by the UNRRA.

In 1948, all the remaining people in Valivade were taken by train to Bombay and shipped on board the USAT General Stewart to Mombasa. After disembarkation, the people were sent by train to Kampala and driven by trucks to a Polish settlement in Koja, situated in the jungle, on the banks of Lake Victoria. Like all the other people, we were accommodated in straw-roofed clay huts. My brother and I continued our education at the high school and mother commenced employment at the local post office. She also involved herself in local cultural activities. While in Africa the responsibility for the Polish refugees was given to a new organisation, IRO and the authorities had to decide on the future of the DPs in Koja.

In late 1949, a delegation sent by the Australian government had arrived in Koja and after medical examinations, most people qualified for migration to Australia. The emigrants had to sign a two-year contract with the Australian government and agree to undertake any employment that the authorities saw fit. After the expiry of the contract, the authorities reserved the right to decide if the immigrant would be allowed to receive the 'permanent residents' status. In late January, 1950, people from Koja and Tangeru camps in Kenya embarked the *USAT General Langfitt* in Mombasa and sailed for Fremantle in western Australia. While on board, the passengers were forced by the American crew to work in the kitchen, mop the stairs and do other chores. When some of the passengers objected about this treatment, the Americans punished all the passengers by dumping the breakfast overboard. The sleeping quarters accommodated about 150–200 people and the ship was not fitted with air-conditioning systems.

On 14th February 1950, the ship docked at Fremantle harbour where a funny narrow-gauge train was waiting, ready to transport the immigrants to Northam migration centre. The new Australians, as they were called at the time, were accommodated in corrugated iron barracks in extremely primitive conditions. People were fed at local canteens and after a short time were sent by the authorities to their new jobs.

We were transported to Melbourne and were soon directed to the Westinghouse factory as unskilled labourers. None of us could communicate in English and in general, and so, all the 'New Australians' were treated in a somewhat hostile manner by the resident Australians. Mother was assigned to the telephone-receiver production unit, Jerzy and I to a power-transformer winding section. We rented half a house nearby and paid a weekly rent of 8 pounds to the landlord. The salaries earned by the family were: mother about 12 pounds a week, Jerzy about 8 pounds and me about 6 pounds a week.

The three of us enrolled in a rather unsuccessful, radio conducted, English language programme for New Australians, but the main source of learning the language were our factory mates. I wish the Australian government had let the young people further their education instead of sending them to factories to work. After completing our two-year contract, mother continued for some time working in the Westinghouse factory, Jerzy commenced employment with the PMG, and I began working at a photographic studio.

At the same time, I commenced evening photographic courses at Melbourne Tech.

The three of us also involved ourselves in local Polish community activities. We boys participated in a rover scout group and mother organised cultural activities. In mid-1950s, she started working as a secretary for the *Polish Catholic Weekly* and remained there until her retirement. By then she had a good command over English, which she had learned by reading newspapers and books.

In 1961, I married a young lady of Polish origin who migrated with her parents from the UK. We have two daughters, Ewa and Izabella. Both children had tertiary education and are now working in a professional capacity; they are independent, in their own dwellings. For the last 26 years, I have been employed by the University of Melbourne in charge of the Clinical Photography and Audio Visual Section. Mother stayed active and in good health. In 1970, she moved to her own granny flat which was attached to our house. In 1973, she was diagnosed with a rare type of cancer and within five weeks she died on 11th April 1973. Jerzy completed university studies and commenced working for the Australian Wool Corporation. He also married a lady of Polish decent and they had one daughter Halinka. In his mid-thirties, he developed a serious heart condition and on 10 August 1990, he died suddenly of a massive heart attack.

Roman Gutowski

Roman Gutowski (see Photographs 34 and 35) chose to be repatriated to Poland once he found his mother quite accidentally. He speaks very little English, but has ensured that both his children learnt English in spite of growing up in Communist Poland. The interview was carried out in Warsaw in 2004.

I was too young to remember any details of how I reached India. I have only a few snatches of memories from Balachadi. Ferdynand Burdzy had a farm with all kinds of animals and it was an honour to be of help there, which I had for one year. We played football made of old clothes, sometimes at night. Usually the next morning we got a spanking. My name was on the list of boys going to the USA. My friend got a letter from his mother in Poland saying amongst other things, 'Mrs Gutowska and her daughters are now sharing the house with us'. As a joke, he sent my picture saying, 'I too share my dormitory with a Roman Gutowski'. When the lady in Poland laughingly showed the picture to her housemate, she recognized me as the son she had left at the orphanage in Bukhara in early 1942, since she could no longer feed him. Ostensibly, when she had gone back to check on him a few days later, she was told, 'He died.'

I am told my father was an officer in the Polish Army, who was amongst those killed in Katyn. After my mother 'discovered' me, I changed my travel option to Poland. I was issued the Displaced Person's documents [see below] which was supposed to be the embarkation card and travel documents to destination. I travelled on board the ship *Alcantara* to Italy in 1947 and onwards by train. My oldest sister came to receive me. On seeing me once we reached Warsaw, my mother welcomed me with the words, 'Oh my dear son! Why have you returned to this poverty?' All I could say was, 'To be with you after all these years.'

Tomsaz Gutowski

Tomasz Gutowski, 45, is the son of Roman Gutowski. An engineer by profession, he lives in Warsaw with his wife and two children. He speaks partially on behalf of his father and gives a perspective of the next generation. The interview was carried out in Warsaw in 2004.

When I was in primary school in 1981–82, Poland was still communist, so we were being told that the Germans had invaded Poland and the Russians came in to rescue and help, which we knew was not true. We knew the truth from our families. My maternal grandmother was a History and Latin teacher, and my paternal grandmother had her experiences to talk from. And, of course, my father and his experience of being taken to India during the War! I also had home education with books that included an independent history of Poland which was published in the UK. There were many people who, if they had any chance of knowing anything, knew that the history being taught at school was all rubbish. The home history was kept strongly at home and could not be discussed in school or media.

In 1984, I was in a secondary school that allowed liberal thoughts. So, my ideas and opinions about the Polish history was one amongst many. At that time I was a supporter of the Solidarity Movement— the original one that had started in the port city of Gdansk by Lech Walesa. So, the real history of wartime Poland was open knowledge, but no one spoke openly.

My first meeting with Reverend Peszkovski was under the aegis of scouts. We had a little discussion during a camp and he told us the way things had really been. Later, I went up to him and told him that my father had been in India. He remembered my father from his India days and was simply delighted to meet me. In fact, I helped my father to dig out all his old friends from India in the UK and the USA during my travels there, and they all had their reunion in 1992 after almost 50 years.

The intervening years had not been easy for most of them. I know about my father's and can guess and empathise with the others. My grandmother who was meeting my father after six years greeted him with, 'Son, why did you come back to this poverty?' She had lost everything during the War, had survived Siberia and

Kazakhstan somehow, and had presumed her son dead after having to leave him in the orphanage in Samarkand because she had no means to even feed him. The letters that they exchanged while my father was still in India, waiting to come back, make the most heartbreaking reading. Of course, they are all in Polish. The family went through very hard times even after the War. My father had chosen to get drafted into the Army and spent several years there inspite of having excellent grades in school that guaranteed a place in the university straight away, due to the financial condition of the family at that time. It was some years before he could go back to university and study civil engineering and then made a good career for himself.

We had the other side of the family too, who had suffered losses in other ways during and after the War and later. There were uncles and cousins who were deported to Siberia *after the War* [emphasis added]. Those people faced bans on education and jobs subsequently and lost out so much. Those are another set of stories, and now in democratic Poland they don't have any special pension. Every family in Poland has suffered and has so many such stories of suffering.

When we were young, our father would tell us stories about adventures in Siberia and India—the bears, the frost, the drive through Afghanistan and peacocks and tigers and cobras in India. At that time, there was no Discovery Channel; so it was all exotic adventure stories for us. It was only when I was older that I began to understand the huge tragedy behind all those stories.

But we are happy that we have been able to put a lot of things behind us and are comfortable. I hope my father is happy. He has worked very hard all his life and made sure that he has excelled. He has been successful professionally, working abroad and for foreign companies at a time few Polish people could. Recently I had the honour of cooperating with him professionally when he was supervising the construction of one of the biggest office buildings in Warsaw.

In fact, my father at 70 is now one of the youngest survivors of the time in Siberia and India. He was only six or seven years old when he was taken to India, so he has very few academically significant memories of that period. The people who were teenagers then would have deeper memories, but they are all aging and passing on. Time is an extremely critical factor for anybody wanting to do a significant study on the subject.

Zygmunt Mandel

Zygmunt Mandel[1] (see Photographs 36 and 37) is Jewish by denomination and now lives in Israel. He is amongst the few Jewish children who were a part of the kinder transports to Balachadi. It is estimated that at least 18 of the 600 children arriving in Balachadi were Jewish.

He was born on the 22 January 1928 in Krakow, Poland, to Dr Zygmunt Mandel, a lawyer and Barbara (Basia) Rosenberg and lived in Krakow till September 1939 with his mother, stepfather, Mr Zygmunt Rappaport (Dr Mandel had died a few months before Zygmunt Mandel's birth) and older sister Lilka, who was eight years older than him. The family was well heeled, and Mandel recalls a very well provided and comfortable lifestyle and upbringing.

He left Krakow on Sunday, 3 September 1939, on foot, with backpacks on the shoulders and has never returned since. His personal odyssey took him to Kowel and Lwow in Poland, Tesma—a punitive settlement for 'unstable elements' north of Yekatrinberg in the Taiga region, Bokhara, Samarkand and Ashkabad in the former Soviet Union, Quetta, Balachadi and Bombay in undivided India and finally Israel, where he reached on 24 April 1943 and has lived there ever since.

He lost both his parents to malnutrition and typhus at Bokhara. He himself was the first to contract the disease and spent several weeks in hospital to return and find out that his mother too had died of the same disease in another hospital. Soon his stepfather too died. A neighbour dropped him off at the Polish orphanage in Samarkand. In July 1942, Mandel moved to Ashkabad, in Turkestan, as part of a group of about 30 children from the orphanage who were to become a part of a much larger group headed to India. At Ashkabad, he met Edmund Ehrlich,[2] a Viennese Jew, who too was a part of the entourage designated to travel to India. Mandel and Ehrlich are friends to this day.

Mandel was a part of the second group of Polish children who made the overland Ashkabad–Meshed–Zahidan–Birjand journey reaching Quetta in undivided India in September 1942. There was an extended halt for several weeks at Quetta since the river Indus was in spate. The group stayed in military cantonment and were often invited to the homes of several British officers.

In September 1942, Mandel, Ehrlich and ten other Jewish children who were a part of the second transport of Polish children to India, reached the Balachadi camp along with the rest of the group. Some of the Polish members of this group are Tadeusz Dobrostanski and Weislaw Stypula. His memories of Quetta and Balachadi are similar to those of Franek Herzog or Weislaw Stypula—individual clean beds, plenty of food, medical attention and a strong sense of relief at being taken care of.

With some initiative from Edmund Ehrlich and a bit of support from the dentist who visited the Balachadi camp from Bombay periodically (possibly Dr Hamburger), soon Mandel, Ehrlich and ten other Jewish children left for Bombay, accompanied by Mr Cynowicz, a representative of the JRA, who arranged for Certificates of Entry to Palestine for each of them. In Bombay they were all temporarily 'adopted' by European–Jewish families. Mandel and Ehrlich were adopted by Lotte and Walter Daus, industrialists (see Appendix 14 for route and compatriots).

In April 1943, Erlich Edmund (15 years), Gilert Pola (15 years), Goldluft Ilona (9 years), Goldluft Janusz (6 years), Hoch Rozalja (15 years), Hoch Rachel (7 years), Magnuszewer Abraham (15 years), Kaufman Fima (13 years), Rozengarten Cila (17 years), Szpalter Maria (15 years), Szpalter Elza (17 years) and Mandel (15 years), chaperoned by a young rabbi, Shor Elias, boarded a cargo ship bound for Suez through the Arabian Sea, the Gulf of Aden and the Red Sea. From Suez they travelled by train to Haifa and arrived there on 24th April 1943 where they were met by Mrs Henrietta Sold, head of the Youth Department of the JRA (Aliat HaNoar). The event was duly carried by the media (only newspapers then) ostensibly to help relatives, if any, to find them.

In Eretz Israel, the group attended the Agricultural School in Magdiel. Walter Daus's brother, Fritz, and his wife, Lotte, remained as their surrogate family till the very end of their life. In October 1945, Mandel, enlisted in the British Army, remaining in active service till the end of the year. At the end of 1947, he enlisted in the Israeli Army, remaining in service till the beginning of 1953 and, thereafter, as a civilian employee of the Army till he retired in 1993.

Ehrlich became the general manager of King David Hotel in 1956 and later, till his retirement, he was the General Manager of The Laurent in Paris. The two have lost track of their other compatriots from India.

In 1958, Mandel married Hadassah (see Photograph 36) and they have two sons, Roee and Giora, and four grandchildren, Tom, Ittai, Amit and Shira. Hadassah died in June 2009.

Polish Women Who Stayed on in India

Barbara Krawiec

Barbara Krawiec became Barbara Shinde till she returned to Poland in the 1950s after separation.

Danuta D

Danuta (see Photograph 38) married Salim Mujawar of Wai and became Danuta Mujawar. She lives in Bombay after a long stint as a school teacher in Wai, Ratnagiri district of Maharashtra. She is now a practising beautician.

Franceszka Stasch

Franceszka Stasch got married and came to be called Franceszka Kail and lived in Bombay till they immigrated to Australia in the 1960s, as written by her daughter Vanessa Kail who resided in Melbourne at the time of this research.

Romualda Bogielski

Romualda got married to Flight Lieutenant RH Chawdhary of the Royal Indian Air Force and spent the rest of her life moving from base to base as an officer's wife. She remembers the warmth with which Jam Saheb Digvijaysinghji received her when they were stationed at Jamnagar. She recalls that he always extended very special courtesies to her and spoke of the Polish Nawanagaris. Later, she became a successful entrepreneur and now lives a retired life in the Mussoorie hills with her second husband, Mr Lall, another Indian.

Wanda Nowicka

Wanda Nowicka married Vasant Kashikar of a staunch Brahmin family in Kolhapur, embraced Hinduism and became Malati Vasant Kashikar.

She even became a vegetarian and remained thus for as long as they were a part of the joint family. She is now an active member of the API and is their representative in Kolhapur. See Photograph 39.

Zofia Krawiec

As she lay recuperating in the hospital in Iran after her peregrinations from L'vov in Poland, Cupid struck for Zofia. A few weeks after she had been discharged and was back at the camp in Abadaan, Captain (Dr) Frederick Mendonca, Royal Army Medical Corps from India, came one day to request Mr Marcin Krawiec for the hand of his daughter in marriage. He had received orders to move back to India and did not want to go without Zofia. Zofia and Captain Mendonca were married some weeks later at Ahwaaz. She travelled in a troop ship, sharing a cabin with an Anglo-Indian nurse, who teased her constantly and quite convinced her that she and Captain Mendonca would have spotted children as she was white and he coloured. So petrifying was the idea that when the ship halted at Karachi, she tried to get away from both of them, but Captain Mendonca caught up with her and assured her that that would not be the case.

They disembarked at Bombay and stepped into a new life. India has been her home ever since (see Photograph 40).

Her older sister Janine remained in Iran, where she married John Fiore, an American soldier and later immigrated to the USA. She lives now in Tampa, Florida. Marcin and Franceszka Krawiec stayed in Valivade till they returned to Poland and farmed in the collective fields of the village. Zofia's oldest sister, Filomena, and her husband went to East Africa, from where they returned to Poland and raised a large family.

NOTES

1. Excerpts from the personal testimony of Zygmunt Mandel which could not be published due to some unforeseen circumstances.
2. Edmund Ehrlich leads a very private life in Paris and declined a request for an interview towards this research and publication.

Author's Note

⟨ॐ⟩

The departure from India marked the end of the Indian leg of the journey of the Poles deported to the USSR. With only about 10 per cent of the Polish population in India opting to return to Poland after the War, most of them were yet to reach a place in the world they could call 'home' for the rest of their lives.

None of the survivors of the Soviet deportation mentioned here, or otherwise, has received any compensation from any government—Soviet or Polish—for all the losses suffered by them and their families till the time of this going into print. While some applications have been sought by the Polish government, no tangible compensation has yet been accorded. No trials were ever conducted for the war crimes of deportation of 1.7 million civilians or the Katyn forest massacre of 15,000 Polish officers. Adequate information about the deportees and POWs were not given to humanitarian agencies like the International Red Cross in contravention to the Geneva Convention of 1929, as applicable at that time. With no responsibility fixed and no one ever indicted by the world community, this episode comes through as one of the greatest unresolved human rights violation of our times and a blemish in the history of mankind.

In Britain, the Polish people were discouraged from mentioning the suffering at the hands of the Soviet Union. There is no mention of it in any of the memorial monuments, except in the plaque at St Andrews Bobola Church. The movement for the awareness about the Katyn forest massacre was taken up in Poland by Reverend Z Peszkovski, who himself narrowly missed being executed in Katyn as a young officer in the Polish Army, only after a democratic government came into place in 1989.

In fact, even the GOI prefers little mention of the former Soviet Union in the public declaration of this history, which leaves several unresolved questions in the minds of the common people of India whose source of knowledge of world events is the British and American media. Usually, it is assumed that they fled the infamous Nazi persecution; this is much to the annoyance of the members of API.

The role played by the semi-autonomous Princely States in pre-Independence India in contributing towards preserving Polish national life is unique and unparalleled. Financially, Indians contributed about ₹600,000 in the period 1942–45.[1] This amount raised through charity for the upkeep of Polish orphan children amounts to 6,444,241 pound sterling[2] or 6,765,607 euros[3] in 2008 terms. The Polish Children's Fund continued to receive the promised subscription from numerous sources in spite of the financial difficulties caused during the famine of Bengal and drought in Madras.

The offer by Jam Saheb Digvijaysinghji to accommodate the orphaned Polish children was a primer for the rescue of the rest of the Polish population, whether or not they were supported financially by India. Though some role by India was envisaged while planning the move of the Polish Army from Buzuluk to Yangi Yul in 1941 and the British Military Command in India was one of the recipients on the intensive communication[4] that marked the period, the concrete offer to accommodate the Polish orphans by Jam Saheb Digvijaysinghji of Nawanagar was the first of its kind. The first group of orphaned Polish children left USSR in March 1942 and reached India in April 1942 and were settled in Balachadi by July 1942, well before the second evacuation of August 1942. These children reached India directly. Polish population from the second evacuation spent time in Persia before they reached India. In fact, Lieutenant Colonel Ross's final report to MERRA in September 1942 mentions the closure of the transit camp at Meshed as 'A small transit camp has been in existence at Meshed since the summer of 1942. It was originally intended for the reception of Polish orphans released from the Soviet Union and travelling overland to *destinations in India* [emphasis added] via Zahidan ... as many as 675 have travelled with their guardians to India by this route.'[5]

The file NAI, 276(8)-X/42 containing the first three reports by Captain AWT Webb, which have yielded a wealth of information about the setting up of the Balachadi camp, were located at the National Archives of India (NAI), New Delhi. A marking on the cover page of the file identifies it for destruction in 1962. The non-availability of the linked files is a testimony to the sheer luck by which this lone file has survived to tell the tale. It is almost comparable to Lieutenant Z Peszkovski surviving the Katyn forest massacre to be able to uphold its validity now.

Webb's report states that the British GOI accepted to accomodate 500 Polish children on the condition that they were to be maintained on charitable funds raised in India and their expenses underwritten by the Polish government-in-exile in London. It must be noted here that no place could be found in British India or elsewhere in the world for 500 orphaned Polish children till Jam Saheb of Nawanagar stepped in with his offer of Nawanagar as a destination for not only those 500 children but also another batch of 500 children and another batch of 2,000 subsequently.

It is noteworthy that the Polish government-in-exile was looking for a place to move their people and not their money as they had fair amounts of it at that time. It was a destination that was important at the time and not financial support. All wealthy nations and dominions across the world shied away from offering a destination to the hapless Poles at that time. It is imperative to note here that though the Polish government-in-Exile in London had underwritten the entire financial responsibility for the Balachadi camp, it was not called upon to honour it during the existence of the Balachadi camp from 1942–46, since receipts from charitable funds raised in India covered the duration of stay adequately.

Financial commitments made in India were honoured in spite of a downturn in economic situation and the growing volatility of the political situation. The Bengal province experienced a severe famine in 1944, as also some parts of the Madras Presidency. Gandhi gave the clarion call of 'Quit India' at that time.

As mentioned in 'A Polish Village on an Indian Riverbank', the house of the Tatas donated money towards the Polish Red Cross Hospital in Bombay.[6] This charity was extended at a time when India herself was a country of meagre resources, reeling under wartime shortages and fighting to free herself from British yoke. It is not only demonstrative of generosity but also the fact that the Indian Independence Movement was merely anti-British administration and not xenophobic.

Hence, the importance of the bold offer of Jam Saheb, offering Nawanagar as a destination for Poles, can neither be underestimated nor diluted. He not only offered Balachadi, but also made available Chela and involved the rulers of Patiala and Baroda, with whom he had a good rapport in the COP, to help the Poles with a destination in their states when there was no place for them anywhere in the world, and they were dying en masse sandwiched between the German and the Soviet policies. Maharaja Yadavindra Singh of Patiala too extended an invitation for 3,000 Polish people, a similar offer which was also made by Baroda state. These offers were the bedrock towards the formation of the Valivade camp in the politically pliant Princely State of Kolhapur.

All other destinations for the Poles—Africa, Lebanon, New Zealand—opened after Nawanagar. Persia was a transit country and they too were reluctant to host the Poles initially, as is clear from Sir R Bullard's communication. War-duration domicile was accepted as an idea and provided later. The Country Club camp in Karachi was the transit camp for Poles evacuated out of Persia and headed to destinations all over the world. It may not be misplaced to say that a majority of the Polish diaspora worldwide has a small Indian connection somewhere, which has played a critical role in their preservation.

The adoption of the Polish children by Jam Saheb Digvijaysinghji paved the way for 81 children to go to the USA and build a life for themselves there in the free world, after initial assistance by missionaries.

It is also important to note the presence of Jewish children in Balachadi. At least 18 Jewish children reached Balachadi in the transport for the Polish orphans, which bring out two important points: there was presence and persecution of the Jews in the former USSR and the composite nature of the Polish evacuation process. India has been a home to the Jews in distress since times immemorial, and this is one more example of the Indian hospitality towards the Jewish community. The presence of Jewish children at the Polish orphanages and their evacuation to Balachadi raises pertinent questions about the presence of claimed anti-semitism.

The removal to Palestine, of the children arriving at Balachadi, within weeks of their arrival by the JRA who organised entry documents to Palestine, hospitality by rich members in Bombay and a chaperone for the children, demonstrates that the Jews were ready with plans and systems for mass evacuation from all over the world, quite unlike the Poles in general where evacuation took place due to personal heroism. A comparison of the numbers of non-Jewish people evacuated by Jewish organisations vis-à-vis the number of Jewish people evacuated through Polish relief measures would open up a new area of study.

There was no political outrage about the presence of Polish refugees, and in fact, the Poles received the sympathies of Mahatma Gandhi. He understood the stance of Moscow vis-à-vis Poland and predicted quite accurately in 1946 that Moscow would not spare the 16 Polish representatives arrested on charges of espionage. The last group of Poles from the

Valivade camp were present during the funeral of Gandhi held all over the country. The scouts from the camp formed a special contingent when the ashes were received for immersion in river Panchganga.

It is unfortunate that the Poles could not leverage this sympathy and goodwill for permanent residency in India, but they definitely did not encounter any hostility of any kind during their stay in India. The Poles were well received by all walks of Indian gentry at that time—the elites, as demonstrated by Jam Saheb and the offers of destination by other Indian rulers, and common people, including simple villagers as demonstrated by Dr Joshi, Dr Ashani, the merchants of the Valivade camp and Suleiman Khan and Vasantbapu Pawar referred to earlier in the text.

It is in response to this warmth experienced by the survivors, that those from Balachadi have a greater affinity for India in comparison to the others. They were the first to return and install a commemorative monument at the site of their former school as a token of gratitude. It is another matter that the school is rather cut off due to its distance from the city and being a property of the Ministry of Defence, has the status of a defence property whereby access to and visibility of the commemorative monument is extremely restricted. With ever-stringent security drills in the age of terrorism, no foreign nationals are allowed in a defence property; hence, the former residents are not allowed there in a rather ironic situation. It was demonstrated during the visit of Stefan Klosowski from Canada. Klosowski, a person for whom the original camp was built in the first place, was declined permission to stay. It was the personal magnanimity of the principal that allowed him to visit from dawn to dusk for two days to see the place that brought him to India all the way from Canada.

The Balachadi children were orphans and cherish the chance of survival that they got in India. They are relatively small in number and most are not so conversant in English. Also, being orphans, they had to start life from a much lower level, without much education and support; hence, they are not that wealthy and financially well established. It was the children of Balachadi in Warsaw who initiated the first memorial monument in India to mark their gratitude. Their testimonies are not adequately available in English and may soon be lost forever. They are not vociferous about recording their history in the manner and style of western historians, after spending decades surviving in a communist environment. From the piecemeal accounts available and Captain Webb's report, it seems that the camp at Balachadi was run on charitable funds raised in India throughout, not invoking the guarantee the Polish government had given to make up the difference in expenses and the amount raised by charity. Those settled in the western countries are few and far between. The author was able to contact Tadeusz Dobrostanski in Australia, Franek Herzog in the USA, Stefan Klosowski in Canada and Marian Raba in the UK. But they are few and far between and not in a position to form a separate association. They prefer to remain in the ambit of the API 1942–48, though hugely outnumbered by the Valivade residents, who have a markedly different perspective. The Jewish children are conspicuous by their silence.

The children of Balachadi treasure their association with Maharaja Jam Saheb, who took more than passing interest in them and visited the camp often in an attempt to make them feel comfortable. It was more emotional in nature. A very emotional Marian Raba in Leicester said,[7]

> He welcomed us to Nawanagar saying he was Bapu, father, to all, which meant a lot to us. He lived upto it by involving himself in our lives and taking pride in our achievements, and later we heard that he had even adopted us to prevent our forcible removal to communist Poland. In his farewell speech he said that he would always be Bapu to us and we could return to Nawanagar anytime in our lives.

Weislaw Stypula describes India, Balachadi in particular, as his 'second homeland'. Jam Saheb's financial contribution to the camp is not recorded in the account books formally, hence, not meeting the requirements of a modern scientific recording of events and their analysis. Wieslaw Stypula insists they are mentioned in the Polish reports, now housed in the New Archives of Warsaw. A researcher with knowledge of Polish language will be able to throw better light on the subject.

The Valivade group of Polish refugees in India emanated from the second evacuation out of the Soviet Union, and the group was ten times as large as the Balachadi group. In addition, they had at least one parent or relative to care for them, which had a considerable effect in the difference in perception about the land and its hospitality. The Valivade camp was financed by the Government of Poland, with HMG acting as their agents. This group settled in the western world and learnt fluent English and the western techniques of recording events. They are all now fluent in English and can record their history in English in complete contrast to the children of Balachadi. For the former Valivade residents, India was a pleasant interlude from the harshness of the Soviet Union and the return to responsible adult life after India. The interaction of the royal family with the campers from Valivade was also extremely restricted due to the governing rules of the British GOI.

Thus, the author often encountered the jibe, 'Why are you so interested in details about Balachadi? It was Valivade that was the bigger camp.' This study is not about majority numbers, but the hospitality of an Indian ruler at a critical time that unwittingly provided the British with a politically viable solution to the awkward relationship between the Poles, British and the Soviet Union at a delicate time of the War alliance.

This international example of the traditional Indian philosophy of *Vasudhaiva Kutumbakam* (the whole world is one's family) remains relevant in the modern and current context of unrest around the world.

NOTES AND REFERENCES

1. B.L-I&OC, L/P&J/8/415, Cypher telegram No. POL 8701, Webb to Gilchrist, dated 1 July 1947, 260.
2. http://www.measuringworth.com/ukcompare/result.php (accessed 21 January 2010). Price index: Share of GDP. This measure indicates opportunity cost in terms of the total output of the economy in 2008 terms.
3. Currency converter fxtop.com/en/cnvhisto.php (accessed on 25 January 2010).
4. K Sword, *Deportation and Exile, Poles in the Soviet Union 1939-48.* (London: St Martin's Press with School of Slavonic and East European Studies, 1994), 63.
5. BNA, FO 371/ 42781, W 8364, Ross Report on Polish Refugees April 1942–December 1943 (MERRA report), 22.
6. TCA, DTT Collection, Minutes of 57th, 69th and 74th meetings.
7. M Raba, video interview to the author, UK, May 2005.

Photographs

CRO

Section 1: Arrival

1. The last postcard from Father (Lieutenant Colonel F Herzog) from Starobielsk

Note: This postcard was never delivered to us in Lubaczow. We had been deported to USSR on 13 April 1940. Note the methodical crossing out of our old address in Lubaczow and adding of our new address in USSR in spite of the deportation and general chaos prevailing at that time. Both addresses indicate the general region where both had been moved to.

Franek Herzog's collection.

2. Polish boys in Bandra, 1942

Franek Herzog's collection.

Section 2: India Years

3. Franek, Balachadi, 1942

Franek Herzog's collection.

4. Tadek Herzog and Henry Bobotek, Balachadi, 1943

Franek Herzog's collection.

5. Marian Rozanski, Jerzy Dobrostanski, Franek Herzog, Zbigniew Suchecki, Jerzy Krzyszton, Steven Balaram and Mrs Janina Dobrostanska, Balachadi, 1945

Franek Herzog's collection.

6. End-of-year report for 1943–44 from Balachadi

Nr. *4*   Rok szkolny 19*43*./*44*.

SŚWIADECTWO SZKOŁY POWSZECHNEJ

Nazwisko i imię *Herzog Franciszek*

urodzon *y* dnia *28 kwietnia* 19.. r.   w *Chorzowie*

powiatu .... religii (wyznania) *rzym. kat.*

uczęszczał .... do klasy *piątej* .... i otrzymał ...... za r. szk 1943 44

oceny następujące :

sprawowanie	*bardzo dobry*
religia	*bardzo dobry*
język polski	*dobry*
język	*dobry*
historia	*dobry*
geografia	*dostateczny*
nauka o przyrodzie	*dobry*
arytmetyka z geometrią	*dobry*
rysunki	*dostateczny*
zajęcia praktyczne	*dobry*
śpiew	*dobry*
ćwiczenia cielesne	*dobry*
Decyzja Rady Pedagogicznej	*promowany do VI. klasy*

Opuścił .... dni szkolnych .... w tym nieusprawiedliwionych ....

PUBLICZNA SZKOŁA POWSZECHNA III ST. IM. ŚW. ANDRZEJA BOBOLI PRZY
ZAKŁADZIE WYCHOWAWCZYM W OSIEDLU DZIECI POLSKICH BALACHADI
JAMNAGAR W INDIACH

Opiekun Kl.... klasy   Kierowni...... Szkoły

Skala ocen : bardzo dobry, dobry, dostateczny, niedostateczny.

L. O. i S. Sz. Druk Nr. 7
Św. Szk. Powsz.

Franek Herzog's collection.

7. End-of-year report for 1945–46 from Balachadi

Koedukacyjne GIMNAZJUM *ogólnokształcące*
Balachadi - Jamnagar

Nr. 15   w *Indiach*   Rok szkolny 194.5/.46

ŚWIADECTWO GIMNAZJUM

OGÓLNOKSZTAŁCĄCEGO

Franciszek   Herzog

(Imię i nazwisko)

urodzony dnia *28 kwietnia*   roku 19*31* w *Chorzowie*
województwa *Śląskie*   wyznania *Rzym - Kat* uczeń
klasy *pierwszej* otrzymał za   rok szkolny 19*45/46*

oceny następujące :

z zachowania się	*bardzo dobry*
z religii	*bardzo dobry*
z języka polskiego	*dostateczny*
z języka łacińskiego	*dostateczny*
z języka angielskiego	*dobry*
z języka	
z historii	*dobry*
z geografii	*dostateczny*
z biologii	*dobry*
z fizyki z chemią	
z matematyki	*dobry*
z zajęć praktycznych	
z ćwiczeń cielesnych	*bardzo dobry*
z przysposobienia wojskowego s.przt	*bardzo dobry*
z rysunków	*dobry*

U. O i S. Sz. Druk Nr 6
(Sw Gimn.)

Franek Herzog's collection.

8. The youngest children at Balachadi with Indian caretaker, 1942

Courtesy of Tadeusz Dobrostanski.

9. Dr Ashani, Mr Joshi, Fr Pluta and Polish nursing staff, Balachadi, 1942

Courtesy of Weislaw Stypula.

10. Sabina Kotlinska's picture, page 160, Rama Varma (Appan) Tampuran, War Publicity Officer, 'Cochin', 1944

Sabina Kotlinska
(Polish Refugee Girl adopted by
Cochin Government)

Courtesy of Mythri Prasad, Cochin.

11. Programme sheet of a function by the children, Balachadi, 1944

Courtesy of Weislaw Stypula.

12. Jam Saheb with Polish children, Jamnagar, 1944

Courtesy of Tadeusz Dobrostanski.

13. Polish refugees arriving from Russia, 1942

Courtesy of Jan Siedlecki.

14(a). Letter from a complete stranger (front)

Hatchlands
Netterbury
Briminster
GB.
Dorset

Friday June 6th 1945.

Dear Mrs Harasymiow –

I expect you will be very surprised to get a letter from an unknown RAF officer in England. I have just returned from Germany where I was a prisoner since 1940 : during the last few months of the war, when all Germany was in complete chaos, a certain number of RAF prisoners were moved to a camp at Luckenwalde (30 miles south of Berlin) where were some 600 Polish officers transferred from internment in Hungary – among them your husband. When I left, he asked me to write and tell you that he was very well and safe and that he intended

14(b). Letter from a complete stranger (reverse)

to return to Poland immediately the Russian authorities gave permission. This permission can only be a matter of days — until the transport system is again in working order. He also told me to add — since he thought it might amuse you — that I was myself in India as a child of 15 months. I knew your husband quite well — he was always cheerful in spite of the disgraceful conditions in this camp and I thought he bore his imprisonment much easier than many of his companions. Being only 25 myself, I always felt sorry for the older men; but your husband refused to be depressed and was always optimistic. The Russian authorities in the camp seemed very friendly and had promised to move the Polish officers home as soon as possible. I left Luckenwalde myself on May 22nd.

Yours sincerely. John Bushell. Flt RAF.

Courtesy of Stanislaus Harasymow.

15. Book on Indian theme developed by Madam W Dynowska

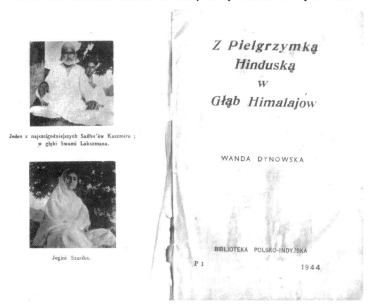

Book courtesy of Stanislaus Harasymow.

16. Franek (extreme left) and Jerzy Krzyszton (extreme right) with two Portuguese scouts in Goa, 1947

Franek Herzog's collection.

17. Polish girls with Wanda Dynowska and Subramaniam – 1

Courtesy of Jan Seidlecki.

18. Polish girls with Wanda Dynowska and Subramaniam – 2

Uczestnicy wycieczki: Irka Adamczyk, Marysia Brink, Pacia Cariuk, Danka Czechówna, p. Wanda Dynowska, Józef Ezman, Marysia Ganczar, Irka Janczewska, Janka Jankowska, Mila Kamińska, Irka Kaziewicz, Alina Kurzawska, Janusz Kurzeja, Wojtek Kwiatkowski, Lucia Ligajówna, Hanka Nadańska, Lucia Ostrowska, Irka Piotrowicz, Danka Raczyńska, Czesia Sobol, Hela Suszkowna, Janka Szafrańska, Marysia Szczyrska, Halina Śliwińska, p. Zofia Wilczyńska, Jadzia Wróblewska.

Courtesy of Tadeusz Dobrostanski.

19. Shamrao Gaikwad and Roma, engagement picture, 1948

Courtesy of Shamrao Gaikwad.

Section 3: Reminiscences and Reflections

20. Father's (Lieutenant Colonel F Herzog) symbolic grave at the Polish Military Cemetery, Charkov, Ukraine, 2000

Franek Herzog's collection.

**21. Stefan Bukowski (late), Jam Saheb Junior, Kira Banasinska
and Wieslaw Stypula at Jamnagar palace reception, 1989**

Courtesy of Weislaw Stypula.

22. Monument at Balachadi

Bhattacharjee collection.

23. Reunion 2004. Members of API 1942–48 with His Excellency Ambassador Anil Wadhwa and Reverend Z Peszkovski at Katowice, Poland

Courtesy of Danuta Pniewska.

24. Hershad Kumariji, 2010

Courtesy of 'Outlook'.

25. Hershad Kumariji in Polish costume, 1944

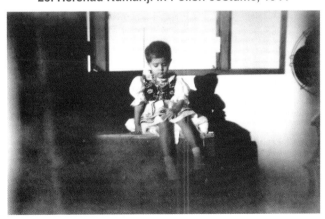

Courtesy of Hershad Kumariji.

26. Alina Baczyk Haus with spouse and family, Ephrata, USA, 2007

Back Row: Son Christopher F Haus and Dana H Haus (daughter-in-law); Frank R Haus and Alina Baczyk Haus; Teri R Haus (daughter-in-law) and Son Jere R Haus; Son Mark A Haus.
Front Row: Grandchildren Danielle Marie Haus and Spencer Christopher Haus.

Courtesy of Frank and Alina B Haus.

27. Alina and Henryk Baczyk, Balachadi, 1944

This photograph, from the Bonshek family collection, is used, with permission and was first published in Heniek: A Polish Boy's Coming of Age in India During World War II, *by Anna Bonshek, 2010, Prana World Publishing, Australia.*

28. Marian Raba, Leicester, UK, 2005

Bhattacharjee collection.

29. Henry and Marian Raba with Tarvinder Singh of Malaria Institute, New Delhi, Balachadi, 1943

Courtesy of Tadeusz Dobrostanski.

30. Reverend Z Peszkovski and the author, Warsaw, May 2004

Bhattacharjee collection.

31. Lieutenant B Pancewicz, Janina Dobrostanska, Janina Ptakowa and Lieutenant Z Peszkovski with scouts in Balachadi, 1943

Courtesy of Tadeusz Dobrostanski.

32. Tadeusz Dobrostanski, Melbourne, Australia, 2003

Courtesy of Tadeusz Dobrostanski.

33. Tadeusz Dobrostanski, Quetta, 1942

Courtesy of Tadeusz Dobrostanski.

34. Roman Gutowski in front of Jam Saheb School, 2004

Bhattacharjee collection.

35. Polish children at the beach in Balachadi, 1943

Roman Gutowski in front row with handkerchief on the head. Tadeuz Dobrostanski and Lucian Pietrzykowski in the foreground. Apolonia Kordas, Danka Gracz and Janina Dobrostanska in the last row.

Courtesy of Tadeusz Dobrostanski.

36. Zygmunt and Hadassah Mandel, Israel, 2004

Courtesy of Zygmunt Mandel.

37. Zygmunt Mandel, Janina Dobrostanska, Dr Brune, Ms Kowalewska, Quetta, 1942

Courtesy of Tadeusz Dobrostanski.

38. Danuta Mujawar and granddaughter, Bombay, 1997

Courtesy of Danuta Mujawar.

39. Vasant and Wanda (Malati) Kashikar, Kolhapur, India, 2003

Bhattacharjee collection.

40. Christine Rebello, Nikola Rebello and Zofia Mendonca, Pune, 2001

Courtesy of Christine Rebello.

Appendices

(ORO)

1. List of Polish children in Balachadi camp, India, 1942

POLSKA WALCZĄCA
(FIGHTING POLAND) 1942.

The list of names of Polish children evacuated
from the Soviet Union to India 1942.

POLISH CHILDREN'S CAMP BALACHADI

Dzieci polskie w Indiach

(Continued)

(Continued)

Courtesy of Tadeusz Dobrostanski, Australia.

2. Censored telegram, 1943

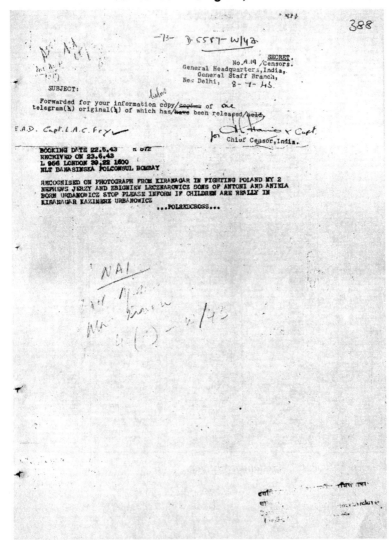

SECRET.
No.A.19 /Censors.
General Headquarters, India,
General Staff Branch,
New Delhi, 8-7-43.

SUBJECT:

Forwarded for your information copy/copies of one
telegram(s) original(s) of which has/have been released/held.

E.A.D. Capt. L.A.C. Frey

for Chief Censor, India.

BOOKING DATE 22.5.43
RECEIVED ON 23.6.43
L 966 LONDON 30.22 1600
NLT BANASINSKA POLCONSUL BOMBAY

RECOGNISED ON PHOTOGRAPH FROM KIRANAGAR IN FIGHTING POLAND MY 2
NEPHEWS JERZY AND ZBIGNIEW LECZNAROWICZ SONS OF ANTONI AND ANIELA
BORN URBANOWICZ STOP PLEASE INFORM IF CHILDREN ARE REALLY IN
KIRANAGAR KAZIMIRZ URBANOWICZ
...POLREDCROSS...

Courtesy of National Archives of India, New Delhi.

3. Linlithgow's appeal to Indian princes for funds for Polish children, 1942

386

To THE PRINCES (*vide* List attached).

The Viceroy's House, New Delhi,
December 15th, 1942.

(310-G./41.)

MY DEAR ————,

In response to an appeal received from the Polish Government through His Majesty's Government, the Government of India agreed to receive and, to the extent to which private hospitality might make possible, to maintain for the duration of war five hundred Polish refugee children many of whom are orphans and all of whom have undergone many hardships. The first party consisting of 160 children reached India in the middle of April 1942 and is now, through the kindness of His Highness the Jam Saheb, in a camp on the sea-coast at Balachedi in the Nawanagar State, Kathiawar. A second party of 220 children which arrived at Quetta in August, has also reached Balachedi. The remainder will follow.

2. A part of the expenditure so far incurred has been met from a grant which I made from my War Purposes Fund and from subscriptions received as a result of an appeal issued by the Indian Red Cross Society, but the greater part has been met by advances from public revenues which under an agreement made by the Polish Government will be refunded by that Government if subscriptions received in India are insufficient.

3. In addition to these five hundred children, there are several thousand other Polish children in a similar plight in Russia and Persia. The Polish Government have recently asked the Government of India to permit as many as can be evacuated to enter India where their maintenance will be guaranteed by the Polish Government. In the circumstances I feel that we should do what we can to treat as the guests of India at least the first five hundred children.

4. It is estimated that the average monthly cost of maintaining one child will be Rs. 60 (a sum which covers supervision, board, lodging, clothing, education and medical facilities) and hence if only five hundred persons in the whole of India were prepared to contribute a monthly sum of Rs. 60 each and so, as it were, "adopt" one child during the time of its residence in India, India would have completely discharged the duties of host to these unfortunate guests. I am therefore approaching Governors of Provinces in the hope that they may be able to secure the financial "adoption" of some

(Continued)

387

2

of these children by individuals or institutions. I have also had a Committee constituted to administer the funds which may be raised.

5. My object in writing to you is to enlist Your Highness' sympathy and help in a cause which I feel sure will appeal to you and to ask you whether Your Highness' State could agree to "adopt" one or more of these unfortunate children. I feel sure that their cause will make its own appeal without any further advocacy on my part. If Your Highness feels able to make a regular contribution for the purpose indicated, it may be sent through my War Purposes Fund for the benefit of the Polish Account Committee.

Yours ————,

LINLITHGOW.

Courtesy of National Archives of India, New Delhi.

4. Expanding the offer, Randall to Gibson, 1942

FOREIGN OFFICE, S. W. 1

(W 11294/87/48)   20th August, 1942.

COPY SENT 31 AUG 1942 TO INDIA

6251 1942

Dear Gibson

Will you please refer to my letters W 9800/87/48 of the 15th July and W 10764/87/48 of the 15th August regarding the respective offers of the Maharajahs of Patiala and Nawanagar to take 5,000 Polish children into the territory under their rule. I am now enclosing telegrams received from Kuibyshev and Tehran asking whether certain Polish children in the Soviet Union can be received in any of the larger Indian States. These children are excellent material, and will be very valuable for the future Poland. If there is no objection on the part of the Government of India to the offers of the Maharajahs of Patiala and Nawanagar being accepted, we should like to inform Kuibyshev as soon as possible that there is a prospect that these boys can be accommodated in their States. Before, however, we could proceed to settle details of evacuation the financial and transport aspects of the problem would need to be examined.

I am sending a copy of this letter to W.L. Fraser (Treasury).

Yours sincerely,

Alex E. Randall

REG. POL. DEPT. 24 AUG 1942 INDIA OFFICE

J.P. Gibson, Esq.,
India Office.

Courtesy of British Library, London.

5. Gratitude from Poland, E Raczinsky to Anthony Eden, 1943

/110-N 19-1/412

*The Under Secretary of State,
India Office*

COPY.
(W 10625/283/48).
No.792/90.

POLISH EMBASSY,
LONDON.

~19th July, 1943.

Sir,   29-7-43

       I have the honour to express on behalf of the
Polish Government their sincere and deepfelt thanks
for the interest taken in the welfare of Poles
evacuated from Russia and particularly for the
generosity of the Indian Government, the Indian
Princes and Indian organisations in undertaking to
maintain large numbers of Polish children for the
duration of the war. The sympathetic attitude adopted
by the Indian Government and the community, and their
deep understanding of the plight of these children are
highly valued by the Polish Government and will always
be remembered with gratitude by the Polish people.
By their decision to offer shelter on hospitable
Indian soil to thousands of Polish children, India
has rendered possible their preservation for Poland,
where important tasks will await them in the future.

       I have, etc.,
          (Sd.) E. Raczyński.
           Polish Ambassador.

Copy sent Sir O O'malley.

COPY SENT
17 AUG 1943
TO INDIA

The Rt. Hon.
  Anthony Eden, M.C., M.P.,
    Principal Secretary of State for Foreign Affairs,
      Foreign Office,
        S.W.1.

30

(Continued)

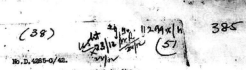

(38)

385

No. D. 4285-G/42.

A copy of the undermentioned paper is forwarded to the -

Residents - Hyderabad, Mysore, Central India, Rajputana,

Western India, Punjab States, Baroda, Kashmir,

Gwalior, Madras States, Eastern States,
External Affairs Department,

for information.

2. The Rulers of the following States have been addressed -

Baroda, Gwalior, Hyderabad and Berar, Jammu and Kashmir, Mysore, Bhopal,
Kalat, Travancore, Udaipur (Mewar), Bahawalpur, Bharatpur, Bikaner,
Cochin, Cutch, Jaipur, Jodhpur, Kotah, Patiala, Tonk, Alwar, Dhar,
Jodhpur, Idar, Rampur, Bhavnagar, Cooch-Behar, Jind, Junagadh,
Kapurthala, Nabha, Porbandar, Rajpipla, Faridkot, Gondal, Morvi and
Tehri-Garhwal.

By order, etc.,

for Secretary to HIS Excellency the
Crown Representative.

Political Department,
New Delhi,
The 22nd December 1942.

Forwarded from the Office of the Private Secretary to His
Excellency the Viceroy No.6290-G/42, dated the 16th December 1942,
with enclosure.

6. Polish boys from Bombay travelling to the UK, 1944

431

12

Passport Control Department,
Foreign Office,
Broadway Buildings,
Westminster, S.W.1.

VR. 43555.

11th September
1944.

Dear Silver,

I attach a list of Polish boys at
present in Bombay who are to come to this
country for training for the Polish Marine
Service. I should be grateful if you would
kindly inform the appropriate authorities in
India that these boys may, on application, be
granted visas for the United Kingdom, endorsed
"Authorised by Home Office No.Gen.320/18/16".

Yours sincerely,

(Sd.) P. Beck.

C.H. Silver, Esq.

(Continued)

430

LIST OF CANDIDATES FOR THE POLISH MARITIME SCHOOL IN LONDON.

(BOMBAY GROUP).

SURNAME	CHRISTIAN NAME	DATE OF BIRTH	PLACE.
BACZYK	Henryk	23. 2.1926	Wolkowysk
BIERONSKI	Tadeusz	18.11.1928	Sawaluszki
BOZEK	Stanislaw	26. 2.1927	Zgubice
BRAUMULLER	Alfred	21. 2.1927	Krakow
BUC	Jaroslaw	23. 3.1929	Wolkowysk
BURY	Eugeniusz	11. 1.1927	Orchowice
CZARNECKI	Zanon	13. 8.1928	Rukojnie
DEREN	Mieczyslaw	5.11.1928	Jankowce
FRACH	Zbigniew	29. 6.1929	Grembobin
GANCZAR	Kazimierz	28.10.1928	Lamy
GAUDYN	Stanislaw	1.11.1927	Delatyn
GRZESZUK	Antoni	17. 4.1926	Lozy
HERZOG	Tadeusz	28. 7.1926	Wilno
ISKRA	Marjan	22. 9.1930	Stary Rachow
JANKIEWICZ	Waldemar	18. 9.1928	Pulsudczyzna
JAROSZ	Jerzy	10. 3.1927	Ruda
JERMAK	Wladyslaw	30. 8.1927	Luck
KAPALA	Franciszek	20. 5.1928	Zofiowka
KAZMIEROW	Stanislaw	8.12.1927	Moscice
KEMPA	Jan	8. 1.1929	Gliniki Gorne
KOTLARCZYK	Zbigniew	8. 6.1930	Stanislawow
KRECZMANSKI	Boleslaw	19. 6.1928	Borszczow
KWIATEK	Wiktor	26.12.1928	Wola Kurybutow ka

Courtesy of National Archives of India, New Delhi.

7. Status of adoption, HH Eggers to Gilchrist, 1947

FILE COPY.   INDEXED

Tel. No.: Whitehall 1234   TREASURY CHAMBERS,
    Your Reference................   GREAT GEORGE STREET,
Treasury ReferenceO.F.91/4/53.   LONDON, S.W.1.

P O L
8103   3rd May, 1947.
1947

.ear Gilchrist,

        With reference to your letter POL7757/47 of May 9th
about the legal guardianship of Polish orphans in India, the
following is an extract from Webb's letter of December 19th for
which you ask:-

        "It appears that two groups of persons in
    "Kolhapur and Nawanagar State respectively have been
    "appointed as legal guardians by State Courts and that
    "the proceedings have been regularised by a formal
    "document.   These documents forbade the guardians to
    "remove their wards from the Courts' jurisdiction with-
    "out its permission and, in the case of the Orphans at
    "Balachadi, that permission is now being sought
    "retrospectively for the removal of the Orphans from
    "Balachadi to Kolhapur.   I understand that there is no
    "legal difficulty in the way of obtaining this permis-
    "sion and that it is intended by the Poles to follow
    "a similar procedure if and when the children go to
    "Australia.

        "I am informed that the best legal advice has been
    "taken and that, in the opinion of an eminent Bombay
    "lawyer, the formal documents are water-tight from a
    "legal point of view."

        I am sending a copy of this letter to Hancock.

                        Yours sincerely,

                        H. H. Eggers

Courtesy of British Library, London.

8. Finances raised in India for Polish children, 1943

449

INDIA OFFICE,
WHITEHALL,
LONDON, S.W.1.

15th July, 1943.

Dear Sir Walford,

With reference to our telephone
conversation today and also to your
correspondence with the Foreign Office, of
which copies have been sent to us,
regarding assistance to the Poles in India,
I write to suggest that the sum of £2,000
as a first contribution to the Viceroy's
fund for Polish evacuees would be highly
appreciated by the Viceroy, not only for
the measure of extra help that it will
make possible, but also as a token of the
recognition for the splendid work that the
Government of India have done for the Poles.

It may be of interest to you to know
that as a result of an appeal made in India
by the Viceroy for funds to support the
first 500 Polish orphans to reach India,
promises have been received for the sum of
Rs.3,93,120 or about £29,500.

I would suggest that the money
should be applied on behalf of Polish
evacuees at the discretion of the Viceroy
as suggested in Randall's letter of the 13th
July. In due course we should hear how it
has/

Sir Walford Selby, K.C.M.G., C.B.,
C.V.O.,
Polish Relief Fund. 31. Belgrave Square. S.W.1.

(Continued)

450

-2-

has been spent and doubtless any
further needs of the evacuees will
to be brought to our - and your - notice.

Yours sincerely,

(Sd.) R. N. GILCHRIST

Courtesy of British Library, London.

9. Financial summary by Captain AWT Webb, 1944

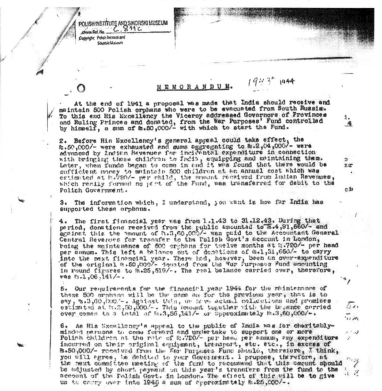

M E M O R A N D U M.   1943 1944

At the end of 1941 a proposal was made that India should receive and maintain 500 Polish orphans who were to be evacuated from South Russia. To this end His Excellency the Viceroy addressed Governors of Provinces and Ruling Princes and donated, from the War Purposes' Fund controlled by himself, a sum of Rs.50,000/- with which to start the Fund.

2. Before His Excellency's general appeal could take effect, the Rs.50,000/- were exhausted and sums aggregating to Rs.2,04,000/- were advanced by Indian Revenues for incidental expenditure in connection with bringing these children to India, equipping and maintaining them. Later, when funds began to come in and it was found that there would be sufficient money to maintain 500 children at an annual cost which was estimated at Rs.720/- per child, the amount received from Indian Revenues, which really formed no part of the Fund, was transferred for debit to the Polish Government.

3. The information which, I understand, you want is how far India has supported these orphans.

4. The first financial year was from 1.1.43 to 31.12.43. During that period, donations received from the public amounted to Rs.4,91,660/- and against this the amount of Rs.3,60,000/- was paid to the Accountant General Central Revenues for transfer to the Polish Govt's account in London, being the maintenance of 500 orphans for twelve months at Rs.720/- per head per annum. This left a balance out of donations of Rs.1,31,660/- to carry into the next financial year. There had, however, been an over-expenditure of the original Rs.50,000/- donated from the War Purposes Fund amounting in round figures to Rs.25,519/-. The real balance carried over, therefore, was Rs.1,06,141/-.

5. Our requirements for the financial year 1944 for the maintenance of these 500 orphans will be the same as for the previous year, that is to say, Rs.3,60,000/-. Against this, we have actual collections and promises estimated at Rs.2,50,000/-. This amount together with the balance carried over comes to a total of Rs.3,56,141/- or approximately Rs.3,60,000/-.

6. As His Excellency's appeal to the public of India was for charitably-minded persons to come forward and undertake to support one or more Polish children at the rate of Rs.720/- per head per annum, any expenditure incurred on their original equipment, transport, etc. etc., in excess of Rs.50,000/- received from the War Purposes Fund should, therefore, I think, you will agree, be debited to your Government. I propose, therefore, at the next committee meeting of the fund to recommend that this amount should be adjusted by short payment on this year's transfers from the fund to the account of the Polish Govt. in London. The effect of this will be to give us to carry over into 1945 a sum of approximately Rs.25,000/-.

7. It may be mentioned that contributions in the present financial year have been somewhat less than in the previous year. This is due to the famine conditions in Bengal and the stringencies in Madras, which have caused a number of earlier subscribers to express their inability to continue their donations.

8. In conclusion, it can be said that India has maintained 500 Polish orphan children during the year 1943, will be able to repeat this in 1944 and it is hoped, will continue to support these children till their return to their own country.

9. As regards future donations, much depends on the economic conditions of this country. But quite a number of subscribers have pledged themselves to continue their donations indefinitely.

Sd. A.W.T.Webb.
O.S.D.

Courtesy of Polish Institute and General Sikorski Museum, London.

10. Contribution by Indian public for Polish children, 1947

451

FILE COPY.

INWARD TELEGRAM

(260)

8701

1947

(If in any case the communication of the contents of this document to any person outside British or B. Government Service is authorised, it must be paraphrased).

Allotted to Political Department.

CYPHER

From	Government of India, External Affairs and Commonwealth Relations Department
To	Secretary of State for India
Dated	New Delhi, 22.55 hours, 1st July, 1947.
Received	07.20 hours, 2nd July, 1947.

No. 5094.

Gilchrist from Webb. Your telegram No. 8277 28/6. Polish orphans.

2. Government of India regret inability to accept any financial liability for Poles vide their telegram No. 3265 of 9/4/1946. Would remind that Indian public contributed some six lakhs rupees for maintenance of these orphans, an amount which otherwise would have been chargeable to H.M.G.

3. Regarding adult Poles wishing to emigrate Australia. On advice of Mr. A.R. Peters of Australian Emigration Department who visited Delhi

POL DEPT.
4 JUL 1947
INDIA OFFICE

/in

(Continued)

452

in March last, names of only 58 Poles (chiefly Jews
in possession of capital) were recommended for
entry permits. No reply received and a reminder
has issued. Most of these 58 Poles are not (repe
not) on strength of Kolhapur Camp.

11. Looking for places for the Poles, Anthony Eden
to Leo Amery, 1942

(W 8236/87/48).

M: Gibon
M: Patrich

Foreign Office.
S.W.1.

6th June, 1942.

POL
4258
1942

My dear Leo,

The Poles are pressing us hard again over their civilians in the Union of Soviet Socialist Republics, whom they represent as living in harrowing conditions, diseased and threatened with death from starvation. Our own reports on the condition of those Poles who have reached Persia recently confirm much of what the Poles tell us, and the Polish Ambassador in Kuibyshev has begged his Government to appeal to us and the United States to help in removing 50,000 Polish children.

Although we have consistently made it clear to the Poles that the problem of their civilians in Russia is for themselves to settle with the Russian Government, we have done a good deal to help with supplies. Our humanitarian interest is re-inforced by certain political considerations. The Poles argue that between the German extermination policy and the fate of their people in the Union of Soviet Socialist Republics the basis of their national life is being destroyed, and Sikorski has told me that the condition of his people in Russia is an important obstacle to a full Polish-Russian understanding. We have left the Poles in no uncertainty regarding the limitations which transport, supply and overriding military considerations impose on us, but with this renewed appeal I should like to be in a position to say to the Polish Government that the possibilities of help were being urgently reviewed. And, for the most immediate help, I can think of nowhere to turn but India. You arranged some months ago that India should receive 500 Polish children, and the Viceroy has given generous

/ assistance

The Right Honourable
L. S. Amery, M.P.

Source: BL-120c letter file

XI

(Continued)

371

assistance over the initial expenditure. · A general appeal which we made in an official note to your Department on the 8th April was answered negatively in an official letter Pol/3134/42 of the 21st April.

I now write to say that, while I appreciate the increased difficulties which beset India since the date of that letter, I should be extremely grateful if you felt able to review the position. The Poles have shown by the first despatch of children to India that the route is practicable; they say they can increase transport facilities. It would greatly assist me in dealing with them if it were possible to say that the Government of India would undertake to give hospitality to Polish children additional to those already received. I do not know whether local conditions make it practicable, but it has been suggested that as a great proportion of the Polish children are Catholics an appeal for billets to convent schools and colleges, as well as private homes, might have a favourable response. However this may be, I am most reluctant to give the Poles an unqualified negative without asking whether you could lay their pressing need before the Viceroy. I shall be most grateful for any help or suggestions you can offer.

12. India as transit/destination (Randall to Gibson), 1942

15 - 24,000 to over
be accounted for in Africa
above like he in Africa

H. Gibson

✓

(W 15133/5130/G).
SECRET.

FOREIGN OFFICE, S.W.1,
17th November, 1942.

9473
1942

Dear Gibson,

We must, I fear, once more ask for the assistance
of the India Office over the problem of the Polish
civilians in Persia. Although the East African
colonies have taken them in up to practically their
limit of accommodation, and 1,000 are to be received
in Southern Rhodesia, there are still some 25,000 for
whom an alternative destination must be found. Their
continued presence in Persia is a serious embarrassment,
military, political and economic, and we receive
repeated reminders of the urgent necessity of getting
as many as possible removed. We thought we had found
a complete solution when we induced the Mexican
Government to receive them; then, when that hope
faded on account of insuperable difficulties of
shipping from the Persian Gulf to America, we again
thought we should solve our problem to a substantial
extent with the moving of 25,000 Italian prisoners of
war from East Africa to the United States so leaving
places to be filled by not less than 12,000 Poles.
This hope, too, is dashed by the impossibility of
obtaining military escorts for the prisoners to cross
the Atlantic, and by the extreme difficulty of
shipping, the details of which I need not describe here.

As the result of a discussion with the War Office
and Ministry of War Transport we have discovered that
the most promising solution, from the point of view of
shipping, involves the use, if it is at all possible
to arrange it, of India either as a destination or a
transit territory, or both. A substantial transport
of Poles from Persia is at present taking place via
India; I understand this could, so far as shipping is
concerned,

18 OV 942
INDIA OFFICE

J.P. Gibson, Esq.,
India Office.

(Continued)

concerned, continue almost indefinitely. But the
agreed limit of reception in Africa is getting near.
On the other hand, removal from Bombay to America,
probably in large numbers in one or two ships,
might be practicable in the next few weeks and the
suggestion has been made that if a reserve camp
could be built up near Bombay then all opportunities
could be taken as they arise to remove the Poles.
Alternatively, or as a complement to this suggestion,
there is the idea that, as Nawanagar and Patiala
have been so helpful in providing war-duration
accommodation for Polish children, it might be
possible to push these doors a little more widely
open and get a substantial number of the adults
included. There is, finally, the suggestion that
other ~~Native~~ *Indian* States, such as Mysore or Hyderabad,
might be appealed to. Their help could be invoked
on both humanitarian and political grounds. By
allowing their territory to be used to accommodate
these Polish civilians for the duration of the war
they would not only relieve a vast amount of
suffering, but would give most valuable help to the
united war-effort, at present embarrassed by the
presence of these unfortunate people in Persia.

We should therefore be grateful if the India
Office could urgently consider recommending to the
Government of India

    1) the provision of a large transit camp near
Bombay; 2) the possibility of getting the rulers of
Patiala and Nawanagar to include a good number of
                                 adults/

adults in their hospitality, already so much appreciated
for the Polish children; 3) the possibility of an urgent
appeal to other rulers of states which are not too
unsuitable climatically for the reception of Polish women
and children.

I am sending a copy of this letter to Commander
C.A. Jenkins (Admiralty); Colonel Evelyn Smith (War
Office: Prisoners of War Section); Lieutenant-Colonel
Wright (War Office: Q.M.2); Colonel Bainbridge (War
Office: S.D.2); Dixon (Ministry of War Transport);
J.N. Wood (Ministry of War Transport); Sir Harold Satow
(Foreign Office: Prisoners of War Department);
Kimber (Dominions Office); and Sidebotham (Colonial
Office).

Yours sincerely,
A.W.G. Randall

13. Unused visas of Alicja M Edwards

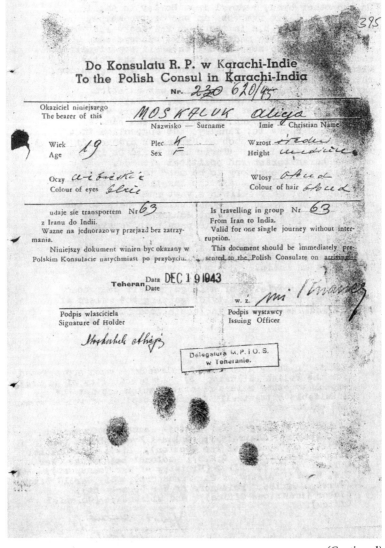

395

Do Konsulatu R. P. w Karachi-Indie
To the Polish Consul in Karachi-India

Nr. 220 620/45

Okaziciel niniejszego The bearer of this	MOSKALUK alicja	
	Nazwisko — Surname	Imie — Christian Name

Wiek 19
Age

Plec K
Sex F

Wzrost średni
Height

Oczy *niebieskie*
Colour of eyes *blue*

Wlosy *blond*
Colour of hair *blond*

udaje się transportem Nr 63
z Iranu do Indii.
Ważne na jednorazowy przejazd bez zatrzymania.
  Niniejszy dokument winien być okazany w Polskim Konsulacie natychmiast po przybyciu.

Is travelling in group Nr 63
From Iran to India.
Valid for one single journey without interruption.
  This document should be immediately presented to the Polish Consulate on arriving.

Teheran Data DEC 1 9 1943
Date

w. z. *signature*

Podpis wlasciciela
Signature of Holder

Podpis wystawcy
Issuing Officer

Delegatura M. P. i O. S.
w Teheranie.

(Continued)

396

Do Konsulatu R.P. w Brytyjskiej Afryce Wschodniej.
To the Polish Consul in British East Africa
Nr. 508/42

Okaziciel niniejszego
The bearer of this   *MOSKALUK*   *Alicja*

Nazwisko — Surname   Imie — Christian Name

Wiek / Age   *19*   Plec / Sex   *K / F*   Wzrost / Height   *sredni / medium*

Oczy / Colour of eyes   *niebieskie / blue*   Wlosy / Colour of hair   *blond*

udaje sie transportem Nr. *48*   Is travelling in group Nr. *48*
z Iranu do Brytyjskiej Afryki Wschodniej.   From Iran to British East Africa.
Wazne na jednorazowy przejazd bez zatrzy-   Valid for one single journey without inter.
mania.   rupion.
Niniejszy dokument winien byc okazany w   This document should be immediately pre-
Polskim Konsulacie natychmiast po przybyciu.   sented to the Polish Consulate on arriving.

Teheran   Dnia / Date   FEB 20 1943
III

Moskaluk Alicja   w. z.
Podpis wlasciciela   Podpis wystawcy
Signature of Holder   Issuing Officer

508/42

14. Zygmunt Mandel papers

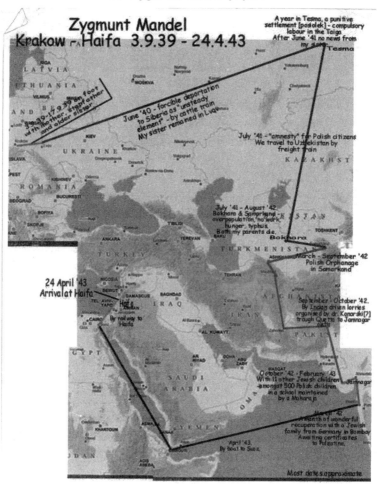

(Continued)

לקה העליה של הסוכנות היהודית לא"י

רשימת עולים שבאו לא"י

הקליה	הקרובים בא"י וכתבתם	מס. הרשיון	מצב	גיל	השם	המשפחה
	ויצה, הורו - ליאון ילדה	פולין	ב–3	18	אדפונגר	ארליך
	ורדה, הורו -	"	ב–3	16	פולה	גילום
	עלית הבוער, סנדיאל	"	ב–3	9	אילובה	גולדלרום
	לוון, מ' שפיטבצון, תל-אביב	"	ב–3	8	יבוק	"
	רחוב הרפ"ס 6	"	ב–3	16	רוזליון	ר ב ן
	סבנקן הורים - יצ"ב	"	ב–3	7	ד א ל	"
	גדוזה, קברצת	"	ב–3	15	זיגברונד	
	קוקירו, עלית הבוער	"	ב–3	15	אברהם	קלרושנר
	גולופטק, הורו -	"	ב–3	18	פימה	
			ב–3	17	צילה	רוזנגרטן
			ב–3	18	מרים	שפלר
			ב–3	17	אלונה	"
	סקולה, חיים הר,	א		33	אליאס	ש ו ר

בולגריה

		ג	64	כפים	אברהם
		"	49	זיקפרויה	"
		"	12	אידירור	קלסקי
		ג	35	לודניק	"
		"	42	מרים	
		"	40	אמונר	
		"	18	מנואל	
		"	16	רובה	
		ד	18	אורי	

	תולים	ב–3	17	אנלי	ארדיטי
		ב–3	16	אריס	בכר
		ג	26	דרד	
		"	22	לבנה	
		"	28	ריכרד	
				אסתר	
				חיים	
				זוגבגרל	
				ירוסף	
				לראי	
				מסיל	
				גבר	

(Continued)

List of children who came to Israel [Palestine] on 24.4.43 from Bombay.
[compiled from The Jewish Agency records]

Erlich Edmund	15
Gilert Pola	15
Goldluft Ilona	9
Goldluft Janusz	6
Hoch Rozalja	15
Hoch Rachel	7
Mandel Zygmunt	15
Magnuszewer Abraham	15
Kaufman Fima	13
Rozengarten Cila	17
Szpalter Maria	15
Szpalter Elza	17

We were "chaperoned" on our way from Bombay by Rabbi Shor Elias [33] who
came, if I remember correctly, to India by way of a jail in Afganistan

Courtesy of Mr Zygmunt Mandel, Israel.

Bibliography

ॐ

Primary Sources: Archival Files

National Archives of India (NAI), New Delhi

EAD File no. 186/-X/40 (Secret)
EAD 276-X/42/Secret
EAD 276(8)-X/42/Secret
EAD 218(72)-G/44

Tata Central Archives, Pune

Sir Dorab Tata Trust Meetings Minutes
Banasinski Papers

Kolhapur Administration Reports, Kolhapur

1943–45 Reports

British Library—India & Oriental Collection (formerly India Office Library), London

R2/952/76 C-70/43
W 11294/87/48
OF 91/4/53
L/P&J/8/413
POL 6251 1942
R2/952/76 C-70/43
L/AG/40/1/169 (PRC/A-25)
L/AG/40/1/131 (RRO A-5)
L/P&J/8/415
L/AG/40/1/169/PRC/A-25
L/P&J/8/414/Coll 110 N3
POL 8103
POL 9244

British National Archives (BNA) (formerly Public Records Office), Kew, London

CAB/111/310
PREM 3/354/1
WO 193/216
WO 204/8711
WO 204/8711
FO 371/29214
FO 371/ 32630
FO 371/42882
FO 371/36736
FO 371/31079
FO 371/ 42781
FO 371/34584 C 8076
FO 371.51153
T 160/1204 8H177

Polish Institute and General Sikorski Museum, London

C-811c
C 811d
Banasinski Papers

Archiwum Akt Nowichy (AAN) or The New Archives, Warsaw

Letter No. W 9800/87/48 dated 15 July 1942, Maurice Peterson to Count E Raczynski, State Archives of Poland, Warsaw
File 417

Secondary Sources

Books Consulted

Anders, W, *An Army in Exile* (London: Macmillan, 1949).

Applebaum, A, *Gulag—A History* (New York: Penguin, 2003).

Association of Poles in India 1942–48, *A Short History of Poles in India 1942–48, In Light of Reminiscences and Documents*, Polish (English translation underway) (London, n.d.).

Bak, E, *Life's Journey* (New York: East European Monographs, 2002).

Banasinska, K and G Verghese, *Autobiography of Kira Banasinska* (Mumbai: Kotak & Co., 1997).

Bhatti, A and V Johannes, *Jewish Exiles in India* (New Delhi: Manohar, 1999).

Carr, EH, *What is History?* (London: Penguin, 1990).

Copland, I, *The Princes of India in the Endgame of Empire 1917–47* (London: Cambridge University Press, 1997).

Dalai Lama, *Freedom in Exile, Autobiography of Dalai Lama* (London: Abacus, 1990).

Davies, N, *Heart of Europe—A Short History of Poland* (London: Oxford University Press, 1984).

———, *Rising '44* (London: Macmillan, 2003).

Dear and Foot (eds), *The Oxford Companion to WW II* (London: Oxford University Press, 1995).

Djurovic, G, *The Central Tracing Agency of the International Committee of the Red Cross* (Geneva: International Committee of the Red Cross, 1986).

Edwards, AR, *And God was our Witness* (Montana: Self Published, 2002).

Fundacja Archiwum Fotograficzne, *Exiled Children (Tulacze Dzeici)* (Warsaw: Fundacja Archiwum Fotograficzne, 1995).

———, *Polish Schooling in War-time Exile* (Warsaw: Fundacja Archiwum Fotograficzne, 2004).

Grant, AJ and H Temperly, *Europe in the Nineteenth and Twentieth Centuries 1789–1950*, 6th edition (London: Longman, 1952).

Jacob, JFR, *Surrender at Dacca-Birth of a Nation* (New Delhi: Manohar, 1997).

James, L, *Raj: The Making & Unmaking of British India* (London: Abacus, 1997).

Krolikowski, L, *Stolen Childhood—A Saga of Polish War Children* (New York: Father Justin Rosary Hour, 1983).

Lala, RM, *Beyond the Last Blue Mountain—Biography of J.R.D. Tata* (Bombay: Tata Press, 1992).

Prasad, B (ed.), *Official History of the Indian Armed Forces in the Second World War 1939–45*, Vol. 5–Campaign in Western Asia (New Delhi: Combined Inter-Services Historical Section (India and Pakistan), Orient Longmans, 1958).

Raczynski, E, *In Allied London* (London: Weidenfeld & Nicholson, 1962).

Rawicz, S, *The Long Walk* (Connecticut: The Lyons Press, 1988).

Rodrigues, M, *Battling for the Empire* (New Delhi: Penguin, 2003).

Sarkar, S, *Modern India 1885–1947*, 2nd edition (London: Cambridge Commonwealth Series, 1989).

Solomon, S, *Hooghly Tales* (London: David Ashley Publishing, 1998).

Stypula, W, *W Goscinie U "Polskiego" Maharadzy (Guests of the "Polish" Maharaja)* (Warsaw: Orion (22)615 54 01, 2000).

Sword, K, *Deportation and Exile, Poles in the Soviet Union 1939–48* (London: St. Martin's Press with School of Slavonic and East European Studies, 1994).

Umiastowski, R, *Poland, Russia and Great Britain 1941–45—A Study of Evidence* (London: Hollis & Carter, 1946).

United States Holocaust Memorial Museum, *Flight and Rescue* (Washington: United States Holocaust Memorial Museum, 2001).

Other Published Material

Basu, M, 'Mother Courage', Pune Newsline, *The Indian Express*, Pune, 15 August 2005.

Bhattacharjee, A, 'Sophie's World', Foray, *The Pioneer*, New Delhi, 10 June 2001.

Neizgoda, A, '1000 children of the Maharaja', *Polityka*, Warsaw, June 2, 2001.

Polak w Indiach, No. 18-19, 15 Sept.-1 Oct. 1944.

Puranik, SS, 'Why the Poles do not want to leave India', *The Maratha*, Pune, 10 January 1949.

Robbins, KX, 'The Camp for Polish Refugee Children at Balachadi, Nawanagar (India)', *Journal of Indo-Judaic Studies* (1998), Washington.

Tokarski, K, 'Wanda Dynowska- Umadevi: A Biographical Essay', *Journal of Theosophical History* (1994), California State University, Fullerton.

Oral History

Personal Interviews

The place indicates where they normally reside and where the interview was conducted.

1. Ashani, Kirit; Jamnagar
2. Bartosz, Zbigniew; Warsaw
3. Bereznicka, Teresa; Manchester (interviewed at Kolhapur)
4. Bhagubapu; Balachadi
5. Bock, Hubert; Manchester (interviewed at Kolhapur)
6. Buras, Zbigniew; Luton, UK
7. Byrski, Maria K; Warsaw
8. Chendinski, Andrej; Warsaw
9. Gaikwad, Shamrao; Kolhapur
10. Gaikwad, Vijaysingh; Kolhapur
11. Glazer, Teresa; London
12. Gonzaga, Maria; Mumbai
13. Gutowski, Roman; Warsaw
14. Harshad Kumariji; New Delhi
15. Hoogewerf, Margaret; Mumbai
16. Huppert, Karol; London
17. Ingle, Ramrao; Kolhapur

18. Jacob, JFR, General; New Delhi
19. Kashikar, Wanda; Kolhapur
20. Khan, Suleiman; Balachadi
21. Kleszko, Weislawa; London
22. Klosowski, Stefan; Quebec, Canada (interviewed at Balachadi)
23. Maresch, Eugenia; London
24. Mendonca, Zofia; Pune
25. Nesrikar, Nirmala; Kolhapur
26. Pawar, Vasant Bapu; Kolhapur
27. Peszkovski, Z, Reverend; Warsaw
28. Pniewska, Danuta; London
29. Raba, Marian; Leicester, UK
30. Siedlecki, Jan; London
31. Singhji, Shatrushalaya; Jamnagar
32. Stypula, Wieslaw; Warsaw
33. Szydlo, Daniela; London
34. Truchanowicz, Jagwiga; Warsaw
35. Vara, Dinesh; Jamnagar

Interviews by Correspondence (including emails)

1. Adamczyk, Wesley; USA
2. Baczyk, Henryk; Australia
3. Baczyk-Haus, Alina; USA
4. Bak, Eugene; USA
5. Charuba, Barbara; Canada
6. Chhina, Hardev Singh; Chandigarh
7. Dobrostanski, Tadeusz; Australia
8. Dziurinski, Janusz; USA
9. Edwards, Alicja, R; USA
10. Harasymow, Stanislaus; Australia
11. Herzog, Franek; USA
12. Kail, Vanessa; Australia
13. Krawiec, Janina Fiore; USA
14. Majewski, Casimir; USA
15. Mandel, Zygmunt; Israel
16. Trella, Boguslaw; Australia
17. Trzaska, Leszek; Poland
18. Wisniowski, Stefan; Australia
19. Wolski, Marek; UK

Index

About the Author

☙❧

Anuradha Bhattacharjee is Fellow, Centre for Culture, Media and Governance, Jamia Milia Islamia, New Delhi. Prior to this, she was Assistant Professor, Mudra Institute of Communication, Ahmedabad (MICA). A Fellow of the Charles Wallace India Trust (2004), she was a journalist with the *Times of India* (1991–94) and the *Pioneer* (2000–02). She was Research Fellow under the Kasturbhai Lalbhai Chair for Social Entrepreneurship at Indian Institute of Management, Ahmedabad (IIMA) in 2006.

This work has been culled out from her doctoral thesis, 'History of Polish Refugees in India 1942–48', submitted to the University of Pune, which was awarded the Bendre Prize for Best Dissertation (2006).